PRISON ABOLITION FOR REALISTS

PRISON ABOLITION FOR REALISTS

Anna Terwiel

UNIVERSITY OF MINNESOTA PRESS
MINNEAPOLIS • LONDON

Portions of chapter 5 were previously published in "What Is the Problem with High Prison Temperatures? From the Threat to Health to the Right to Comfort," in *New Political Science: A Journal of Politics & Culture* 40, no. 1: 70–83. Copyright 2018 Caucus for a New Political Science. All rights reserved. Republished by permission of the publisher. www.dukeupress.edu.

Published by the University of Minnesota Press
111 Third Avenue South, Suite 290
Minneapolis, MN 55401-2520
http://www.upress.umn.edu

ISBN 978-1-5179-2039-5 (hc)
ISBN 978-1-5179-2040-1 (pb)

A Cataloging-in-Publication record for this book is available from the Library of Congress.

Printed in the United States of America on acid-free paper

34 33 32 31 30 29 28 27 26 25 10 9 8 7 6 5 4 3 2 1

For L.N.

Contents

Preface

How else could we respond to harm and violence besides relying on the criminal legal system to send people to prison? We often assume that this question has no answer because we must put criminals somewhere, but our own experience might suggest the inadequacy of this response and point beyond it. As abolitionist legal scholars and critical criminologists remind us, only a fraction of criminal lawbreaking is reported to the police or results in a conviction.[1] This means that intervention by the criminal legal system is generally an exception, not the norm. Most of us have directly or indirectly experienced both "criminalizable events" (acts that technically constitute crimes, from illicit drug use to assault) and alternative forms of conflict resolution or efforts at accountability and repair, however small or incomplete. What could these experiences teach us about possible alternatives to criminalization and punishment?

As I have been reading and writing about prison abolition, I have also been collecting stories of improvised efforts at justice and repair, shared with me by friends, relatives, colleagues, and acquaintances. I was told about a treasurer who took money from the association's bank account to finance his drug addiction. When the members found out, they ousted him from the treasurer position but did not press charges. Instead, they reached an agreement for gradual repayment of the stolen funds. I heard many stories about sexual violence, of victims/survivors confronting their abusers years or decades afterward. Alone or with others, in person, in writing, or on the phone, they issued demands: for an acknowledgment or an apology, for the person to enter therapy, to never be in contact again. In these cases, pressing criminal charges often did not seem feasible: The abuse happened too long ago and would be too difficult to prove in court, or the idea of testifying and being cross-examined in court seemed too daunting.

These stories inform this book's argument that prison abolition is a realist political project. Abolitionists are often dismissed as dreamers or moralists who have unworkable ideas, but over the course of years of exploring abolitionist theories and practices, I have found this characterization to be deeply misleading. The abolitionist thinking articulated in a range of formats and settings—academic publications and general audience ones, talks and webinars, social media posts and podcasts—has overwhelmingly struck me as attuned to lived experiences of harm and violence while refusing to accept existing punitive practices as necessary, inevitable, or just. Prison abolitionists refuse complacency, but they do not promise a "heaven-on-earth that will never come to pass."[2] Some of the abolitionists discussed in this book say little about the kind of society they envision, while others offer normative visions of "abolition democracy" and are clear-eyed about the practical obstacles in their way and the need for tactical and strategic action to overcome them.

Most of all, abolitionists are realists because they reckon with the realities of the criminal legal system. Rather than assume that prisons make us safer or justify their existence, abolitionists confront what they do and don't do and question their legitimacy. We know that Black, Latinx, and Indigenous people are incarcerated at the highest rates; that incarceration inflicts suffering, shortens lifespans, and strains or ruptures family and social ties; and that it typically leads to reincarceration.[3] Abolitionists find these realities intolerable, but theirs is not simply a moral critique that prisons are bad or evil. Importantly, their critique is political. Exactly who or what is served by the deployment of state violence, and at what cost? What racial and economic hierarchies are upheld, what kinds of state power are legitimated, and what kinds of citizenship are affirmed and normalized? Conversely, many abolitionists ask: What other responses to harm are possible? What visions of democracy, justice, and freedom are foreclosed or obscured by our collective investment in state punishment? How can we win?

This book aims to illuminate the political thinking developed by prison abolitionist scholars and activists. I write as a white, nonincarcerated political theorist of abolition, moved by a desire to understand abolitionist political thought in its complexity and convey its relevance to the academic field of political theory and to our political thinking at large. Because my academic practice is textual interpretation, my account of abolition is based on abolitionist writings rather than interviews or ethnographies. I describe prison abolition as *realist* to capture its attentiveness to empirical realities and also to preempt its dismissal as irrelevant to the "real" world of politics and to "serious" political theory. (Deeming a project or demand "unrealistic" is a powerful way to dismiss it, even though history is full of examples of the seemingly impossible or highly unlikely becoming reality.) This book further uses concepts from queer and democratic theory to identify a broad but significant political difference between abolitionist approaches. What I call *paranoid* abolitionism[4] advances a strong critique of prisons and other kinds of confinement but does not develop an alternative vision of freedom, democracy, or justice, or advocate for political action or institutions that could realize them. It can even turn away from collective efforts to build power, instead generating a *politics of purity* focused on eradicating carcerality from the self. *Agonistic* abolitionism, in contrast, is willing to get its hands dirty and combines radical critique with efforts to build new democratic institutions. I identify agonistic abolitionism in the work of Angela Davis and in the community accountability efforts of the radical feminist and abolitionist group Communities Against Rape and Abuse (CARA), and I use this approach to advocate for strategic abolitionist engagements with law and the state. The final chapter argues that a *right to comfort* could both ground demands for air-conditioning to protect incarcerated people from extreme heat and help us imagine the kinds of lives that abolition democracy seeks to make possible for all.

My work as a political theorist is connected to practical efforts to challenge mass incarceration. While writing this book, I have been codirecting Trinity College's Prison Education Project (TPEP), which offers credit-bearing college classes to incarcerated people in Connecticut at no cost to the students. I think of this work as a small way to support incarcerated people, challenge unequal access to higher education, and advance a vision of education as a public good we all deserve. At the same time, this effort risks shoring up the legitimacy of jails and prisons in the eyes of the public as sites of humane treatment and rehabilitation. It thus presents a version of dirty-hands politics. If the risks seem to me to be worth taking, that is largely because incarcerated people tell me that college classes provide them with glimmers of meaning and hope, as well as relief from the boredom and monotony of life behind bars. I first taught in prison through the Prison + Neighborhood Arts/

Education Project (PNAP), which offers arts and humanities classes at Stateville Maximum Security Prison and connects students with people outside the prison by exhibiting their art, poetry, and essays in Chicago galleries.[5] These exhibits both disrupt students' isolation and increase public knowledge of incarcerated people, prisons, and their conditions.[6] Teaching with PNAP confronted me with the profound violence of imprisonment and showed how committed collective action is possible and can orient us toward a different world. I hope this book's account of prison abolition might do the same.

Introduction

Prison Abolition for Realists

There might be no surer way to dismiss prison abolition than to claim it is unrealistic. Sometimes, abolitionists are assumed to have strong moral critiques of prisons but no sense of how to put their ideas into practice. Other times, they are said to hold an idealized view of human nature, overlooking the fact that some people are a danger to others. They are also accused of political naiveté, of failing to grapple with public support for "tough-on-crime" policies. Either way, the idea that prison abolitionists are out of touch with reality often shuts down serious engagement with their ideas and practices.

This book develops a different perspective on prison abolition as a realist political project. I argue that prison abolition is *realist* because it reckons with how criminal legal institutions actually function and with the limitations of efforts to reform them. It takes seriously lived experiences of violence, and informal responses to it, improvised by people with varying outcomes and perceptions of success. Prison abolition is *political* because punishment is a key function of the state. It is a form of state violence, "lawful harm" as Locke calls it, that is inflicted on some for the purported benefit of others.[1] State punishment does not simply protect democratic citizens, however: It also deskills and disempowers them, while deepening divisions between those deemed innocent and deserving of rights and others deemed threatening and disposable. The centrality of punishment to the political order means that abolitionists' critiques extend far beyond policing and prisons. As Angela Davis puts it, the abolitionist aim is not just to dismantle prisons but also to build "abolition democracy."[2]

One contribution of this book, then, is to situate prison abolition in the realist political theory tradition. Realism in political theory is an approach to the study of politics that is grounded in the empirical realities of political life.[3] This focus on what is actually happening "on the ground" distinguishes realism from *ideal theory,* which starts from hypothetical circumstances to develop insights about political problems. Ideal theorists might assume that people comply with the law and that people's basic needs are met, for instance, to develop theories about justice that they then adapt to the real world, with its lawbreaking, inequality, and deprivation.[4] Realism's focus on political life further distinguishes it from approaches that privilege *moral and philosophical reasoning.* Kant, for instance, famously wrote that "all politics must bend its knee before the right," thus subordinating politics to morality and reducing political theory to applied moral philosophy.[5] As early as Plato, philosophers have turned away from the political realm to develop the "principles, concepts, ideals, and values" that they think politics should express, or else to define the "conditions in which power can be justly exercised."[6] From this perspective, the task of political theory is either to prescribe what political life should look like, based on what is morally right or philosophically just, or else to consider whether existing arrangements are justified. Realists, in contrast, argue that political theorists should focus on understanding the distinctive features of political life, which include disagreement and contestation, struggles over power, and rule. For realists, the task of political theory is not "to resolve institutional questions, to get politics right, over, and done with" but rather to prepare us for the ongoing challenges of politics and help us navigate them.[7]

Theorizing prison abolition as a realist political project, I challenge understandings of realism as resigned to existing circumstances or pessimistic about the prospect of political transformation.[8] It is true that some self-described realists reject the pursuit of justice, for instance, and argue that stability and order are all we should hope for.[9] In their wish to stay true to empirical political realities and avoid the dangers of well-intentioned but unfeasible utopian schemes, they offer an overly narrow account of the real and the realistic and produce a sense of resignation to the present. But realism need not entail such resignation. "If realism means a commitment to describing what we see," Bonnie Honig and Marc Stears write, "then surely realists must concede that politics includes violence and consensus, agreement and strife, murderousness and reasonableness . . . If we attend to these realities, we may find ourselves inspired to strive for more than modus vivendi. . . . We may seek justice."[10] Honig and Stears name their approach *agonistic realism* and my interpretation of prison abolition builds on their work. My take on realism also resonates with earlier thinkers in the realist tradition who combine a clear-eyed assessment of political realities with aspirations for change.[11] Hobbes is often invoked to warn of the dangers of disorder, but Machiavelli offers a more complicated picture. *The Prince* famously disparages "imagined republics" like the well-ordered city Plato conjures in the *Republic.* Abandoning "what is done for what ought to be done," Machiavelli says, is likely to lead to political ruin.[12] Yet his critique of political moralism does not lead him to abandon hope for political change: He calls for a prince to unite Italy.[13] Marx, too, is a realist: He offers an account of politics grounded in power relations and struggle, rejecting abstract philosophical and moralistic approaches, and he nonetheless imagines and fights for revolutionary change.

Prison abolition, I will show, departs from both abstract normative theorizing and from realist tendencies to underestimate possibilities for positive change. Abolitionists reckon with the empirical realities of punishment and the lived experiences of the people and groups subjected to it. They displace idealized accounts of criminal justice and liberal democracy with stark accounts of racial criminalization and state disinvestment and abandonment. People in race-class subjugated communities often encounter the criminal legal system and the broader political order not as democratic or just but rather as violent, extractive, and largely unaccountable.[14] At the same time, abolitionists affirm the possibility of revolutionary change. In so doing, they challenge what many see as the conservative tendencies of realism and widespread pessimism or despair on the American Left about emancipatory politics.[15] Leading scholar-activists of the movement, such as Angela Davis and Ruth Wilson Gilmore, situate prison abolition in a long history of Black freedom struggles against slavery and other forms of racial oppression. In these iterations, abolition shares its joint attentiveness to, and struggle against, racial oppression with the broader field of African American political thought and especially with the Black Radical Tradition.[16] Both Davis and Gilmore also see struggles against gender oppression as a core part of both the Black Radical Tradition and contemporary prison abolitionism.[17]

A second contribution of *Prison Abolition for Realists* is to theorize differences within realist prison abolition and argue for an approach I call *agonistic abolitionism.* In discussing abolitionist writings that span more than fifty years and two continents, I show abolition itself to be a contested term and site of struggle. Typically, abolitionisms are differentiated by their object of critique. Thus, *prison* abolition targets prisons, *penal* abolition targets state punishment generally, and *carceral* abolition challenges confinement both within the criminal legal system and in other forms such as psychiatric hospitalization, although these categories often overlap in practice.[18] Abolitionist approaches might also be distinguished based on the political ideology that informs them, for instance anarchism, socialism, or liberalism. *Prison Abolition for Realists* uses these approaches but also offers a new way to conceptualize differences in abolitionist thought and practice. I draw on queer theorist Eve Kosofsky Sedgwick and democratic political theorist Bonnie Honig to distinguish between *paranoid, purist,* and *agonistic* modalities of abolition. Paranoia, here, is not a clinical diagnosis.[19] When I describe abolitionist approaches as paranoid I do not mean that they are incorrect, based on false premises, or pathological. Rather, following Sedgwick, I describe paranoid approaches as ones that offer expansive diagnoses of the prison or the carceral, are wary of proposed alternatives, and seek to stave off disappointment. Paranoid thinking and feeling is valuable but insufficient for a democratic abolitionist politics, I argue. It is *valuable* because it reveals the magnitude of the problem at hand and resists easy fixes. Most abolitionist thinkers discussed in the book take issue not simply with jails and prisons but also with the broad structures in which they are embedded, such as the "prison industrial complex" (Davis), the neoliberal "anti-state state" (Ruth Wilson Gilmore), and the "disability gulag" or "institutional-industrial complex" that disappears people with disabilities into nursing homes and other residential institutions (Liat Ben-Moshe). All are, in my view, rightly suspicious of reformism. Paranoid thinking is *insufficient* for an abolitionist politics, however, because its strong critique relies on suspicion and negative affect and cannot generate the hope and courage to create and support concrete alternatives with their inevitable shortcomings and disappointments. Paranoid thinking thus tends to leave us in an impasse.[20] Without a sense of what abolition is *for,* we either end up resigned to the status quo or withdraw from political struggle to pursue change inside the self, what I describe as a *politics of purity.*

In its agonistic modes, in contrast, prison abolition is both a radical critique of prisons *and* sustains work toward a more democratic order. It is both critical and affirmative, committed to both tearing down and building up. Agonism (derived from the Greek word *agōn,* meaning "contest," "struggle," or "gathering") is a kind of realism that sees contestation as a fundamental and permanent feature of democratic politics. It counters idealizations of popular unity, political consensus, and impartial justice and reminds us that every settlement will generate "remainders."[21] It does not follow that agonism values contestation over agreement, subversion over stability. Rather, both are needed, precisely because even the best politics produce remainders to which we are answerable. Politics, as Honig puts it, always "consists of practices of settlement and unsettlement, of disruption and administration, of extraordinary events . . . and mundane maintenances."[22] At their best, democratic actors, institutions, and theories acknowledge this reality and remain open to challenges, indebted to others. The task of political theory, from this perspective, is not to close political debate by providing the correct answer or drafting the right policy, but rather to press for the best advances in justice and equality while committing to the kinds of care or response that follows from finding out their likely implication in violence or injustice.

My hope is that the distinction between paranoid, purist, and agonistic approaches can support and strengthen abolitionism by clarifying its core concepts and approaches and illuminating its internal tensions. Anything less will not simply fail to be persuasive; it may misdirect or thwart transformative political practices that are badly needed now. Though I develop the categories of paranoid, purist, and agonistic abolitionism by discussing specific thinkers—Michel Foucault, Liat Ben-Moshe, and Angela Davis—I do not argue that any of them can or should be reduced to these categories. Rather, I focus on dominant notes in each thinker to make visible a difference in theoretical approach that has considerable practical implications for abolitionist politics. Paranoid and agonistic impulses might well exist side by side in abolitionist theory and practice, and even in the space of a single text. My aim is to alert us to these different impulses to advance both the political theory and practice of prison abolition.

Beyond its analysis of prison abolition, this book affirms a vision of political theory as attuned and responsive to the possibilities and demands of the present, starting with the persistent crisis of racialized mass incarceration. I hope that political theorists may gain further appreciation of prison abolition as a political project and of realism as a useful theoretical lens, including for radicals and revolutionaries. Political theory has been slow to reckon with prison abolition, and most abolitionist scholarship has developed in and across other disciplines.[23] But the main topics of abolitionism—

justice, power, equality, domination, democracy—are political theory's core topics, and one of my interests is in seeing what happens to political theory when the prison is at its center rather than on its margins. This requires unseeing like a state, and theorizing from below, both practices that scholar-activists and social movement actors do so well.[24] To abolitionist practitioners, I hope to offer a theory-informed perspective that rings true to their experiences and that may help navigate the joys and challenges of abolitionist politics. I begin, here, with three reasons to approach prison abolition as a realist political project.

The Realities of Criminal Punishment

Prison abolition is realist because it analyzes punishment as it actually operates. In so doing, it resists the focus on justification that characterizes many philosophical approaches to punishment, as well as the idealizing and moralizing discourses that often attach themselves to popular discussions of criminal justice. There is an extensive scholarly literature, for instance, on whether punishment should properly be understood as retribution for past wrongdoing that affirms responsible personhood (a Kantian position), a means of deterring future wrongdoing both by specific people and by the public at large (a utilitarian or consequentialist argument), a technique to transform the wrongdoer into responsible selfhood (the rehabilitation ideal), a means to reduce or eliminate a person's opportunities to do certain kinds of harm (the incapacitation approach), a way to express societal outrage about the violation of an important norm (an expressivist argument), or some combination of these.[25] Discussions about justification are important. Punishment is a form of state violence that should not be imposed lightly. Prison abolitionists must grapple with the question of whether and when it is acceptable to use force or impose obligations on others. And scholarship on the justification of punishment helps guide the form that punishment will take while also providing grounds for critique. Critics of the death penalty, for instance, often argue that capital punishment does not deter crime, while others defend imprisonment because it effectively incapacitates, and still others critique it because it does not prioritize repair. Brutal prison conditions that seem acceptable as a form of retribution may be unjustifiable to those who believe prisons should promote rehabilitation.

At the same time, debates about whether prisons and punishment are justified take our attention away from important questions of *how* they actually work in practice and *why* they work the way they do. Realists acknowledge that moral considerations play a role in politics, but they caution against overestimating that role or limiting political theory to moral inquiry. Thus, Angela Davis and Michel Foucault both reject the idea that the shift from public torture to imprisonment in the late eighteenth and early nineteenth centuries resulted from increased moral development.[26] More important factors, they argue, were the emergence of rights-based political orders, which allowed punishment to be conceptualized as rights deprivation, and economic needs for a disciplined workforce. Both authors also caution against framing the shift from public torture to prisons as progress. The issue is not that prisons are just as bad as, or even worse than, physical torture. Rather, Foucault and Davis are concerned that progress narratives obscure what is different and new about prison-based punishment. In *Discipline and Punish,* Foucault famously frames this difference as one between sovereign and disciplinary power. Torture, he says, enacts sovereign vengeance on the body of the condemned to terrorize the onlookers; imprisonment combines various disciplinary techniques to transform the criminal's "soul."

The prevalence of thinking that legitimizes or idealizes punishment helps explain why Foucault is such an important thinker for a political theory of abolition. *Discipline and Punish* historicizes punishment and challenges its idealization with a focus on the concrete techniques used in nineteenth- and early to mid-twentieth-century correctional institutions in Western Europe and the northeastern United States. These include continuous surveillance and tight restrictions on bodily movement, activities, and interpersonal contact, facilitated by cellular confinement and a highly regimented organization of time. These techniques are informed by specific forms of knowledge, Foucault shows, most centrally an understanding of punishment as correction or rehabilitation and an understanding of crime and madness as social dangers rooted in individual deviance and abnormality. Though Foucault starts with ideal expressions of disciplinary punishment—the written timetable of a penitentiary, Jeremy Bentham's imagined panopticon, architectural blueprints—he moves from there to the practical functioning of correctional institutions. Ideals of rehabilitation, which cloak state punishment in the mantle of cure, in practice justify permanent suspicion and surveillance of people deemed deviant, resulting in the creation of a marginalized underclass of "delinquents" marked by a criminal record and subjected to repeated incarceration. Ideals of perfect disciplinary order obscure the unpredictability of correctional officers' discretionary power and the corruption, smuggling, and other lawbreaking endemic to correctional institutions.[27] Repeated efforts to reduce high reincarceration rates through prison reform have yielded only marginal results, Foucault observes, implying that it is *unrealistic* to expect the criminal legal system to produce fundamentally different outcomes in the absence of changes that include correctional institutions but also far exceed them.

Contemporary U.S. prison abolitionists have critiqued elements of Foucault's historical account, but they too focus on the concrete functioning and effects of past and present U.S. punishment systems. Davis shows that Foucault misses how punishment and the political order as a whole are thoroughly racialized and gendered.[28] U.S. penitentiaries were originally largely reserved for white male citizens deemed capable of redemption while enslaved people, white women, and other noncitizens were subjected to private violence. At the same time, penitentiaries and punishment were not altogether distinct from slavery. Forced labor, the whip, and political exclusion marked both plantations and prisons.[29] These continuities intensified after the Civil War, when Southern states used racial criminalization and convict leasing to reestablish white domination and control over Black labor. Davis is one of the key theorists of criminalization as a mechanism of anti-Black oppression in the aftermath of racial chattel slavery, a dynamic also theorized by Saidiya Hartman and Michelle Alexander and dramatized in Ava DuVernay's documentary *13th*.[30] All four consider how the wording of the Thirteenth Amendment, which abolished slavery in 1865 "except as punishment for a crime," left room to use the criminal legal system as a mechanism of reenslavement and helped link criminality and Blackness. Black people have consistently been incarcerated at higher rates than whites, and racial disparities deepened in the late twentieth century as carcerality expanded, to the point that by the 1990s almost a third of young Black men were in prison. Indigenous and Latinx people, too, are incarcerated at far higher rates than white people. Meanwhile, women have for years been the fastest growing group behind bars.[31]

The presumed justification for the hyperincarceration of Black, Indigenous, and Latinx people is that these groups commit more crimes, but the reality is more complicated.[32] The "War on Drugs" has been concentrated in poor Black neighborhoods even though Black and white Americans use and sell criminalized drugs at similar rates.[33] Both within and beyond the drug war, people of color are policed, prosecuted, and convicted at higher rates than white people.[34] Meanwhile, long-standing policies of racial segregation and public abandonment have created areas of concentrated disadvantage that increase the likelihood of serious interpersonal violence, including murder.[35] This is one of many instances where racial and class oppression, and state and interpersonal violence, are inseparable. As Marie Gottschalk observes, "it is extremely hard—perhaps impossible—to disentangle the race effects from the class effects in violence because there are virtually no white neighborhoods as poor as the poorest black neighborhoods."[36] The racialization of poverty further means that Black, Indigenous, and Latinx people are much more likely to be affected by laws that "criminalize poverty" and punish survival practices such as sleeping in or otherwise occupying public space.[37] They are also more likely to lack the money to pay for cash bail and to be detained in jail while their criminal cases unfold, which increases pressures to accept a guilty plea, even as a criminal record makes securing a stable income and housing more difficult.[38] Finally, it is widely acknowledged in critical criminology that only a fraction of all lawbreaking is punished by the state, and that marginalized groups are punished most frequently.[39] Given that lawbreaking is found throughout the population while most people in prison are poor and/or non-white, Angela Davis suggests that race and class are greater predictors of state punishment than crime is.[40] Like Foucault, Davis shifts the focus from what the criminal legal system says about itself to its actual past and present functioning and effects, which perpetuate and deepen inequalities of race, class, gender, and sexuality.[41]

Davis's and Foucault's critiques of punishment may give the impression that abolitionists prioritize the fate of the criminalized over that of crime victims, but as feminist abolitionists in particular remind us, the criminal legal system fails victims too. In fact, abolitionists challenge the opposition of victim and aggressor, pointing out that many people who harm others have previously been harmed themselves. Most women who are incarcerated have experienced sexual or intimate partner violence, for instance, and women who are punished for harming or killing their partner often describe the violence as self-defense against abuse.[42] Feminist analyses of sexual and intimate partner violence also disprove the notion that crime is unusual and that criminals are distant others. Rape and sexual assault are staggeringly common, especially for Black and Indigenous women, and in the vast majority of cases, the attacker is someone known to the victim. The domestic sphere, then, is the most dangerous place for women.[43] As feminist theorists have demonstrated, it is also where the criminal legal system is least likely to intervene.[44] Meanwhile, as Iris Marion Young shows, the narrative that women need protection by benevolent "masculine protectors" against the threat of evil men props up the very heteropatriarchal and racialized power relations that make women vulnerable to violence to begin with.[45] Moreover, masculine protectors tend to limit their services to "good" or "innocent" women: those who are cisgendered, straight, white, and middle class. Sex workers, and women who are poor, undocumented, non-white, or queer/trans more often experience police as a threat to their safety and livelihoods than as a source of protection. As the INCITE! and Critical Resistance Statement points out, reliance on police and prisons to keep women safe also takes energy away from community organizing and other grassroots responses to harm and can reinforce women's isolation and sense of powerlessness.[46]

Refusing to accept rampant sexual violence that is at once ignored and compounded by the criminal legal system, abolition feminists have taken action on their own. In the past two decades, grassroots "community accountability" and "transformative justice" initiatives that aim to fight sexual and gender violence without the state have emerged across the country. Activists work together to develop collective responses to harm aligned with both feminist and abolitionist values, seeking to stop abusive behavior and transform the conditions that enabled it without calling the police or sending anyone to prison. At first glance, these efforts might look unrealistic and even dangerous. Individuals lack the authority to impose punishments on or otherwise coerce others, and exercising that power anyway could undermine the rule of law and liberal rights. There is indeed a risk that grassroots efforts may come to wield excessive and unaccountable power over others, without due process but powered by the formidable force of moral righteousness. In the United States, the history of lynching provides a dark example of mob violence, in which white lynch mobs sometimes framed their actions as retributive justice for sexual violations of white women.[47] Even the history of revolutionary and insurgent politics, in which this book argues most contemporary prison abolitionism belongs, contains troubling conceptions of "popular justice": public shaming, kneecapping, summary executions.[48]

We would be wrong, however, to see only the dangers of feminist justice and accountability efforts and ignore their democratic promise. Abolition feminists are right that the lack of a collective response to most sexual and gender violence discredits the criminal legal system and the justice and safety it claims to offer. And as abolitionist legal thinkers have long pointed out, letting state officials and legal professionals monopolize the rendering of justice, narrowly defined as punishment, disempowers and de-skills citizens even if such justice were to be equally applied to all. Laypeople may lack legal training or the authority to punish but they have other skills or could learn them: to acknowledge harm done, work toward repair, and engage in community organizing and activism work to pursue more structural changes. In fact, when it comes to forms of harm that typically happen within existing social relationships, such as sexual violence, people closest to the victim (and perhaps the aggressor) are arguably best positioned to respond. About two-thirds of sexual assault survivors disclose the assault to someone close to them, such as a friend or family member; reporting to police is rare.[49]

The Realities of Liberal Democracy

Prison abolitionists' focus on the empirical realities of punishment entails a realist approach to liberal democracy and the contemporary U.S. state. Both abolitionist and mainstream scholars agree that punishment is not simply a reaction to crime but rather a practice driven by a host of variable factors, including policy- and lawmaking, policing and prosecution practices, and judicial decision-making, which may all be influenced by political rhetoric and media representations of crime and punishment.[50] The massive expansion of the U.S. criminal legal system since the 1980s cannot simply be explained by rising crime rates.[51] Nonetheless, the number of people behind bars grew from about two hundred thousand in the late 1960s to more than 2.4 million people in the early 2000s, making the United States the world's largest jailer, both in absolute numbers and relative to its population size. One in five of the world's prisoners is detained in the United States, a number that was one in four just a few years ago.[52] The impact of the criminal legal system is widely felt, albeit unevenly. One in three Americans has a criminal record, one in thirty-two adults is under correctional supervision (incarcerated, sentenced to community service, or on probation or parole), and one in nineteen African Americans of voting age is disenfranchised.[53] The expansion of punishment has transformed American politics, Gottschalk explains: "It has altered how key governing institutions and public services and benefits operate—everything from elections to schools to public housing."[54] Abolitionist scholars have been among the first to theorize the explosion of punishment as symptomatic of new and profoundly antidemocratic state-building, resulting in a "prison nation" (Beth Richie), "penal democracy" (Joy James), or "anti-state state" (Ruth Wilson Gilmore).[55]

The growth of the criminal legal system, these scholars point out, has gone hand in hand with the shrinking of the state's social welfare and regulatory functions. This neoliberal state-building project has been defended by both major parties as a way to limit government, but it has merely changed what the state does and doesn't do. In the context of powerful anti-state ideology, Gilmore and Gilmore argue, "tough-on-crime" policies bolster state legitimacy by claiming to provide much-needed protection from dangerous criminal elements.[56] Punitive policies thus compensate for the state's abandonment of the poor and its dismantling of labor protections and the broader social safety net, and they also provide an outlet for state capacities that can no longer or only with great difficulty provide social support. Importantly, the contemporary state presents a starkly different face toward different groups. It is laissez-faire toward the wealthy, and authoritarian and punitive toward poor and racialized groups.[57] Prison conditions are often abysmal. Sexual and physical violence, substandard medical care, overcrowding, and extreme isolation are widespread.[58] This Janus-faced state undermines democratic principles in multiple ways: The differential treatment of citizens violates the principle of equal citizenship, and encounters with police have been shown to diminish people's trust in government, their sense of standing, and even their likelihood to vote.[59] State-based felon disenfranchisement laws exclude millions of adults from voting, and criminal records have been used to exclude people from public benefits ranging from food stamps to student loans. For Andrew Dilts and Michelle Alexander, the mass criminalization of people of color upholds an illiberal, white supremacist construction of citizenship.[60] Dilts theorizes this citizenship as a form of standing, marked by the rights to vote and earn, and dependent for its meaning on the disenfranchisement and dispossession of others.

Prison abolitionists condemn the injustice of this punitive order, but they do not treat it as an aberration. That is to say, they do not treat the state as "a momentarily misguided parent who forgot her promise to treat all her children the same way," as Wendy Brown describes the moralistic Left.[61] Rather, abolitionists start from the assumption that the criminal legal system as it actually functions enjoys significant support, at least among key interest groups. The challenge is not how to fix a broken system, but to identify who benefits from the status quo and how to disrupt those interests. This is why abolitionists tend to reject descriptions of the prison system as "failing." Foucault, for instance, declares in a 1976 lecture, "I believe that, paradoxically, far from the prison failing, it has been succeeding pretty well."[62] The prison has not succeeded in its stated mission of reducing crime and correcting criminals, but Foucault suggests it has served other economic and political functions. Imprisonment divides the working classes and maintains social order, while criminalization creates profitable markets in forbidden goods and services. Through the notion of a "prison industrial complex," Davis draws attention to the economic opportunities provided by prisons in the form of jobs and corporate profit.[63] In the contemporary United States, jails and prisons routinely outsource services from phone calls to health care to the private sector, which pushes their cost onto incarcerated people and their loved ones.[64] U.S. Immigration and Customs Enforcement (ICE), meanwhile, relies heavily on for-profit corporations to detain immigrants. The American Civil Liberties Union (ACLU) reports that in 2023 more than 90 percent of people held in ICE detention were housed in private facilities.[65] Some local communities compete for prisons because they promise to generate jobs and tax revenue.[66]

More generally, abolitionists examine the political order from below. They center the coercive arm of the state rather than its electoral or legislative institutions as its central functions, and the viewpoints of the people subject to policing and punishment rather than the officials exercising those powers. In so doing, they challenge the mainstream of both political theory and American politics.[67] While political scientists often lament citizens' lack of political knowledge, abolitionists take seriously the perspectives and analyses of people in race-class subjugated communities, who often describe the U.S. political order as one marked by unfreedom, disempowerment, and injustice, undemocratic features exemplified by overpolicing, underprotection, and mass incarceration.[68] From this perspective, Black freedom dreams were never realized and the United States remains marked by the afterlives of slavery.[69] That the Civil War ended chattel slavery but did not inaugurate freedom is a perspective first offered by formerly enslaved people in the Reconstruction era. As Saidiya Hartman recounts in *Scenes of Subjection,* the supposed liberation of enslaved people in fact was a shift in forms and techniques of bondage, from the direct physical violence of the whip to racial subjection ensured by debt, discipline, and criminalization, supplemented by white terrorism.[70] This reality was obscured in most public discourse but astutely described by formerly enslaved people like Andy McAdams, who observed that though "'they [*sic*] was plenty of land that did not belong to anyone except the government . . . we did not get nothing but hard work, and we were worse off under freedom than we were during slavery, as we did not have a thing—could not write or read.'"[71]

Abolitionists' attentiveness to lived realities of unfreedom grounds their realist approach to the law. They challenge as fanciful the idea that legal declarations of equality can end entrenched inequalities, pointing out that the Civil Rights Act of 1964 did not end deep racial disparities in wealth, health, and life expectancy.[72] They also challenge liberal representations (and justifications) of punishment as an abstract, legal, and lawful process—the suspension or revocation of rights—and insist on its corporeality and violence. Naomi Murakawa, for instance, challenges how liberal legalism, combined with undue faith in proceduralism, works to make state violence unproblematic. "The carceral state," she writes, "exerts extreme coercive power in forcing a person to wear an ankle bracelet, to live in a cell, or to die by lethal injection, but this naked violence is licensed by adherence to rights [and] secured through race-free administrative protocol."[73] The conception of criminal punishment as a rights-based process, in other words, does little to protect punished people from "extreme coercive power," but it does a lot to legitimize that power and obscure its violence. Similarly, legal scholar Colin Dayan has theorized how the punitive suspension of rights creates a condition of "civil death," a legal status that subjects people to subordination, dispossession, degradation, and premature death. "When the state decided to punish criminals psychically without executing them," she writes, describing solitary confinement, "a bold reimagining occurred. Hell came into this world."[74] People subjected to long-term solitary confinement describe the punishment as torturous, a violent destruction of one's capacity to maintain a stable sense of reality.[75] Litigation for better prison conditions has yielded fraught results, abolitionist philosopher Lisa Guenther shows. Supreme Court rulings have banned some practices (such as isolating people in the dark, without clothes, or without access to a flush toilet), but not solitary confinement as such.[76] As a result, the constitutional protection from "cruel and unusual punishment" promised by the Eighth Amendment in practice does not protect against forms of punishment widely considered to constitute torture.[77]

The Real Limitations of Reform

Guenther's lucid assessment of Eighth Amendment litigation exemplifies the third reason why prison abolitionists are realists: They offer sophisticated assessments of the limitations of reform. This contribution is missed by commentators who deride abolitionists for offering "a heaven-on-earth that will never come to pass."[78] True, abolitionists do not share the pessimism that is, for some, a hallmark of realism. They believe that a radically more democratic world is possible and worth striving for, but this does not make them naive about what would be required for such change to occur. Abolitionists start from a reckoning with the empirical realities of the present and the forces that produce it and try to make space for something new and not yet thinkable to emerge. In this way, they break from realism's tendency to be "confirmatory," as Honig and Stears put it. Conventional realism, in their words, "protects us from doubt. It offers a picture of the world that we seem to know, and in the process confirms our status as knowing subjects by reaffirming that picture as true. . . . Its message is that things are as we think they are."[79] Given political realism's debt to Hobbes, the "reality" that these theories present is often that political order is so fundamental and disorder so threatening that it is worth maintaining even at high costs to democracy. Abolitionists are more attuned to and less tolerant of that cost, and more appreciative of how radical politics can benefit from the power of disorientation and uncertainty.

For abolitionists, it is reformers who are naive about the prospect of making the U.S. criminal legal system a humane and effective protector of public safety. As abolitionist organizer and writer Mariame Kaba writes,

> we must reject all talk about policing and the overall criminal punishment system being "broken" or "not working." By rhetorically constructing the criminal punishment system as "broken," reform is reaffirmed and abolition is painted as unrealistic and unworkable. Those of us who maintain that reform is actually impossible within the current context are positioned as unreasonable and

> naïve . . . This is in the service of those who benefit from the current system and works to enforce white supremacy and anti-Blackness.[80]

Kaba here takes the familiar abolitionist—and realist—stance that prioritizes empirical realities and outcomes over stated intentions and goals. The claim that the criminal legal system *malfunctions* (that it is "'broken' or 'not working'"), she shows, is a way to dismiss its actual empirical effects and reaffirm its stated goals.[81] It also keeps us attached to the hope and expectation that better results are possible, that a return to "proper" functioning, ensured by our ongoing investments and efforts to repair, would produce desired outcomes. We might say that representations of the criminal legal system as "broken" foster what Lauren Berlant calls cruel optimism: an attachment to institutions or practices that rarely deliver on their promises and impede human flourishing.[82] As critical race theorist Derrick Bell knows, such regularly disappointed optimism easily gives way to despair.[83] Cruel optimism also makes it difficult to imagine or explore other courses of action, which are marginalized by the framing of the object of attachment (the criminal legal system, civil rights law) as the only reasonable approach. Meanwhile, the possibility that the seeming "malfunction" benefits significant groups is occluded. The consensus that the criminal legal system needs reform obscures a conflict, Kaba suggests, between those who find the status quo attractive or acceptable, a "good enough" approximation of liberal democracy, and those who find in its white supremacy and anti-Black racism cause for refusal and radical change.

If the prospects for reform are dim, how could radical change be realized? The contemporary U.S. prison abolition movement is often accused of moralism. Roger Lancaster, for instance, claims that "'prison abolition' (as opposed to sustained prison reform) is one of a number of slogans that cultivate a strong in-group sense of rightness and morality but hobble the socialist left and render it ineffective."[84] Some contemporary abolitionist projects are indeed moralistic. As Elizabeth Bernstein shows, efforts to abolish commercialized sex, labeled human trafficking and understood as modern-day slavery, have tended to locate the problem in nefarious men and the solution in increased criminal law enforcement, border control, and strengthened families.[85] Missing in this "prostitution abolitionism," Bernstein argues, is a critique of the structural causes that lead many women in the global South into clandestine migration and sex work: the inequalities of global capitalism, national borders, and policing. Many nineteenth-century slavery abolitionisms, too, treated racialized chattel slavery as a moral evil that should be forbidden rather than as an institution sustained by economic, political, and social forces that should be dismantled.

In fact, abolitionism as a realist politics is a *cure* for moralism. Prison abolitionists couple moral condemnation with structural critique of the forces that produce racialized mass incarceration and other forms of captivity.[86] Ruth Wilson Gilmore's *Golden Gulag,* for instance, theorizes the prison boom in late-twentieth-century California as the result of capitalist crises that generated surplus land, workers, and state capacity. Her political-economic analysis calls for collective organizing to (re)direct the social wage toward social well-being, not for the punishment of "evil" lawmakers, prison wardens, or corporations. Similarly, Davis explains that her prison abolitionism does not seek "the isolated dismantling of the facilities we call prisons and jails. That is not the project of abolition. We proposed the notion of a prison industrial complex to reflect the extent to which the prison is deeply structured by economic, social, and political conditions that themselves will also have to be dismantled."[87] Davis's statement reveals the far-reaching transformative goals of her abolitionism, described here as a radical project to eradicate the roots of incarceration. Prison abolitionists thus not only provide lucid critiques of the limits of reformism; they also reinvigorate revolutionary theory and praxis with their determination to "change everything."[88]

Abolitionists' revival of "total critique" is rooted in local, sometimes interconnected, activism and organizing. Some organizations have national visibility, such as the activist group Critical Resistance with branches in Oakland, Los Angeles, Portland, and New York City; the youth organization Black Youth Project 100 with ten chapters across the Midwest, South, and Northeast; or National Bail Out, a Black-led abolitionist collective that coordinates "Mama's Day Bail Outs" to release Black mothers and caregivers held in pretrial detention across the country.[89] Other abolitionist organizing is less visible: initiatives to offer arts and humanities classes to incarcerated people and exhibit their art and writing in community galleries,[90] small-scale efforts to provide books to incarcerated people,[91] campaigns to "ban the box" (inquiries into people's history of arrest and criminal conviction) on college and employment applications,[92] student groups working to divest university endowments from corporations that profit from punishment,[93] and feminist efforts to prevent and respond to sexual violence without involving the police.[94] These efforts are often presented as small steps toward the radical goal of abolition. My local bail fund, for instance, opens its instruction sheet for volunteers with the statement: "So you've volunteered to post bail—thank you for your time and energy! The work is vital to our efforts to abolish the prison industrial complex."[95]

Abolitionists' critique of reform, then, is not simply a critique of incrementalism. It is far more realist than that. Gilmore, for instance, holds on to the possibility of revolutionary breaks with the past, but she resists envisioning such breaks as "single cataclysmic event[s]." "The chronicles of revolutions," she writes, "all show how persistent small changes, and altogether unexpected consolidations, added up enough weight, over time and space, to cause a break with the old order."[96] For Gilmore, revolutionary breaks are accomplished gradually, through small changes that reverberate and coalesce in unpredictable ways and that continue as a process beyond the supposed revolutionary event. The dramatic revolutionary imaginary never adequately described how profound large-scale change happens, Gilmore suggests: We have long devalued the importance and potential of small and partial changes. Gilmore also works with the concept of "nonreformist reform," adapted from French Marxist André Gorz. In the 1960s, Gorz critiqued the French Communist Party for holding on to a belief in revolution through armed insurrection, which Gorz believed was no longer credible in Western Europe. The only way to revolution, he argued, was through gradual and small-scale "non-reformist reforms": demands made in light of what *should be* possible rather than reforms that affirm the basic legitimacy of the existing capitalist system. Nonreformist reforms aim to build workers' power, rather than make capitalist hierarchy more tolerable.[97] Where workers' demands for higher wages are reformist, for instance, the demand for control over working conditions is non-reformist because it challenges the presupposition that the wage relationship entitles employers to control the labor process and prepares workers for new struggles.[98] Gorz grants that nonreformist reforms could be co-opted by capitalism, but he insists that they could also advance socialism by showing what it is *for* and by building the collective power needed to realize its revolutionary politics.

In sum, some of the key thinkers of the movement show that abolition is a political and not just a moral project, that it is politically savvy and pragmatic rather than naive. My theorization of prison abolition as realist counters its misrepresentation and dismissal in both political science and American political discourse at large. As Mariame Kaba noted earlier, such misrepresentations and dismissals do significant political work. They help perpetuate existing policing and punishment practices by affirming the sense that there is no alternative. In political theory, facile dismissals of abolitionism also perpetuate the marginalization of Black and feminist approaches, which are often grounded in lived experiences, attend to intersecting oppressions, and promote activism toward radical change.[99] For Patricia Hill Collins, Black Feminist Thought constitutes a distinct intellectual tradition that has long been suppressed in the discipline, in part by narrow constructions of theorists as professional scholars employed in the academy. Those constructions, Hill Collins notes, exclude activists (from Sojourner Truth to Mariame Kaba) as well as texts published outside of peer-reviewed journals and university presses with great impact on scholar-activist communities (from *This Bridge Called My Back* to *The Color of Violence*). By taking prison abolition seriously as a realist project, this book challenges narrow racialized and gendered conceptions of what political theory looks like.

Toward an Agonistic Abolitionism

Prison abolition is not only realist and political; it is also plural. Abolitionists disagree about how best to analyze prisons and which tactics and strategies are most likely to accomplish their aims. As realists, however, all abolitionists face the challenge of developing theories and practices that advance radical change without succumbing to what Bernard Williams calls "the subversion of the wish": the kind of wishful thinking that becomes an empty optimism.[100] The challenge is felt most acutely by those thinkers and activists for whom abolition is a revolutionary project to "change everything," as Gilmore has titled a recent book, and not "merely" the radical transformation of the criminal legal system that some earlier European abolitionists pursued. How to change everything, knowing that such change will not happen all at once, nor once and for all, nor only for the good? If everything must go, what is there to affirm or fight for? And if abolitionist change is incremental, what distinguishes it from reform?

This book charts a strong tendency to preserve the radicalism of abolition through negative tactics and critiques. Approaches that focus on what is wrong with the present and demand the removal or limitation of imprisonment often seem safe or safer than constructive action and positive demands, which could be co-opted, fail to break fully with the carceral, or turn out to have serious problems of their own. After all, the prison was once a radical challenge to punishment practices centered on torture, and look where those good intentions and ideals got us. An agonistic abolitionism acknowledges the risks of cooptation and disappointment but disputes that negative reforms provide a safe alternative, or any alternative at all. It reminds us that refusing to specify what abolition is *for* carries political risks of its own. Abolitionist opposition to police and prisons could be co-opted by right-wing neoliberal agendas eager to diminish state institutions in favor of private power and control, for instance, as in the case of private security forces.[101] When they are not paired with affirmative visions and experiments, abolitionist critiques can also produce a sense of political impasse and resignation, a claim I develop through my discussion of paranoid critique. In short, an agonistic abolitionism affirms Foucault's dictum that everything is dangerous as well as abolitionists' hopefulness that we can and must do better.

A focus on negative tactics dates back to the "first wave" of prison abolitionism in the 1960s. It marks the work of Thomas Mathiesen, sociology professor and cofounder, in 1968, of the Norwegian anti-prison organization KROM.[102] His book *The Politics of Abolition* offers a highly abstract theory of change informed by a detailed account of the development and activities of KROM, which began as an organization with 164 members led by a board of mostly academics.[103] In Mathiesen's account, the group initially focused on achieving specific prison reforms (more visits, less censorship, more furloughs) through collaboration with prison authorities and gradually took up a more negative and adversarial stance, pursuing political collaboration with prisoners against the wishes of prison authorities and pushing for changes that would reduce imprisonment.[104] Mathiesen narrates this development as a maturation toward a policy of abolition. The group tried to get rid of existing detention practices, prevent the establishment of "alternatives" with the same function as the old forms of detention, and challenge the "ideologies and myths which the punitive system relies on."[105] "KROM developed into a typical 'no-organization,'" he says approvingly. It faced harsh criticism "for being negative and destructive, and for not wanting to advance 'constructive alternatives,'" but for Mathiesen, these were the very characteristics that made it abolitionist. The demand for alternatives is inherently conservative, he says, because "in order to be an 'alternative' . . . a proposed new arrangement must satisfy the same objective as the arrangement you wish to get away from—and if possible, in a more effective way."[106] Abolitionism, in contrast, refuses existing paradigms and seeks to make space for something new and yet unknown, what he calls "the unfinished."[107]

For Mathiesen, negativity and the refusal to propose alternatives are political strengths. They preserve the radicalism of abolition and protect it from cooptation into reformism. He considers nonreformist reforms, theorized by Gorz, but ultimately rejects them because "none of [Gorz's] examples . . . are *guaranteed* against being absorbed by and consolidating the system."[108] The only changes Mathiesen characterizes as abolitionist and endorses without hesitation are what he calls "negative reforms," which "abolish or remove greater or smaller parts on which the system in general is more or less dependent."[109] He is right that nonreformist reforms risk being absorbed into "the system," but are negative reforms immune to such absorption and guaranteed to deliver abolitionist outcomes? Mathiesen's own account suggests otherwise. First of all, KROM found it impossible in practice to demand only negative reforms. The group's program included short-term demands for "positive" reforms such as higher wages for incarcerated workers, Mathiesen recounts, because these demands were popular among prisoners.[110] "KROM must necessarily view it as its task to work for all real improvements for prisoners," he grants, "including those which do not abolish and unmask."[111] Second, abolitionist reforms may indeed "unmask" social problems hidden by the prison, as Mathiesen claims, but such unmasking has uncertain political effects. This uncertainty is revealed in the closure of Norwegian labor camps for people convicted of public drunkenness.[112] The closure, fought for by KROM, did make the broader public more aware of the interrelated problems of alcoholism, poverty, and a lack of stable housing, but it also empowered a conservative backlash committed to removing previously confined people once again from public space. Mathiesen's simultaneous commitment to negative reforms and his awareness of their limitations leaves him in an impasse. Perhaps, he muses, "the most important 'result' of our political struggle will be the extended knowledge we have acquired concerning *the difficulties of remaining unincorporated*."[113] He ends the book by stressing that the future of abolition and revolution is "difficult and uncertain."[114]

From an agonistic perspective, negative reforms are part of abolitionist politics but cannot be all of it. Undeniably, abolitionists must seek to close detention centers, fight for incarcerated people to be released, and resist new prison and jail construction—this is a point on which all the authors discussed in this book agree. In the United States, Critical Resistance (CR) and the California Prison Moratorium Project have helped prevent new prison construction in Delano, California, and activists have campaigned for years to close the notorious Rikers Island Jail in New York City and prevent the construction of new "state of the art" facilities to replace it. In Massachusetts, Families for Justice as Healing and the National Council for Incarcerated and Formerly Incarcerated Women and Girls have introduced a bill to pause all jail and prison construction for five years.[115] Yet negative reforms alone will not do. In the United States, the history of deinstitutionalization, the focus of chapter 2, is perhaps the most compelling reminder of this fact. The massive closure of psychiatric hospitals and other large disability-related institutions of confinement in the middle of the twentieth century was not accompanied by the creation of adequate resources for the formerly institutionalized and other people with disabilities, which left them vulnerable to both houselessness and to other forms of forced confinement, notably in jails and prisons. The presence of houseless people with severe mental illness in public spaces like the New York City subway, meanwhile, is fueling a backlash against deinstitutionalization and calls for a "return to the asylum."[116]

It makes intuitive sense that abolishing something requires making a clean and uncompromising break with it, but that imaginary oversimplifies political realities. Inspired by Foucault's insight that there is no outside to power, agonistic abolitionism orients us toward a different imaginary of change: change wrought through subversion and conspiracy, reclaiming and repurposing, experimentation and revision, rather than through binary choices—to be for or against, inside or out.[117] This is the abolitionism of "nonreformist reforms": one that is no less radical for being incremental, and no less valuable for being ongoing. In fact, it may well be more politically effective than seemingly "purer" approaches. The promise of this kind of messy and drawn-out politics of the ordinary is that it expands the terrain of abolition to sites and practices often dismissed or discounted by abolitionists, such as law, rights claims, and the state, and facilitates coalition-building. This is not a rejection of more strident modes of abolitionism, such as those theorized by the late Joel Olson and Joy James.[118] But this book, at this moment, seeks to valorize an abolitionist politics of the ordinary that draws attention to modes of engaging both with and against institutions.

Chapter Overview

I begin with Michel Foucault, arguably the thinker who has done most to steer abolitionism toward a politics of negation. Unlike Mathiesen, Foucault does not explicitly defend so-called negative reforms, but both his activism and scholarship on prisons rely on discontent and disorientation to generate change without specifying or building alternatives. The activist Prisons Information Group (GIP) Foucault cofounded in 1971 used "intolerance" of prisons as its rallying cry, and Foucault describes both the GIP and *Discipline and Punish* as efforts at "problematization." I draw on Eve Kosofsky Sedgwick to theorize the main facets of Foucault's abolitionism as a form of *paranoid critique.* My claim is not that all of the GIP's efforts or all of Foucault's writings are paranoid in Sedgwick's sense of the term, but rather that paranoid thinking predominates in Foucault's prison-related writings and activism. It is important to illuminate this mode of thinking, I argue, because it informs a distinctive abolitionist politics that has both strengths and weaknesses. On the one hand, Foucault's broad definition of carceral power, practically coextensive with modernity itself, advances abolitionism by expanding the terrain of abolitionist critique far beyond jails and prisons. Moreover, Foucault shows that punishment and other historically contingent operations of power *produce* seemingly natural categories of people, such as criminals, deviants, or the mentally ill, and that this production legitimates surveillance, confinement, and state abandonment. Because power relations are unstable and historically contingent, this state of affairs could at least theoretically be transformed, but Foucault is deeply attuned to the risk that seeming breaks from carcerality are mere repetitions of the same. The difficulty, then, is how to move from this kind of paranoid critique to abolitionist action that is necessarily partial and impure, entangled with the forces it opposes. Reliant solely on the affect of intolerance and on methodological suspicion, paranoid abolitionism risks collapsing into either the resignation often ascribed to traditional realism, which knows that attempting radical change is futile, or else into a *politics of purity* anxious to rid itself fully of what it opposes.

Chapter 2 identifies paranoid abolitionism in the work of critical disability theorist Liat Ben-Moshe. Ben-Moshe's *Decarcerating Disability* (2020) is the first book-length study of deinstitutionalization from an abolitionist and crip perspective. The historical example helps make the case that prison abolition is a *realistic* project because massive decarceration has happened before: In a few decades in the mid-twentieth century, most large residential disability institutions closed their doors. It also shows that abolitionist change must go further than jails and prisons, and do more than close down carceral locales. Ben-Moshe acknowledges the need to build a new society, and she critiques neoliberal austerity for thwarting efforts to provide the formerly institutionalized with affordable housing, health care, and other basic resources. Yet the paranoid style of her abolitionism, I argue, is ill-equipped to support the construction of alternatives because it cannot say what it is *for.* Like Foucault, Ben-Moshe is deeply attuned to carcerality and to the risk that well-intentioned initiatives reproduce troubling power relations. Both authors affirm uncertainty and unknowing as ways forward, rather than offer a positive vision of an abolitionist society. But where Foucault tends toward political resignation, I argue that Ben-Moshe's abolitionism is ultimately pulled toward what I call a *politics of purity.* This approach refuses confinement and institutionalized care under all conditions and seeks to rid the self of "carceral logics." This abolitionism might successfully stave off reformism and liberal co-optation, but I question whether it can energize the collective action needed to defeat the forces that treat disabled and criminalized people alike as disposable.

A democratic politics of abolition must combine critique, questioning, and negation with collective efforts to bring new realities into being. To theorize the practices, affects, and ideas that might allow us to move beyond the impasses of paranoid thinking, chapter 3 turns to Angela Davis. Davis finds in nineteenth-century struggles against racial chattel slavery, and specifically in Radical Reconstruction as theorized by W.E.B. Du Bois, a historical example to articulate what abolitionism is *for.* Building on the example of Reconstruction, Davis theorizes abolition as a collective struggle to ensure full democratic citizenship for Black people and other historically oppressed groups. This requires not merely the conferral of equal rights but also the creation of social, economic, and political institutions to meet people's basic needs for food, shelter, education, and health care and provide mechanisms for participation in collective self-governance. Reconstruction was incomplete to begin with and eventually overthrown, but the example allows Davis to theorize abolition as both a negative and a positive project, a tearing down and a building up, which is an ongoing project and practice. The historical example of deinstitutionalization, in contrast, is ill-suited for articulating a positive vision of abolition due to its essentially negative character. Large institutions were closed, but the creation of new infrastructures of care was undercut by the rise of neoliberalism.

From the perspective of paranoid critique, Davis's vision of democracy looks suspicious. Socialism, schools, and clinics are all potentially carceral. Davis does not argue that such suspicions are baseless. Rather, she takes these concerns seriously, without giving up on a positive account of democratic governance or public goods. Her abolitionism insists on acting in and on the world, with care not only for the common good but also for the inevitable limitations of our tactics and unintended consequences of our actions. She offers what I call an *agonistic abolitionist politics* that affirms elements of paranoid critique but overcomes its tendency toward political resignation or purity. I use Davis's work to illuminate agonistic abolitionism, which is advanced by many abolitionist thinkers and activists, including at times Foucault and Ben-Moshe. Davis's vision of reconstructing the state and the economy in the service of abolition democracy is not supported by all abolitionists, however. It is rejected by anarchist abolitionists who argue that the state is inherently carceral and anti-Black. Both William Anderson and Dean Spade depict abolitionist state-building as a fantasy that is misguided at best, and dangerous at worst, especially for Black people and other groups that have historically been rendered "stateless"—denied the state's protection. I argue that Davis's agonistic abolitionist politics does not idealize the state but is rather at once suspicious and hopeful, both of the state and of its presumed other, the community.

Chapters 4 and 5 apply agonistic abolitionism to current debates. How should abolitionists respond to gender and sexual violence, and what is the role of rights and rights claims in the project, especially when it comes to addressing terrible prison conditions? Readers who are most interested in how an agonistic abolitionist politics might play out "on the ground" are welcome to skip ahead to these chapters. Chapter 4 focuses on the community accountability efforts of Communities Against Rape and Abuse (CARA), a radical feminist organization led by women of color. Through their example, I theorize feminist grassroots justice and accountability efforts as enactments of the kind of citizenship needed in an abolition democracy. At the same time, I draw on Foucault's paranoid critique to identify the limitations and dangers of these initiatives. Because abolition feminists not only generate collective power but also wield significant and potentially punitive power over others, we need institutional forms that both build and preserve this power and limit it. The work of earlier European abolitionist thinkers contains resources for imagining how reconfigured state institutions and civil law might support community-based justice and accountability work.

Chapter 5 considers the role of rights in abolitionist politics. The theorists discussed in this book all regard rights and rights claims with suspicion, but they do not reject them altogether. Foucault made rights claims to advance political struggle, such as the public's "right to know" about prisons and incarcerated people's "right to make demands." Olson, Davis, and Michelle Alexander, meanwhile, all use rights claims to describe what an egalitarian, participatory abolition democracy would be like. I supplement these authors' calls for fundamental human rights—to education, housing, medical care, and other necessities—with emergent rights claims: claims to rights that are not yet recognized as legitimate. Emergent rights claims, I suggest, could democratize freedoms in unexpected ways and help abolitionists move beyond "negative" reforms, which aim to eliminate or diminish prisons without offering detailed alternatives or a path to realize them. The chapter ends with a consideration of a specific emergent rights claim: the right to comfort. This right, I suggest, could ground solidarity with incarcerated people affected by extreme heat in prisons, and it could inspire new visions of abolition democracy.

1

Abolition in a Paranoid Key

Foucault's Problematization of the Prison

I think that at this point, imagining another system is still part of the system.

—Michel Foucault, "Par-delà le bien et le mal"

Paranoia knows some things well and others poorly.

—Eve Kosofsky Sedgwick, "Paranoid Reading and Reparative Reading"

Michel Foucault has long been known as a formidable critic of the prison. Angela Davis has described his *Discipline and Punish: The Birth of the Prison,* first published in 1975, as "arguably the most influential text in contemporary studies of the prison system," and it remains a key reference in critical carceral studies.[1] The book examines the historical transformation of state punishment from public torture to incarceration in the late eighteenth and early nineteenth centuries. For some, this is a story of increased leniency, civilization, and respect for human rights, but Foucault sees something else: the growth of disciplinary power in modern societies. Prisons use isolation, surveillance, and regimented activities including forced labor to transform individuals and manage unruly groups. These "coercive technologies of behaviour," Foucault argues, are found throughout the social body, including in schools, hospitals, and workplaces, which helps explain broad support for prisons and state punishment.[2] Conversely, Foucault's analysis of carcerality implies that resistance to prisons must be part of a broader project of social and political transformation.

Foucault himself engaged in such resistance in the years leading up to the publication of *Discipline and Punish.* From 1971 to 1973, he was a driving force behind the French Prisons Information Group (GIP), a loose activist collective that aimed to "make known the reality" of the prison to the broader public by allowing incarcerated people to "take the floor" [*prendre la parole*].[3] Upon its founding, the group included "magistrates, lawyers, journalists, doctors, and psychologists," as well as intellectuals.[4] Over the course of its short existence, the group illicitly circulated a survey in twenty prisons, published four pamphlets, held press conferences, gave interviews, and organized rallies. By gathering information about and publicizing what incarcerated people and others found "intolerable" about imprisonment, the group aimed to cultivate "active intolerance" of prisons and related institutions and practices. The GIP offered an open-ended list of intolerables: "prisons, the legal system, the hospital system, psychiatric practice, military service, etc."[5]

Several recent books explore Foucault's scholarly and activist engagements with the prison and enlist them for the contemporary prison abolition project. *Active Intolerance: Michel Foucault, the Prisons Information Group, and the Future of Abolition* (2016) is a collection of essays on the GIP, and *Intolerable: Writings from Michel Foucault and the Prisons Information Group (1970–1980)* (2021) makes the GIP's writings available in English.[6] Both treat the GIP's work as both valuable in itself and as a resource that could inspire abolitionist practices today. "What we have sought to do," the editors of *Intolerable* explain, "is to document the GIP's life in a way that introduces this organization . . . and that also provides an entryway for those seeking resources for fostering diverse and genuinely new forms of resistance to penal society."[7] Other contemporary abolitionists take inspiration from Foucault's scholarship rather than his activism. Chloë Taylor's *Foucault, Feminism and Sex Crimes: An Anti-Carceral Analysis* (2019) reads *Discipline and Punish* alongside *History of Sexuality Volume 1* to theorize abolition feminism, and *Decarcerating Disability: Deinstitutionalization and Prison Abolition* by Liat Ben-Moshe draws on Foucault's genealogies to theorize the abolition not just of prisons but also of psychiatric hospitals and other institutions for people with disabilities.

Given his scholarly interest in, and activist opposition to, prisons and other carceral institutions, it makes sense that Foucault is considered a prison abolitionist. Yet there is also something surprising about how Foucault has been claimed for the contemporary abolitionist project. His scholarship certainly offers dark diagnoses of modern carceral power, but it is nearly silent on the histories of anti-carceral resistance. Despite Foucault's extensive knowledge of prison hunger strikes, protests, and uprisings from Toul prison in France to Attica prison in upstate New York, *Discipline and Punish* only notes obliquely that "in recent years, prison revolts have occurred throughout the world."[8] Political theorists have long expressed concern that Foucault's analyses fall short for understanding collective struggles for change. Banu Bargu, for instance, who theorizes the deadly resistance practices of political prisoners during the Turkish Death Fast movement in the early 2000s, suggests that Foucault is too focused on detailing the workings of disciplinary institutions to attend to the ways prisoners and others manage to challenge or subvert their power. "Resistance to discipline exists (even though Foucault leaves us in the dark regarding how it exists) but remains overshadowed by the functional efficiency and effectiveness of disciplinary institutions for social control," Bargu writes. "Ultimately, we are left with a rather *pessimistic* stance on the possibility of change despite the recognition that multifarious acts of resistance are everywhere present."[9] Some theorists turn to Foucault's later work on care of the self for a fuller account of resistance, but as Ella Myers shows, individual efforts at self-transformation cannot undo how prisons and other disciplinary institutions undermine interpersonal relations of solidarity and collective power.[10] Even the activism of the GIP is puzzling: The group never explained what makes prisons intolerable, and it did not articulate a vision of a tolerable society. When Foucault was asked, in the early days of the GIP, to reflect on "the problem created by the existence of prisons," he replied: "Simply put, I perceive the intolerable. The blandness of the soup or the coldness of winter is relatively bearable. But to imprison an individual just because he has a run-in with the legal system, that is not acceptable!"[11]

This chapter argues that Foucault's activist and scholarly critiques of carceral power occupy a more complicated place in the abolitionist tradition than is commonly realized. The issue is not just that Foucault's analyses of prisons fail to reckon adequately with racism, sexism, or capitalism, as Davis and others have observed, or that the contemporary U.S. prison system differs significantly from that of the 1970s.[12] It is also not simply a matter of Foucault's pessimism, diagnosed by Bargu and commonly defined as an "inclination to emphasize adverse aspects, conditions, and possibilities or to expect the worst possible outcome."[13] One could certainly argue that abolitionists take a pessimistic view of the present: They center the people and practices marginalized in both political life and political theory—the warehoused, the disenfranchised, the policed—and are deeply troubled by their plight and its implications for democracy. As I argued in the introduction, abolitionists' attentiveness to the empirical realities of punishment and confinement, and their theorizing "from below," is part of their political realism. Foucault once described his work with the GIP as "trying to see, to reveal, and to transform into a discourse graspable by everyone what can be unbearable for the least favored classes in the current justice system."[14] But why would an abolitionist like Foucault, who tried through activism to generate "intolerance" of most institutions and who argued that there is no power without resistance, be pessimistic about possibilities for change?

I turn to queer theorist and literary scholar Eve Kosofsky Sedgwick's essay on paranoid and reparative reading to answer this question. In its dominant manifestations, Foucault's abolitionism is not just pessimistic; it is paranoid in the sense that Sedgwick uses the term. Sedgwick describes as paranoid theoretical approaches that anticipate oppression everywhere and trust that exposing or revealing it will have transformative effects. Paranoid theories rightly wish to end oppression and might well be correct about its systematic nature—Sedgwick does not use paranoia in the clinical sense that suggests a break from reality—but their suspicion of any proposed alternative tends to undercut rather than foster political mobilization and experimentation. I theorize Foucault's abolitionism as paranoid to suggest that it both illuminates carceral power in unsuspected places *and* generates conceptual and practical problems that have an enduring hold on the abolitionist project. Specifically, I suggest that, for all its illuminative potential, paranoid abolitionism is ill-equipped to foster incremental action toward a more democratic world. Its far-reaching critique and its suspicion of reforms can generate a kind of resignation to the present, or else a politics of purity focused on ridding the self of what it opposes. Meanwhile, its reliance on negative affect—"intolerance" for the GIP and "problematization" for the later Foucault—obscures the importance of more positive affects for democratic politics. Without a sense of hope for a better future, joy and pleasure taken in working together, courage to intervene and experiment, and forgiveness and repair for when our experiments fail, who would take the risk of collective action?[15]

Chapter 2 examines the hold of paranoia on contemporary prison abolition, as well as a possible escape from its demobilizing effects, through the work of Liat Ben-Moshe. I start, here, with Sedgwick's take on paranoid thinking, before reading Foucault's prison scholarship and activism through this lens. My reading is not exhaustive: Both the GIP's activism and Foucault's scholarship also contain reparative moments and impulses, which could be mobilized for a more agonistic abolitionism. I identify such reparative elements at the end of this chapter and later in the book. First and foremost, however, this chapter considers the dominant tenor of Foucault's texts that are most commonly enlisted for abolitionism, starting with *Discipline and Punish*. The concept of paranoid abolitionism helps explain why a radical critique of carceral power might not readily translate into alternative institution-building, and it invites us to consider what practices, affects, and dispositions might support such translation.

Paranoid Critique

Eve Kosofsky Sedgwick's essay "Paranoid Reading and Reparative Reading, or, You're So Paranoid, You Probably Think This Essay Is About You," first published in 1997, is concerned that theoretical projects from queer theory to feminism to literary criticism have come to privilege a single method of critique: exposing hidden oppression.[16] What Paul Ricoeur diagnosed in the 1960s as a "hermeneutics of suspicion" in the work of Marx, Nietzsche, and Freud has come to be seen as the only non-naive way to practice critique, Sedgwick says. She turns to psychoanalyst Melanie Klein and affect theorist Silvan Tomkins to theorize this methodology as "paranoid reading." Her invocation of paranoia is neither a clinical diagnosis nor a rejection. Ours is "a world where no one need be delusional to find evidence of systemic oppression," Sedgwick writes, and paranoid thinking can yield important insights.[17] We should not, however, assume that the only or best way to practice theory or engage in activism is to embark on a "tracing-and-exposure project."[18] Paranoid reading can be practiced not only by academics but also by political activists, Sedgwick suggests: It is a way of analyzing the world that implies specific courses of action and activates specific affects. Thinking and acting from a paranoid position is one possibility among others, including what she calls "reparative" approaches, and it has mixed political effects.

Sedgwick identifies five characteristics of paranoid critical practice. First, paranoia is *anticipatory*. It thinks ahead to what might happen and tries to eliminate "bad surprises."[19] It is a way of thinking that prefers certainty—even the certainty of pending disaster—over uncertainty and the unknown. Second, paranoia is *reflexive and mimetic*. It is so focused on identifying hitherto unsuspected oppression that it can see or describe nothing else. Paranoid critique thus reflects only the injustice it uncovers. Third, paranoia is a *strong theory* that claims to explain many disparate phenomena. Like all theories, a strong theory is selective. It highlights some events or aspects and downplays others. But the ambitious reach of paranoia, Sedgwick suggests, makes it especially vulnerable to circular reasoning, such as claims that "everything can be understood as an aspect of the carceral, therefore the carceral is everywhere."[20] Fourth, paranoia is oriented toward *negative affects.* Its knowingness, suspicion, and anticipation are defensive strategies to protect against the pain of humiliation and disappointment. These protective strategies are self-defeating, Sedgwick suggests, in that they tend to obstruct the pursuit of positive affects such as joy and pleasure. Finally, paranoid thinking places *faith in exposure:* in demystifying, denaturalizing, and otherwise making visible hidden violence. "Paranoia for all its vaunted suspicion acts as though its work would be accomplished if only it could finally, this time, somehow get its story truly known," Sedgwick writes. "That a fully initiated listener could still remain indifferent or inimical, or might have no help to offer, is hardly treated as a possibility."[21]

Paranoid thinking is deeply attuned to the realities and gravity of systemic oppression and determined to overcome them. Yet the vigilance with which it looks out for manifestations of what it opposes, and its singular focus on laying bare painful realities, Sedgwick suggests, limit its ability to pursue effective change. On the one hand, it cannot see what is meaningfully transformative about "reparative" resistance strategies that pursue pleasure or otherwise try to make life more livable. Seen from a paranoid position, such pursuits are insignificant at best and harmful at worst, Band-Aids that help perpetuate wrongs by making them slightly more tolerable, thereby staving off refusal and revolt. On the other hand, paranoia's own strategy of exposing oppression and intensifying pain is often ineffective. "Some exposés, some demystifications, some bearings of witness do have great effectual force (though often of an unanticipated kind)," Sedgwick writes. "Many that are just as true and convincing have none at all, however, and as long as that is so, we must admit that the efficacy and directionality of such acts reside somewhere else than in their relation to knowledge per se."[22] Paranoid thinking, then, both overestimates the power of truth and underestimates the value of "reparative" efforts to make the world less hostile and to support the survival of oppressed groups.

This chapter argues that Sedgwick's notion of paranoia captures important features of Foucault's prison abolitionism. This is a new claim in abolitionist scholarship, but it is gestured to in Sedgwick's text. Sedgwick twice refers to Foucault's archaeologies of knowledge as paranoid works, and one of her main examples of paranoid scholarship, *The Novel and the Police,* draws on *Discipline and Punish* to analyze nineteenth-century novels as technologies of social control. Sedgwick also raises doubt about the usefulness of paranoid critique for challenging U.S. mass incarceration. "Why bother exposing the ruses of power," she asks, "in a country where, at any given moment, 40 percent of young black men are enmeshed in the penal system" and where several states are reinstating chain gangs?[23] Exposing hidden oppression is of limited use, she suggests, when the oppression is overt and widely accepted, even desired.[24] She is right, but there is still a place in abolitionism for exposing hidden oppression. Not all the harms of current carceral systems are so obvious to all, and justifications of imprisonment as "humane" or simply as "common sense" still hold considerable weight. In this context, showing that "rehabilitative" punishment tends to pathologize lawbreaking and mark convicts as permanently suspicious, for instance, or troubling the segregation and confinement of people with disabilities that is justified in the name of "care," can still help build support for abolition.

This chapter takes up a different concern about paranoid abolitionism: the difficulty of moving from paranoid critique to positive or affirmative visions and demands. Foucault and the GIP offer a sweeping critique of carcerality, understood as a pervasive feature of contemporary society. The GIP aimed to generate "intolerance" of this reality, and Foucault's scholarship seeks to "problematize" it. Both are efforts to distance us from the present, but they do little to orient us toward a different future. While the outlawed Maoist party the Proletarian Left (GP) held "popular tribunals" to render "class justice" and idealized revolutionary China, for instance, the GIP and Foucault did not claim to know what justice is. The Proletarian Left was an important force in French prison politics in the early 1970s, and its history is entangled with that of the GIP: Foucault announced the creation of the GIP at a press conference in Paris that marked the end of a monthlong hunger strike by incarcerated Proletarian Left members.[25] At the same time, Foucault and the GIP gradually developed an abolitionist politics that differs significantly from revolutionary Maoism. While the Proletarian Left privileged the plight of political prisoners, Foucault and the GIP found incarceration in all its forms problematic. Compared to the Maoist group, their paranoid politics thus promises to decentralize and multiply the fronts and forms of struggle and hold space for uncertainty in radical politics. At the same time, their approach lacks any account of what a just or democratic society would look like and struggles to offer specific proposals for transformation. This is at once a conceptual and a practical problem for abolitionism, I suggest: If a paranoid critique of prisons or carcerality is not linked to an affirmative project, radical aspirations risk giving way to inaction and resignation.

Foucault's Abolitionism as Paranoid Critique

To demonstrate how Foucault's abolitionism fits with the concept of paranoid critique, I discuss each of the concept's key features in turn and link them to an aspect of Foucault's scholarship on prisons or his activism with the GIP.

A Strong Theory of Carceral Power

Discipline and Punish presents an analysis of carceral power that moves from archival detail—the daily schedule of a French youth reformatory, writings from nineteenth-century prison reformers—to analytic abstraction that can travel far and wide. Its large explanatory reach qualifies it as a "strong theory" in Sedgwick's parlance, one of the five characteristics of paranoid critique. Great reach also means reductiveness, Sedgwick observes, as well as a risk of being "strongly tautological" and "prov[ing] the very same assumptions with which [the analysis] began."[26] Her example of paranoid tautology, "everything can be understood as an aspect of the carceral, therefore the carceral is everywhere," directly speaks to abolitionism.[27] Of course, for Foucault, power *is* everywhere: This is key to his methodological innovation in the early 1970s, when he began to conceptualize power as a network of unstable force relations that traverses all of society, rather than as a possession held or lacked by individuals and groups. This conceptualization broadens the domain of political inquiry far beyond the "centers of power" that are its traditional focus, to include the body, the built environment, and the everyday. It also shifts the focus from individual subjectivity and intent to the impersonal "micro-physics" of power that acts on and through bodies. Questions of legitimacy—is power held or exercised rightly?—give way to questions of efficacy and technique: *How* is power working, and with what effects? Power does not merely "say no," Foucault argues. It does not only prohibit, inhibit, or drive us away from particular actions.[28] Rather, it also encourages, shapes, and incites us.

If power is everywhere, *Discipline and Punish* suggests that carceral power is almost as widespread in modern societies. This was humorously depicted on a sticker I received at a political theory conference, depicting Foucault's head and two text balloons with the words: "That's a prison." "Yup, that too." *Discipline and Punish* begins with technologies of punishment, but these turn out to be extreme cases of broader power relations: Public torture and executions exemplify sovereign power, and prisons exemplify disciplinary power. The latter existed long before the emergence of the modern prison, Foucault suggests: When states were still holding gruesome public executions, disciplinary techniques were already used throughout society.[29] But because prisons exemplify disciplinary power in its most extreme form, they present a kind of ideal type that helps illuminate disciplinary power in other places. For Foucault, the panopticon prison, designed to enable permanent surveillance of prisoners confined in individual cells, is not just a specific form of prison architecture (the dominant one by 1830, he tells us), but also the "diagram of a mechanism of power reduced to its ideal form," "a figure of political technology that may and must be detached from any specific use."[30] Abstracting prisons into technologies of power, he describes the panopticon as "a type of location of bodies in space, of distribution of individuals in relation to one another, of hierarchical organization, of disposition of centres and channels of power, of definition of the instruments and modes of intervention of power, which can be implemented in hospitals, workshops, schools, prisons."[31] These other institutions may stop short of forcibly confining people in cells, but they rely on similar disciplinary techniques to make individuals productive and obedient and contain the unruly potential of multitudes: isolating bodies in space and subjecting them to hierarchical observation, training, examinations, and normalizing judgment, which compares individuals to a group and evaluates them in relation to it.[32]

Prisons are not only similar to other disciplinary institutions; they are also directly linked to them in what Foucault calls a carceral archipelago, continuum, or net.[33] Though prisons were not the first disciplinary institutions, Foucault argues that once they were established, they infiltrated their surroundings and spread disciplinary power outward.[34] The juvenile detention center Mettray, for instance, opened in 1840, detained not only "young delinquents condemned by the courts" but also children sent there by their parents, presumably to be disciplined.[35] It is a mistake to think of prisoners as "outlaws" who have fallen through the cracks of society, Foucault suggests. Rather, people who are imprisoned have often been found delinquent, deviant, or dangerous by a host of disciplinary institutions and agents, ranging from schools to parents and from foster homes to juvenile detention centers. A "great carceral continuum . . . diffused penitentiary techniques into the most innocent disciplines," he writes, "transmitting disciplinary norms into the very heart of the penal system and placing over the slightest illegality, the smallest irregularity, deviation or anomaly, the threat of delinquency."[36] The use of similar techniques in prisons and other spaces, from the surveillance of prisoners confined in cells to the anxious oversight of children's sexuality in the home or the minute tracking of workers' productivity in the factory, connects deviance and noncompliance to criminality.

Foucault's strong theory of carceral power complicates Marxist accounts of punishment and attendant visions of revolutionary change. *Discipline and Punish* challenges Rusche and Kirchheimer's claim in *Punishment and Social Structure* that the state punishes bodies in accordance with economic demands for labor, for instance, and argues that punishment is just one place where power is exercised over bodies to make them both economically productive and politically "subjected," obedient. Power is not simply exercised by the bourgeoisie or the state *over and against* the working class or citizens; rather, Foucault conceives of a network of "micro-powers" that traverses all of society.[37] He rejects not only the binary of power and powerlessness, important to the Marxist dialectic where the oppression and dispossession of the proletariat equips it to seize power, but he also rejects visions of total revolutionary change. "The overthrow [*renversement*] of these 'micro-powers,'" he writes, "does not . . . obey the law of all or nothing; it is not acquired once and for all by a new control of the apparatuses nor by a new functioning or a destruction of the institutions; on the other hand, none of its localized episodes may be inscribed in history except by the effects that it induces on the entire network in which it is caught up."[38] Foucault here describes a vision of change that results from the cumulative effect of dispersed local struggles rather than from formal control of institutions or top-down decisions to change or destroy them. Moreover, struggles can only change power relations, not eradicate them. One may try to abolish prisons, but for Foucault *there is no abolishing power.*[39]

In sum, Foucault's strong theory of carceral power makes it possible to find prisons or prisonlike phenomena almost anywhere. This expansive diagnosis broadens prison abolition far beyond penitentiaries. *Discipline and Punish* concludes with the claim that the "overall political issue around the prison" is "not . . . whether we should have prison or something other than prison."[40] This is too narrow an approach because prisons dramatize troubling power relations and dynamics that exceed them. "At present," Foucault continues, "the problem lies rather in the steep rise in the use of these mechanisms of normalization and the wide-ranging powers which, through the proliferation of new disciplines, they bring with them."[41]

The GIP similarly called for widespread change far exceeding prisons. One of the first public announcements by the GIP, written by Foucault, exhorts: "Let us become people intolerant of prisons, the legal system, the hospital system, psychiatric practice, military service, etc."[42] The "etc." is at once suggestive and elusive. What do the institutions or practices on the list have in common? What would be similar targets of which we should become intolerant? Schools are not mentioned here, though Foucault opens a 1971 conversation with a group of high school students by suggesting that "the organization of, and the discipline in, high schools" might well constitute unbearable forms of repression.[43] Schools are included on the back cover of the GIP's first pamphlet, which reads: "intolerable: / courts / cops / hospitals asylums / school / military service / the press the tv / the state / and above all the prisons."[44] The open-endedness of the GIP's list could be politically mobilizing: It makes room for others to add to it and expand the struggle. In any case, it aligns prison abolition with broad, perhaps revolutionary social change. At the same time, it also makes more acute the question that neither the GIP nor Foucault answered: If the list of intolerables is open-ended, what is prison abolition *for?*

Faith in Exposure

While the expansive, "strong" theory of carcerality makes it difficult to articulate a positive vision of abolition, Foucault and the GIP's reliance on *exposure* makes such a vision seem unnecessary, or at least not up to theorists to provide. The GIP pursued change by soliciting and circulating "information" about prisons, particularly prisoners' knowledge of incarceration. It hoped that this relaying would spark broader intolerance both within and outside of prisons and generate abolitionist experimentation. Foucault's scholarship, meanwhile, exposes the contingent and troubling nature of contemporary punishment practices to his readers so they might undertake efforts at change. As Foucault explained years after the publication of *Discipline and Punish,* genealogical critique attempts to "separate out, from the contingency that has made us what we are, the possibility of no longer being, doing, or thinking what we are, do, or think."[45] Read through the lens of paranoid reading, these examples indicate Foucault and the GIP's "faith in exposure," their belief that good will come from revealing and denaturalizing oppression. By not positing specific alternatives, this paranoid abolitionism avoids the vanguardism of Maoist prison politics. It decenters the intellectual and changes their function: Rather than tell people what to do or whom to be, Foucault argues that intellectuals should try to unsettle "the systems of thought that have become familiar to us, that appear self-evident." They should then "collaborate with practitioners" to change practices as well as modes of thought.[46] Both the GIP and Foucault effectively defer the task of conceiving abolitionist alternatives to others and present their work as facilitating and inciting such conception. As Sedgwick asks, however, why should we assume that "to make something visible as a problem [is], if not a mere hop, skip, and jump away from getting it solved, at least self-evidently a step in that direction?"[47]

The GIP saw confrontation with the day-to-day realities of imprisonment as a way to break through the abstraction and idealization common in thinking about prisons. As Foucault put it in a 1972 interview, "prisons are the real utopias of a society."[48] He did not mean that prisons are ideal places to be: The GIP had already gathered ample evidence of prisoners' suffering, and it would soon publish a pamphlet theorizing prisons as environments that produce suicidality. Rather, the remark suggests that prisons are widely idealized, imagined as spaces of lawful order where criminals are transformed into disciplined citizens, rather than reckoned with as they actually function. As the GIP states in its founding manifesto, the group wants to make "the reality" of prison known. "We want to know who goes there, how and why they go there; what happens; what life is like for the prisoners and, equally, for the supervisory staff; what the buildings, diet, and hygiene are like; how internal regulation, medical supervision, and the workshops function; how one gets out and what it is, in our society, to be one of those who has gotten out."[49] Really knowing "what the prison is," the manifesto implies, means understanding its material reality, connecting the internal functioning of these institutions to broad social patterns (who goes to prison, how and why). This knowledge includes understanding the day-to-day life of correctional officers as well as of formerly incarcerated people. As the manifesto clarifies, the GIP seeks this information "from those who, in whatever capacity, have an experience of prison or a connection with it" because it is not available in "the official reports."[50] Its first action was to create a questionnaire about daily life behind bars that was illicitly distributed in twenty prisons; the GIP published results in a booklet that would be the first of four in a series called Intolerable [*Intolérable*].[51]

The GIP also hoped that exposing the realities of imprisonment would facilitate and incite collective action. The group said it existed to "give the floor" [*donner la parole*] to prisoners, and it depicted itself as a "relay" of prisoners' perspectives, protests, and demands. Commentators from Gayatri Spivak to Cecile Brich have challenged this self-representation of the group, pointing out that the famous male intellectuals and others involved with the GIP amplified prisoners' speech selectively and in accordance with their own priorities and concerns.[52] Indeed, the GIP did not see giving prisoners the floor as an end in itself, but rather as a means of political mobilization. By changing who is authorized to speak on the prison system, centering the perspectives of those for whom prisons are most intolerable, the group aimed to generate broader discontent with, and refusal of, the present. The goal of the questionnaire, Foucault says, was to enable prisoners to "communicate among themselves, transmit their knowledge, and talk from prison to prison, from cell to cell. We want them to speak to the population, and we want the population to speak to them. These experiences, these isolated revolts must become *shared knowledge and coordinated practice.*"[53] Foucault hoped that shared knowledge of the intolerable realities of imprisonment, previously experienced by prisoners in isolation, would enable collective action to change those realities. As Lisa Guenther puts it, the intolerable is "actively declared and affirmed as the potential for becoming more than it is in the present moment."[54]

Where the GIP used techniques of political organizing to make the prison visible as a problem, Foucault's scholarship relies on archival research and genealogical analysis. In a discussion about how *Discipline and Punish* landed with social workers in prisons, Foucault says his "project is precisely to bring it about that they 'no longer know what to do', so that the acts, gestures, discourses which up until then had seemed to go without saying become *problematic, difficult, dangerous.*"[55] The book complicates a progress narrative of history, starting with the assumption that we have progressed from inhumane to humane punishment. Public torture and the penitentiary punish according to fundamentally different logics, Foucault argues, and they cannot be understood or judged by the same standards. Moreover, the power relations involved in imprisonment are more troubling than they seem. Though prisoners' bodies might not be exposed to brutal violence (at least in principle, if not in fact), they are subjected to constant disciplinary power relations that profoundly affect the self. And since prisons exemplify broader patterns in society, all of us are affected by them. The body, Foucault says, is the prison of the soul. Who we are and might be is shaped and curtailed by the constraints and requirements placed on our bodies.[56] Foucault's account of subject formation problematizes not only humanistic and social scientific accounts of "man," but also the political imaginary of liberal democracy founded on the consent of free individuals.[57]

Later in his life, Foucault would describe his scholarship and activism as efforts at problematization. The GIP, he says in a 1980 interview, had been "an initiative of 'problematization,' an effort to make problematic and doubtful the self-evidences, practices, rules, institutions, and habits that had been sedimenting for decades and decades."[58] Problematization is an effort to cast doubt on something hitherto taken for granted. It takes aim at ideas ("self-evidences") but also more generally at the way things are done and organized, from informal habits to codified rules and institutions, and it implies that things could be otherwise. The GIP, Foucault says, sought to defamiliarize the many ideas and practices that together constitute imprisonment and make it seem normal and acceptable, including existing understandings of criminal justice, the law, and punishment.[59] Such unsettlement is needed, Foucault implies, in the context of decades-long "sedimentation." In interviews as well as published writings, Foucault repeatedly presents the prison-based criminal legal system as in stagnation.[60]

In sum, both the GIP and Foucault's scholarship seek to expose the violence of the present that might be acutely known to the most marginalized but that others may overlook or accept. This impulse can be understood, I have been arguing, as the faith in exposure characteristic of paranoid critique. As Sedgwick caustically puts it, this faith assumes that "the one thing lacking for global revolution . . . is people's (that is, other people's) having the painful effects of their oppression, poverty, or deludedness sufficiently exacerbated to make the pain conscious (as if otherwise it wouldn't have been) and intolerable (as if intolerable situations were famous for generating excellent solutions)."[61] She is right that the transition from exposure to action, and from unsettlement to experimentation, is more fraught than Foucault and the GIP make it seem. As one of Foucault's contemporaries put it, "if one talks to social workers in the prisons, one finds that the arrival of Discipline and Punish had an absolutely sterilizing, or rather anaesthetizing effect on them, because they felt your critique had an implacable logic which *left them no possible room for initiative.*"[62] Exposure might incite creative collective action, but it might also leave us in an impasse, especially when we already anticipate how collective action could go wrong.

Anticipating Bad Surprises

For Sedgwick, paranoid critique seeks to anticipate "bad surprises." Its effort to explain many phenomena with a strong theory and expose oppression in unsuspected places is also an effort to anticipate all occurrences of what is being critiqued. Such anticipation obviously applies to the future, but Sedgwick suggests it expands to the past and present, since "paranoia requires that bad news be always already known."[63] Arguably, the anticipation of carceral power is part of all forms of abolitionism discussed in this book. It is part of abolitionists' critique of reforms, which I theorized in the introduction as one feature of their political realism. Abolitionists describe as *unrealistic* the related ideas that the criminal legal system is "broken" and that reforms would "fix" it and lead to fundamentally different outcomes. The persistent divergence between the stated mission of the criminal legal system and its empirical effects is best understood, they argue, not as a regrettable mistake or a technical inability to deliver intended outcomes, but rather as evidence that other powers or interests (a normalizing society, the prison industrial complex, or a broader institutional-industrial complex) hold sway.[64] Insofar as reforms leave these powers and interests intact, abolitionists do not expect them to make a substantive difference. In this sense, abolitionists commonly take up a knowing attitude—rather than one of surprise—and anticipate that reforms will yield more of the same.

Many abolitionists also endorse or help build alternatives, however. Their anticipation of carceral power does not prevent them from experimenting with specific practices to realize change, such as mutual aid efforts and restorative or transformative justice initiatives discussed in chapter 4. Foucault and the GIP, in contrast, did not engage in or advocate institution building and did not articulate a vision of a society without prisons. Foucault sometimes defended the GIP's silence on alternatives by saying that the group's mission was only to give prisoners the floor, not to propose reforms.[65] He also rejected the vision of intellectuals as enlightened authority figures who should tell people what to do, advocating instead for the "specific intellectual" who tries to use the particular context in which they are embedded to enact change.[66] Still, when Foucault did weigh in on efforts to break with the prison system, his approach was typically to anticipate bad surprises: to expose proposed or actual changes as more of the same, or worse. In Foucault's case, then, the anticipation of carceral power often has demobilizing political effects.

A 1971 conversation with six male high school students provides an example of Foucault's suspicion that activist alternatives are more of the same.[67] One of the students invokes the creation of "free universities" in the United States "as alternatives for the institutions under attack."[68] Free universities emerged in the mid-1960s and early 1970s from political activism by Students for a Democratic Society (SDS) and other groups.[69] They offered free or low-cost classes to the public, outside of the credentialing system of traditional higher education institutions, often on topics related to contemporary political struggles. Foucault responds dismissively: "If you want to replace an official institution with another one that fulfills the same functions, only differently and better, you've already been recaptured by the dominant structure."[70] The remark makes sense: The student invokes the creation of parallel institutions that would *double* [*doubler*] already existing ones. That formulation implies that the changes repeat what already exists, which seems limited compared to an initiative that would inaugurate something radically new and different. Yet the contrast between ideas and proposals that repeat "the dominant structure" (to which Foucault ascribes a tendency to recapture [*reprendre*] would-be radicals) and those that would break with it is also too neat. Do educational initiatives such as free universities really pursue "the same functions" as U.S. public schools? To the extent that community organizations replicate features of dominant institutions (e.g., a curriculum, or distinctive roles for teachers and students), could the experience of organizing or participating in them not have transformative political effects? And do existing universities and other institutions not have some elements worth preserving?

In a 1972 conversation with two leaders of the Proletarian Left, Foucault turns his suspicion to the group's vision of revolutionary change. The lengthy discussion published in English as "On Popular Justice: A Discussion with Maoists" reveals differing conceptions of revolutionary change, especially in the domain of justice.[71] Foucault's interlocutors advocate "popular tribunals" to realize "popular justice" in an orderly and disciplined way. For "Victor" (a pseudonym for Benny Lévy, leader of the Proletarian Left), the Chinese Red Army is a model of revolutionary justice: It is a state apparatus, a dictatorship of the proletariat, that manages the transition to Communism by wielding military and judicial power against class enemies for the benefit of the masses. Foucault, in contrast, argues that popular tribunals, as revolutionary as they seem, in fact reproduce ideas and dynamics of existing, "bourgeois" legal systems. They are part of a state apparatus, he says, that can be wielded as a tool of class domination. Historically, the criminal legal system has maintained class oppression by dividing the working class and turning the majority against an isolated group of criminals who are stigmatized as dangerous.[72] Tribunals also presuppose that justice is rendered through an authoritative judgment by neutral judges whose verdict is not predetermined but reached by applying a universal notion of justice to a particular case.[73] All this runs counter to popular justice, he says, in which there is no neutral third party, the masses refer to their own experience of oppression, and carry out their decision directly.[74]

In paranoid fashion, Foucault exposes and anticipates that what seems revolutionary, whether existing or proposed practices and regimes, in fact reproduces the present. Though in this conversation, Foucault invokes a vision of popular justice that is direct, partisan, and unmediated, this is more meaningful as a critique of the Maoists' revolutionary vision than as an affirmative vision of its own. Neither Foucault nor the GIP ever laid out a sustained vision of justice, popular or otherwise, but Foucault did repeatedly affirm the wish for a radical break with the present. The revolution, Foucault tells the Maoists leaders, "must necessarily involve the *radical elimination* of the judicial system, and anything which could reintroduce [*rappeler*] the penal system, anything which could reintroduce its ideology and enable this ideology to surreptitiously creep back into popular practices, must be banished."[75] Elsewhere, he critiques the Soviet Union for failing to break with the past. "Seemingly new institutions were actually conceived based on elements from the old system," he says. "The Red Army was modeled on the army of the Tsar, the Soviet Union returned to realism in art, to traditional family values: it fell back into norms of 19th-century bourgeois society."[76]

Over the years, Foucault cast doubt not only on revolutionary Marxism but also on prison reform and abolition. In a 1976 lecture delivered at a conference on prisoner rights, Foucault worries that proposed "alternative" methods of punishment inadvertently repeat characteristics of the prison and extend social control.[77] In the lecture, Foucault considers "alternatives" ranging from "model prisons" in Scandinavia to fines and community service. In all these cases, Foucault worries that so-called alternatives actually fulfill the same function as prisons. He repeats the argument from *Discipline and Punish* that prisons' apparent failure to rehabilitate should be understood as the successful production of "delinquency." Prisons create among the poor a population of repeat offenders who cycle in and out of jail for petty crimes.[78] These delinquents are useful to elites, Foucault argues: Their marginalization prevents broader popular uprisings against the political and economic order, while their punishment helps shore up legal prohibitions (of drugs, commercialized sex) that generate bribes and other profit as well as jobs and police and state legitimacy. Ultimately, Foucault suggests, prisons function not so much to fight crime as to *distribute illegalities:* marginalized "delinquents" get punished for relatively minor offenses while elites benefit from criminalization or from participating in white-collar crime. This effect can be accomplished by harsh prisons or comfortable ones, and by imprisonment as well as by alternative sanctions.

Foucault argues that seeming alternatives replicate not only the prison's function but also its assumptions and techniques. In line with his strong theory of carceral power, he takes these to include the belief that work, repentance, and "family" correct criminality.[79] It follows that for Foucault, "alternative" prisons that feature well-paid, interesting prison labor, "prisoner councils" and other mechanisms that give incarcerated people some control over their confinement, and increased contact between incarcerated people and their loved ones—measures that are unthinkable in the contemporary United States—aren't meaningfully different. He sees in prisoner councils not a departure from authoritarian control or an experiment in collective decision-making, but only an attempt to have prisoners accept their punishment and repent.[80] "Today it is not the cell but the decision-making council which is assigned the same objective, that is, of self-punishment as the principle of correction," he writes.[81] Foucault is no more impressed by responses to crime that don't involve confinement. Sanctions such as probation maintain confinement as a threat, perhaps for years on end; court-mandated community service is still forced labor with corrective intent; fines indirectly require people to work; and suspending the right to drive or restricting one's freedom of movement are "other forms of immobilizing" people.[82] Worst of all, these prisonlike practices take place in society and thereby spread carceral power "as a cancerous growth beyond the prison walls."[83]

Foucault's skepticism extends beyond prison reform to the abolitionism of Dutch law professor Louk Hulsman. Unlike Foucault's strong theory of carceral power, Hulsman focuses abolition narrowly on criminal legal processes and punitive confinement. He wants to expand the model of civil law in which individuals or groups encounter each other directly, instead of criminal proceedings in which prosecutors work on behalf of victims and in the name of the people. The juridical notion of "crime," he argues, should be replaced with the more fluid notion of "problematic situation" to give the various parties involved more freedom to define how they understand and wish to resolve the harms and wrongs at hand. The state should play only a facilitating role in the resolution of such situations. When an interviewer describes Hulsman's abolitionism, Foucault says he finds it "very exciting" and important that Hulsman simultaneously reconsiders the foundation of the state's right to punish and the technical means of responding to infractions.[84] But Foucault also reiterates his concerns about carceral continuities, though he admits that he may not be sufficiently informed about Hulsman's work. "Will the notion of problematic situation lead to a psychologization both of the issue at hand and of the response?" he asks. Will there be a "hyperpsychologization" that would constitute the criminal as an "object of psychiatric or medical interventions with therapeutic aims"? Like in the 1976 lecture, Foucault worries that abolition could replicate and spread the prison's tendency to depict offenders as dangerous types in need of cure. As prosecutors, lawyers, psychiatrists, and other experts of the soul lose their privileged position from which to judge problematic behavior and recommend responses, laypeople may follow in their footsteps, potentially in greater numbers and perhaps relying on some of the same psychological discourses and assumptions. In short, Foucault anticipates that efforts to break with the criminal pathologization of people who commit harm may not be successful.

Foucault's anticipation that would-be challenges to the prison actually reproduce carcerality goes back to his analysis of prison reform in *Discipline and Punish.* "Prison 'reform' is virtually contemporary with the prison itself," he writes: "It constitutes, as it were, its programme. From the outset, the prison was caught up in a series of accompanying mechanisms, whose purpose was apparently to correct it, but which seem to form *part of its very functioning*, so closely have they been bound up with its existence throughout its long history."[85] Accompanying mechanisms mentioned by Foucault include inquiries, laws, and policies, as well as reformist organizations such as the French Society for the Improvement of Prisons founded in 1818 and philanthropic groups.[86] Contemporary North American prison abolitionists cite this analysis of reform to depict Foucault as an abolitionist. Chloë Taylor, for instance, asserts that *Discipline and Punish* takes "an abolitionist stance" when it depicts reform efforts as integral to the prison because this implies that a more fundamental challenge to prisons is needed.[87] As we have seen, Foucault indeed repeatedly suggests that existing efforts to challenge prisons fall short. But what, if anything, would pass muster? Are all efforts to "resocialize" someone "carceral"? What about efforts to get someone to take responsibility for their actions? As chapter 4 discusses, both restorative and transformative justice aim, among other things, to change behavior that causes harm. For transformative justice advocates in particular, the pursuit of responsibility or accountability often involves processes of self-transformation.[88] Community members, potentially including friends and family of the aggressor, are often seen as better equipped to enact such change than the state.[89] Is this merely another iteration of the carceral belief that "family" can play a corrective role?

In a 1984 interview, Foucault grants that efforts to transform the penal system need not abandon *all* assumptions [*postulats de pensée*] that undergird criminal punishment.[90] The claim makes sense, but it remains thin. Foucault stops short of affirming a concrete effort or initiative, and without such affirmation, we are left to anticipate the reappearance of carceral power in new guises. As I will now suggest, we can read this absence of affirmation, with Sedgwick, as an example of the "reflexive and mimetic" nature of paranoid thinking.

Reflexive and Mimetic

Sedgwick's analysis of paranoid thinking helps explain one of the most puzzling features of Foucault's scholarship on prisons: his near silence on past and present prison resistance. *Discipline and Punish* contains a vague reference to "recent uprisings" but does not discuss specific events or theorize resistance tactics or their significance. This absence is especially striking when compared to contemporary abolitionist scholarship, which typically seeks to demonstrate that prisons are already being resisted, and abolitionist alternatives built, here and now. Almost all abolitionist scholarship discusses contemporary examples, ranging from violence intervention and prevention work to campaigns to close jails or prisons or prevent the construction of new facilities. Similarly, Hulsman wrote about his family's improvised, restorative response to repeated burglaries of their house to illustrate the potential of already existing communal conflict resolution practices over the inflexible, bureaucratic criminal legal system.[91] Other abolitionist scholars excavate historical examples of abolitionist thinking and activism, such as the 1974 "August Rebellion," an uprising by women incarcerated at Bedford Hills prison in New York, or the 1970s campaign to oppose the creation of a wing for "violent women" at Worcester State Hospital in Massachusetts and the broader "prison/psychiatric state" that both punishes and pathologizes dissent.[92]

Foucault's scholarly silence on prison resistance is striking also because he was so knowledgeable on the topic. The GIP was created after successive hunger strikes by incarcerated Maoists, and the group amplified and commented on several prison protests and revolts, which ranged from work stoppages and hunger strikes to violent prison takeovers.[93] The GIP also dedicated a pamphlet to the revolutionary politics of George Jackson, who was killed in San Quentin prison in the fall of 1971. The assassination, as the GIP named it, helped spark the historic uprising at Attica Prison that would be brutally repressed. Foucault visited Attica the following year and commented that "the only way for prisoners to escape" from the dehumanization and domination of the prison is through "collective action, political organization, rebellion."[94] Yet *Discipline and Punish* may well leave readers with the mistaken impression that actually existing prisons are places of perfect disciplinary order and obedience. Foucault spends so much time discussing the aspirations and justifications for disciplinary institutions—dreams of perfect surveillance that would produce self-surveilling subjects, of orderly labor that would instill habits of discipline, and of indeterminate sentences that would reward rehabilitation—that the book's discussion of how prisons actually preserve and deepen inequality comes as a surprise. And though *Discipline and Punish* argues that prisons produce delinquency and distribute illegalities, it does not consider the many ways prisoners resist their treatment.

Foucault's silence on prisoners' resistance explains why scholars have found his work insufficient for theorizing prison protests. For Allen Feldman, Foucault's account of disciplinary power misses how objectification, violence, and abjection can all be appropriated and returned against the carceral institutions that inflict them. That is what happened during the prison struggles that were part of The Troubles in Northern Ireland, Feldman says, especially during the Dirty Protest, in which incarcerated Irish paramilitaries dirtied their cells with feces and refused to wash in an extended struggle for political prisoner status.[95] Feldman supplements Foucault's account of disciplinary power with an analysis of "self-bifurcation," a splitting of the self that enables body instrumentalization, to explain how prisons inadvertently foster prisoners' ability to resist and subvert carceral control.[96] Similarly, Banu Bargu goes beyond Foucault to account for the self-destructive tactics of political prisoners and their supporters during the Turkish Death Fast movement. Protesters resorted to self-immolation, self-starvation, and suicide bombing in a protracted effort to stop the introduction of U.S.-style supermax prisons. Bargu theorizes the concepts of "necroresistance" and "biosovereignty" to explain these actions: Prisoners did not only self-bifurcate; they also claimed the sovereign right over life and death and resisted the state's biopolitical mandate to "make live." Similarly, abolitionist critical disability theorist Liat Ben-Moshe, whose work is the focus of the next chapter, seeks to expand Foucauldian analysis from "instruments of power to the topography of their resistance."[97] Feldman, Bargu, and Ben-Moshe all develop ways to overcome the limitations of Foucault's account of prisons. But what explains those limitations?

Sedgwick's account of paranoid reading offers a compelling explanation. Paranoid critique, she argues, tends to be so focused on exposing and anticipating instances of what it critiques that it overlooks variation and counter-evidence. This is what she describes as the reflexive and mimetic nature of paranoid thinking: It reproduces in its own writing the omnipresence of its target. From this perspective, Foucault's wish to alert his readers to disciplinary power prevents him from attending to its actual limitations and its availability for appropriation, redirection, and subversion. Foucault affirms these features in the abstract, when asserting that power relations are unstable and carry "risks of conflict, of struggles, and of an at least temporary inversion," but they are missing from his empirical analysis.[98] For paranoid thinking, Sedgwick says, the priority is making sure that the object of critique "at least never arrive on any conceptual scene *as a surprise*."[99] Paradoxically, hypervigilance against carceral power can make us less prepared to recognize, or contribute to, abolitionist possibilities. This observation points us to the final characteristic of paranoid thinking discussed by Sedgwick: its narrow reliance on negative affect.

Paranoia's Negative Affects

For Sedgwick, the suspicion that is so characteristic of paranoid thinking is a defensive strategy to protect ourselves from humiliation and other painful feelings. In this sense, paranoid thinking could be understood as one possible response to the many disappointments of revolutionary politics in the late twentieth century. As Foucault observed in a 1983 interview, "I belong to a generation of people who witnessed the collapse, one after another, of most of the utopias that had been constructed in the nineteenth and at the beginning of the twentieth century, and who also saw the perverse and sometimes disastrous results that could ensue from projects that were extremely generous in their intentions."[100] Some disappointments were recent and personal: Foucault had closely followed the beginning of the Iranian Revolution in 1979, and his hope and excitement for the revolution were dashed when the newly established Islamic Republic violently suppressed dissent.[101] Other events and revelations had steadily undercut Marxist utopias, including Solzhenitsyn's account of the gulag system in the Soviet Union, the disaster of the Chinese Cultural Revolution, and the Soviet Union's invasion of Prague. In the context of utopian collapse, paranoid thinking offers a way to maintain a radical critique of the present and affirm the general possibility of a different world without risking the pain of seeing specific proposals or visions fail.[102] The downside of paranoia's pain avoidance, for Sedgwick, is that it blocks the pursuit of positive affects such as pleasure and joy as it continually surfaces painful truths.

Sedgwick's analysis helps explain why negative affect is so central to the abolitionism of Foucault and the GIP. Under the heading of problematization and active intolerance, both expose hidden or disavowed oppression to provoke or intensify estrangement from, discontent with, and refusal of existing practices, institutions, and discourses. Abolitionist political theorist Andrew Dilts approvingly theorizes the GIP's active intolerance as "abolitionist killjoying."[103] Dilts draws on Sara Ahmed's account of the feminist killjoy who, by refusing to follow gendered conventions and exposing their heterosexism, comes to be seen as a troublemaker who spoils "good times."[104] The feminist killjoy is a negative stereotype, but Ahmed suggests it contains a truth that feminists should embrace: exposing and refusing oppression does cause bad feelings. For Dilts, "becoming an abolitionist killjoy" similarly means "getting in the way of carceral enjoyments," by which he means both material and affective investments in prisons, especially those held by nonincarcerated people.[105] Abolitionist killjoys obstruct not just law-and-order politics but also "the carceral enjoyment of 'prison reform,' taking up the affective labor of naming the prison as a problem that goes far deeper than we might wish to acknowledge. At a minimum, becoming an abolitionist killjoy means insisting on the presence of incarcerated and formerly incarcerated persons around the 'table.'"[106] The abolitionism of the GIP is unmistakable in Dilts's account of the abolitionist killjoy. His emphasis on making the prison visible as a problem, foregrounding the perspectives of (formerly) incarcerated people, and spreading intolerance all resonate with the group's approach.

While negative affects are theorized and affirmed in the GIP and Foucault's abolitionism, positive affects largely go missing from their engagements with the prison. Their approaches may well involve pleasures, such as the joy of forging new friendships through activism with the GIP or the thrill of gaining a new perspective on the present through genealogical analysis, but those are not the affects or experiences they highlight.[107] Similarly, Dilts describes killing joy as a necessary but insufficient part of prison abolition, but he stops short of attending to other abolitionist affects in depth.[108] This narrow focus on intolerance, unsettlement, and disruption resonates with Sedgwick's analysis of paranoid critique, which, she says, tends to oversimplify the affects involved in change. "A disturbingly large amount of theory seems explicitly to undertake the proliferation of only one affect, or maybe two, of whatever kind," she writes.[109] Because negative affects predominate in Foucault and the GIP's abolitionism, there is little room for the positive affects needed to inspire or sustain political action. Lisa Guenther, for instance, argues that Foucault, at the time of the GIP, did not fully appreciate the importance of prisoners' demands for what she calls "creaturely comforts": "little things" like access to transistor radios or more TV channels, flush toilets, art supplies, wall calendars, or sweatpants.[110] Guenther affirms the importance of creaturely comforts not only for prisoners but also for those resisting incarceration on the outside. "In order to participate effectively in radical political struggles for decarceration, activists must not only work hard, but also open ourselves to the creaturely enjoyment of struggle and solidarity," she writes.[111] Paranoid thinking, however, makes it very difficult to pursue joy or to risk positive demands.

Paranoid and Reparative Thinking

For Sedgwick, paranoid thinking is at once valuable and limited, knowing "some things well and others poorly."[112] Similarly, what I have theorized as Foucault's and the GIP's paranoid abolitionism is a political approach with strengths and weaknesses. Its expansive diagnosis of carceral power broadens the potential sites and agents of abolitionist practice and calls for far-reaching change. Its suspicion of both reformist and abolitionist efforts challenges the simplifications of romantic and moralistic accounts of politics, as it acknowledges that neither good intentions, nor moral righteousness, nor firsthand knowledge of oppression can guarantee the success of political actions. These features are valuable for realist abolitionist politics, including the agonistic realism I theorize in chapter 3.[113] At the same time, they make it difficult to envision and support concrete alternatives. Cultivating intolerance and provoking unsettlement might make us want to break with carcerality, but paranoia's suspicious and risk-averse nature makes it difficult to translate such a desire into an affirmative politics.

Not all aspects of the GIP and Foucault fit Sedgwick's account of paranoia, however. As Sedgwick observes, thinkers and projects that feature paranoid thinking also often contain reparative impulses. Where paranoid thinking seeks to anticipate what could happen and is wedded to certainty, reparative thinking is more open to surprise, uncertainty, and therefore hope.[114] Both approaches are realistic and geared toward survival, Sedgwick says, but "the reparative reading position undertakes a different range of affects, ambitions, and risks."[115] Specifically, it pursues pleasure and joy. Where Sedgwick invokes Foucault's *Discipline and Punish* and his earlier *Archaeology of Knowledge* as examples of paranoid reading, she invokes Foucault's later work on care of the self to describe the reparative "concern to provide the self with pleasure and nourishment in an environment that is perceived as not particularly offering them."[116]

Rarely taken up by abolitionists, Foucault's second and third volumes of *The History of Sexuality* theorize ancient Greek and Roman practices of ethical self-making in relation to sexual appetites and other bodily pleasures. These ethical practices did not necessarily aim to provide the self with pleasure—they often included the cultivation of one's ability to *resist* pleasures and maintain self-mastery—but they were intentional efforts to change the self in a desired direction. Notably, Foucault does not treat them with suspicion or anticipate their failure or complicity with oppression, which is how he theorizes the sexual liberation movement in *The History of Sexuality Volume 1*. Instead, he theorizes the basic structure of projects of ethical self-transformation, which his readers have applied to other contexts.[117] Foucault's late writings on "political spirituality" and "counter-conduct" similarly describe practices of self-transformation that open up new possibilities and may amount to freedom.[118] And when we read some of Foucault's remarks about prisons as humorous, they do not seem so negative or suspicious. His remark, for instance, that "the blandness of the soup or the coldness of winter is relatively bearable. But to imprison an individual just because he has a run-in with the legal system, that is not acceptable!" could be a joyful way to own an idea that others will likely see as absurd.

The GIP too contains reparative moments and impulses. The group's desire to serve as a "relay" led it to value building relationships within, across, and outside prison walls. The GIP's "intolerance survey," for instance, was meant to help prisoners "communicate among themselves, transmit their knowledge, and talk from prison to prison, from cell to cell" while also opening up a dialogue with the general public.[119] Distributing the questionnaire to people in prison was illegal, and the process of getting it to circulate already generated new connections both on the inside and the outside. In a 1971 interview, Foucault and GIP cofounder Pierre Vidal-Naquet describe going to the same prison each Saturday to distribute the GIP's questionnaire to people standing in line to visit incarcerated loved ones. Initially, they get a cold welcome, but a few weeks in, a woman responds by angrily proclaiming her frustrations with the prison system. The following week, Foucault and Vidal-Naquet say, when they got to the prison, people were already talking to each other about the questionnaire and "the scandal of prisons."[120] The anecdote could be read as an example of the GIP's paranoid faith in exposure, the belief that confronting people with evidence of violence and oppression foments oppositional political action, against "the scandal of prisons" and for an unspecified alternative. But we could also see in it a reparative appreciation for solidarity or friendship, a sense that coming to a shared understanding is valuable and significant.

More generally, the GIP moved beyond paranoid suspicion and critique by affirming the many prison protests and revolts that erupted during its existence. The protests were often accompanied by lists of demands that the GIP helped publicize and that do not only oppose the existing prison system but also articulate alternative visions of human needs and rights. These demands include changes to the criminal legal system, such as ending life sentences, abolishing criminal records, and entitling incarcerated workers to earn minimum wage, social security, pensions, and paid holidays.[121] They also include demands for better food, showers, a radio in each cell, and "cinema for everyone."[122] The protests, in other words, challenge the rights deprivation of punishment but also take the risk of claiming specific rights. In affirming the protesters' demands, the GIP moved beyond paranoid suspicion, which might judge these demands to be insufficiently radical and anticipate their co-optation, and embraced a reparative pursuit of what Lisa Guenther calls "creaturely comforts." I return to these demands in the final chapter, where I argue that claiming a *right to comfort* could advance an agonistic abolitionist politics. This strange right, I suggest, could at once unsettle the common sense that prisoners deserve to suffer and gesture toward a different vision of democratic citizenship.

In its dominant modes, however, the abolitionism of Foucault and the GIP offers a paranoid critique of carcerality without offering a vision of what abolitionist politics is for. This approach breaks with vanguardism and avoids co-optation, but I suggest it does not readily translate into effective collective action to challenge the carceral state and build a more robust democracy. Specifically, the suspicion and anticipation of paranoid critique can make constructive political action seem like a risk not worth taking, or it can inspire a politics of purity defined by avoiding what it opposes. The latter possibility is discussed in the next chapter, which theorizes the abolitionist politics of critical disability scholar-activist Liat Ben-Moshe. Ben-Moshe theorizes deinstitutionalization—the mass closure of psychiatric hospitals and other residential disability-related institutions—as an abolitionist event. I suggest she both practices paranoid critique and provides a partial answer to a question prompted but not addressed by Sedgwick's analysis: How might we be motivated to let go of paranoid thinking and embrace more affirmative modes of abolitionist politics?

2

The Pull of Purity

Liat Ben-Moshe on Deinstitutionalization and Abolition

> Many no longer resided in institutional settings, but were they free?
>
> —Liat Ben-Moshe, *Decarcerating Disability*

> Given our previous experience with deinstitutionalization, there is no reason to believe that it will be possible to reduce prison populations without getting our hands dirty.
>
> —Bernard Harcourt, "Reducing Mass Incarceration"

In many ways, contemporary U.S. mass incarceration is exceptional. The number of people in American jails and prisons was relatively stable for decades until in the 1970s it began a period of exponential growth. By 2009, prison populations had grown sevenfold (Figure 1), and the U.S. had become the world's largest jailer, far ahead of authoritarian countries like Russia and China as well as liberal democracies like Canada and France.[1] As the U.S. prison system grew, it came to hold more and more people of color. Black people in this country have been confined in jails and prisons at higher rates than whites since the Civil War, but racial disparities intensified in the late twentieth century to the point that by 1995 one in three Black men in their twenties was in jail or prison, on parole, or on probation.[2] The exceptionally punitive nature of the U.S. state helps explain why prison abolitionist thinking and organizing experienced a resurgence in the final decade of the twentieth century. Prison abolition had been advocated before, in the context of the radical freedom struggles of the 1960s and early 1970s, but it had waned in the following decades, which were dominated by neoliberal economic policies, the "war on drugs," and ever harsher "tough-on-crime" policies.[3] The extreme impact of mass incarceration on Black, Latinx, and Indigenous people, meanwhile, helps explain the centrality of race and racism to most contemporary abolitionist thinking. People of color have led the movement, and women, queer, and trans* people of color have brought to light how in contemporary punishment, racism intersects with heterosexism and anti-transness.[4]

Seen from another perspective, however, mass incarceration is not so new. When we broaden our understanding of incarceration beyond jails and prisons to include other sites of confinement, as "carceral abolitionists" do, an important precedent comes into view. An even greater percentage of the U.S. population was confined in psychiatric hospitals in 1955 than in jails and prisons half a century later, at the peak of mass incarceration (Figure 2). In addition to psychiatric hospitals, tens of thousands of people lived in large institutions for people with intellectual or developmental disabilities (IDD), often called "mental retardation" at the time. The inhabitants of these psychiatric hospitals and IDD institutions were not convicted of a crime, but most people in psychiatric hospitals were admitted against their will, and many people with IDD were institutionalized by their families at a young age.[5] Many also lacked the resources to live anywhere else. Like contemporary jails and prisons, these large disability institutions were largely funded and operated by government agencies, and they segregated hundreds of thousands of people from society. If many people have forgotten about this system of mass confinement, that is because it was dismantled, at least in its most visible forms, in a process known as "deinstitutionalization." Starting in the late 1950s, state and county mental hospitals began shutting down, and inpatient populations dropped almost 60 percent in the period 1965–75, and another 30 percent in the five years after that.[6] Large IDD institutions followed suit in the 1970s and '80s. Many formerly institutionalized people moved in with family members or started living on their own. Others moved into different kinds of institutions or forms of shared living: group homes, halfway houses, or nursing homes. Still others became unhoused. Meanwhile, jails and prisons began their rapid growth.

What can abolitionists learn from this precedent? Mass confinement in hospitals and prisons are rarely considered together, and when they are, the takeaway is often pessimistic. Prison abolitionists have historically focused on the specific harms and injustices of punishment and criminalization, disregarding mental health challenges and disability.[7] Sometimes, people with

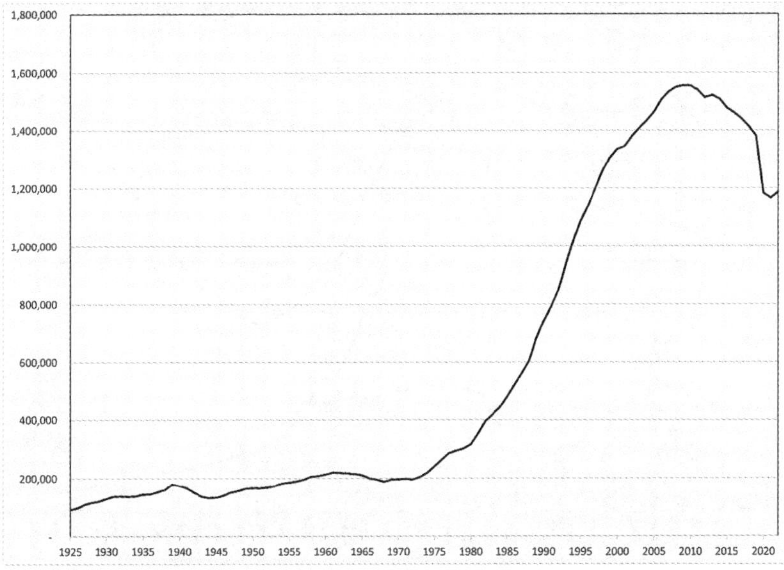

Figure 1. The growth of U.S. state and federal prison populations (excluding jails) from 1925 to 2022. Data source: The Sentencing Project, *Mass Incarceration Trends,* Washington, DC: The Sentencing Project, 2024, 5, https://www.sentencingproject.org/reports/mass-incarceration-trends/.

serious mental illness are treated as exceptions to radical critiques of incarceration, such as when the Attica Prisoner Manifesto argues that prison sentences should be capped at ten years because "if a man cannot be rehabilitated after a maximum of ten years of constructive programs, etc., then he belongs in a mental hygiene center, not a prison."[8] In what is sometimes described as "balloon theory," meanwhile, some researchers argue that if psychiatric hospitalization goes down, prison populations necessarily grow, and vice versa.[9] Even the historical analyses of Michel Foucault, who was critical of both modern psychiatry and the prison system, can be interpreted in such a way. As Bernard Harcourt writes, Foucault's *Madness and Civilization* and other "classic texts of social theory from the mid-to-late twentieth century told a relatively consistent story of the rise and fall of discrete institutions, *and* of the remarkable continuity of confinement and social exclusion—from the lazar houses for lepers on the outskirts of Medieval cities, to the establishment in the seventeenth century of the Hôpital Général in Paris. *There may be, in fact, no true escape from our levels of institutionalization,*" he writes,

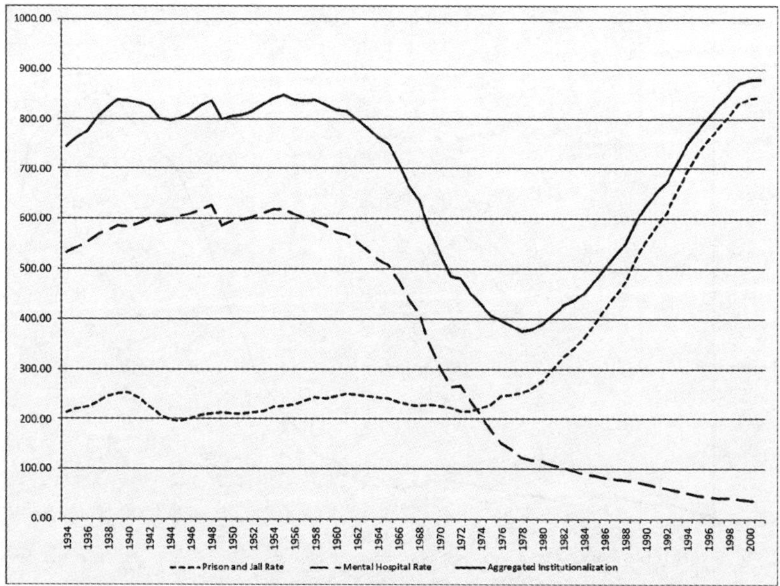

Figure 2. The growing rate of confinement in jails, state and federal prisons, compared to diminishing rates of confinement in mental hospitals in the United States (per hundred thousand adults), 1934–2001. Source: Bernard Harcourt, "Reducing Mass Incarceration: Lessons from the Deinstitutionalization of Mental Hospitals in the 1960s," *Ohio State Journal of Criminal Law* 9 (2011): 53–88, 59.

"and the apparent transfer from mental hospitals to prisons may be another indicator of that ominous fact."[10]

Critical disability scholar-activist Liat Ben-Moshe refuses such resignation in *Decarcerating Disability: Deinstitutionalization and Prison Abolition* (2020), the most sustained abolitionist engagement with deinstitutionalization to date. In an innovative analysis that combines Foucauldian genealogy with critical disability, crip-of-color, and Mad critique, Ben-Moshe invites us to see deinstitutionalization as a hopeful precedent for prison abolition. The mass confinement of a stigmatized group (or groups, if we distinguish between people with psychiatric disabilities and IDD) has been ended before, in the not-too-distant past. Large numbers of incarcerated people have been released, the ideas that justified their confinement challenged, the buildings that housed them razed or repurposed. Moreover, these developments did not happen automatically but were fought for by organized groups, who challenged the diminished rights and routine unfreedom of part of the population and called for their integration in the "community." Seen from this perspective, deinstitutionalization solves an important problem for abolitionists. It provides evidence for their claim that prison abolition is a *realistic* prospect, not an impossible fantasy, because something like it has happened before. "To those who claim that prison abolition and massive decarceration are utopian and could never happen, this book shows that they've happened already, although in a different arena, in the form of mass closures of residential institutions and psychiatric hospitals and the deinstitutionalization of those who resided in them," Ben-Moshe writes.[11] The precedent of deinstitutionalization could embolden abolitionists, she suggests. It provides reassurance that seemingly outlandish ideas can become reality, and that advocating for them might be met with derision in the short term but gain support over time.

Ben-Moshe thus affirms a key claim of this book: that prison abolition should be understood as a realist project. It is neither an abstract moral condemnation of prisons and punishment, nor a dangerously naive pursuit of an impossible dream. Rather, abolitionists reckon with the empirical realities of our society, centering the most marginalized. Prison abolitionists center those who are most subject to policing and most often deprived of rights and warehoused in jails and prisons, and carceral abolitionists like Ben-Moshe and Foucault further consider groups detained and controlled in psychiatric hospitals, nursing homes, and other carceral sites.[12] Abolitionists highlight the harmful and often antidemocratic effects of these institutions and practices, reveal their historical contingency, and excavate resistance practices, to remind us that while our society is filled with unfreedom, *it does not have to be this way.* Their insistence that it is possible and desirable to change institutions that most people see as inevitable distinguishes abolitionists from more conservative forms of realism, which may be more inclined to accept injustice and inequality as intrinsic features of political orders and to view efforts at radical change with suspicion. But as the previous chapter showed, it is difficult even for abolitionists to keep the sense of a different and better future alive. When abolitionist critique becomes "paranoid" as Eve Kosofsky Sedgwick uses the term, it becomes so focused on exposing and anticipating instances of carceral power that it cannot offer a vision of what abolition is *for.* I theorized Foucault's abolitionism as paranoid in this sense and argued that it generates a sense of resignation to the present.

This chapter argues that despite its initial hopefulness about deinstitutionalization, Ben-Moshe's abolitionism, too, is predominantly paranoid in

Sedgwick's sense of the term. In the context of critical disability theory, the very concept of "paranoid critique" might seem suspect. After all, paranoia has historically been conceptualized in psychiatry and psychoanalysis as a pathology: an undesirable departure from healthy functioning that offers a false and even dangerous perspective on the world. Critiquing a style of thinking labeled "paranoid" could reinforce ableist conceptions of mental differences as undesirable illnesses in need of cure, when critical disability theorists see such differences as valuable parts of human existence that can yield unique perspectives on the world. The risk is real. Unlike other recent works in political theory that recuperate paranoia for democratic political projects, this book takes a predominantly critical perspective on paranoid abolitionism.[13] At the same time, like Sedgwick, I do not use "paranoia" as a clinical diagnosis of any thinker, as a state of mind that distorts reality, or as wholly undesirable. Rather, I am concerned about the political effects of thinking from a paranoid position. I do not argue that paranoid thinking is false or unfounded, but rather that it offers few means to escape the oppression it so astutely diagnoses and thus tends to generate a political impasse.

Ben-Moshe's expansive analysis of carcerality could inform a radical abolitionist politics. If jails, prisons, and psychiatric hospitals are all troubling forms of incarceration, then abolitionists must overhaul not only what passes for criminal justice but also what passes for health care and care in general. Ben-Moshe convincingly argues, moreover, that abolitionist change must go beyond changes in *location*—such as moving people with disabilities from large institutions to group homes, or sentencing people to electronically monitored house arrest instead of to jail or prison. Rather, it must seek broader social, economic, and political change to include people with disabilities fully in the polity while still respecting their difference. Furthermore, Ben-Moshe's analysis shows that the failures of deinstitutionalization result in part from neoliberal divestment. As large disability institutions closed their doors, neoliberalism undercut political support and funding for community health care, public housing, and other resources that the formerly institutionalized desperately needed. Deinstitutionalization thus left people with disabilities more dependent on informal or market-based systems, and vulnerable to houselessness and incarceration when these fell through.[14] Ben-Moshe's analysis of deinstitutionalization could therefore ground demands for economic redistribution and state investment in life-supporting institutions and goods.

The mobilizing potential of Ben-Moshe's analysis is undercut, however, by its suspicion and anticipation that carcerality will be reinscribed in any proposed alternative. Rather than risk disappointment, *Decarcerating Disability* refrains from making specific proposals or demands and defines abolitionism in negative terms, as the creation of a "*non*carceral and *non*segregationist society."[15] By turning away from an affirmative political project, this abolitionism also turns away from tactical and strategic questions about how to build power and secure victories, a tendency that is reinforced when Ben-Moshe frames her critique in terms of a "carceral *logic*." Framed as a logic, carcerality seems almost inevitable, susceptible at best to changes in knowledge practices. Indeed, Ben-Moshe argues that abolition is best advanced by letting go of certainty, prescription, professional expertise, and the desire for a clear sense of the future, a kind of unknowing she calls "dis-epistemology," and she calls for "ridding the self of [carceral] logics."[16] Abolition undoubtedly involves self-transformation and new ways of knowing, but Ben-Moshe's own account of deinstitutionalization suggests that such changes must be accompanied by changes to neoliberal political economy. Yet her refusal to affirm specific policies or demands makes it difficult to support a redistributive or anticapitalist politics.

Ben-Moshe's analysis, I argue, ultimately leaves abolitionists in an impasse. On the one hand, the example of deinstitutionalization suggests that shutting down large carceral institutions is possible. To be successful, an abolitionist politics must accomplish more than institutional closures, however. It must also build the resources and infrastructures needed to support the freedom and equal citizenship of formerly incarcerated people. Ben-Moshe affirms this insight in the abstract, but from her perspective of paranoid critique, any concrete alternative nonetheless looks first and foremost like a threat to abolitionism that could reintroduce carcerality in a different form. Her abolitionism both affirms that a radically better world is possible and anticipates that abolitionist victories will be recaptured by the dominant order. This abolitionism secures its radicalism from the threats of reformism and cooptation at the cost of supporting concrete alternatives needed to realize its political vision. In so doing, it generates what I call a *politics of purity* focused on eliminating carcerality and avoiding disappointment but silent on affirmative abolitionist visions and demands.

I begin, here, with a more detailed account of deinstitutionalization, before reading Ben-Moshe's abolitionist analysis through the lens of paranoid critique. I argue that her abolitionism generates an impasse that leads to a politics of purity, and I conclude by sketching some challenges and demands that an affirmative abolitionist politics of disability justice might take on.

A Brief History of Deinstitutionalization

Deinstitutionalization describes a set of developments that began in the late 1950s and continued into the 1970s. State mental hospitals were the first to close, followed more than a decade later by large residential institutions for people with intellectual or developmental disabilities (IDD).[17] These closures reversed a trend of rapid growth in disability-related confinement. The first psychiatric hospital, the Eastern Lunatic Asylum in Williamsburg, Virginia, had opened in 1773 with a capacity of twenty beds.[18] By 1955, psychiatric hospitals held more than half a million people nationwide, and accounted for half of all hospital beds in the United States.[19] Most of that growth took place between 1880 and 1955, when the number of mental hospital patients grew thirteenfold, compared to a threefold increase of the general population.[20] The size of mental hospitals themselves also increased, and by the mid-twentieth century they typically housed thousands of patients, as many as fourteen thousand in extreme cases.[21] The exponential growth of psychiatric hospitalization may have reflected an increase in severe mental illness in this period, but many other factors were at play. Changes in family structure diminished capacities for informal caretaking, and psychiatric hospitals often housed people with no other sources of support, including the elderly and people with syphilis (a disease that, if left untreated, can entail neurological symptoms).[22] Meanwhile, growing support for psychiatric institutionalization and "decreased tolerance for deviant behavior" also contributed to the exponential growth of these institutions.[23]

In addition to mental hospitals, a system of residential "schools" and other institutions purported to care for people with intellectual or developmental disabilities (IDD). As Ben-Moshe recounts, the distinction between "mental illness" and IDD is a relatively recent invention. The practice of "warehousing together all the needy populations lasted in various degrees until the 1930s," but gradually, people deemed to be "mentally defective," "feebleminded," or "mentally retarded" were separated from those deemed mentally ill.[24] Clinical terminology further distinguished the former groups into "idiots," "imbeciles," and "morons," to describe different degrees of reduced mental development.[25]

Eugenic thinking shaped both scientific and popular approaches to disability from the late nineteenth century through the 1940s, depicting both mental illness and IDD as undesirable hereditary traits that risked polluting the national gene pool.[26] Efforts to educate "improvable" people with IDD in specialized residential schools and institutions, or to cure mental illness in psychiatric hospitals, thus became entangled with efforts to protect society from the threat of disability. In 1907, Indiana was the first state to pass a law authorizing the involuntary sterilization of people in asylums and prisons, specifying in a 1917 amendment that such sterilization required a diagnosis of a "mental disease which may have been inherited and is likely to be transmitted to descendants," "various grades of feeblemindedness," or "perversion or marked departures from normal mentality or from disease of a syphilitic nature."[27] Thirty-two more states would enact similar laws, which received legal sanction in 1927 from the Supreme Court. As one Justice wrote in the *Buck v. Bell* ruling: "It is better for the world, if instead of waiting to execute degenerate offspring for crime, or to let them starve for their imbecility, society can prevent those who are manifestly unfit from continuing their kind. The principle that sustains compulsory vaccination is broad enough to cover cutting the Fallopian tubes—Three generations of imbeciles are enough."[28] From the early twentieth century through the 1960s, approximately sixty thousand involuntary sterilizations were carried out in the United States, mostly on residents of disability-related state institutions.[29]

Deinstitutionalization reversed the trend of housing people with disability labels in large state-run facilities. The number of people in mental hospitals peaked at 559,000 in 1955 and fell to fewer than 100,000 by the start of the twenty-first century, despite significant population growth.[30] Large IDD institutions also saw their populations decrease dramatically, from a high of about 194,000 in 1977 to fewer than 70,000 in 2015.[31] Public opinion turned against large disability institutions, and community resources were presented as the alternative. In a 1963 speech to Congress, President John F. Kennedy expressed a plan to "cut by half, within a decade or two, the 600,000 persons now institutionalized for psychological disorders" by providing community-based services for "both the mentally ill and . . . the mentally retarded."[32] This plan was informed by the findings of the Joint Commission on Mental Illness and Health, which had spent five years studying the treatment of mental illness in the United States.[33] Congress soon passed the Community Mental Health Act (CMHA), which created federal grants for the construction of fifteen hundred public and private nonprofit community health centers (CMHCs) across the country. These centers were to provide both inpatient and outpatient services as well as education on mental health. Some formerly institutionalized people moved into smaller institutions, group homes, or nursing homes, while others lived independently or with family.

What explains this drastic turn against large disability institutions? The emergence of new psychiatric drugs in the 1950s and '60s, especially antipsychotic medication like Thorazine, is often mentioned as a key cause, but as Ben-Moshe points out, it cannot explain the closure of large IDD facilities, often omitted from popular and scholarly accounts of deinstitutionalization.[34] In contrast, there is a broad consensus that deinstitutionalization in both mental health and IDD was facilitated by the growth of the federal social safety net. Limited disability insurance benefits were first introduced in 1956, and Medicare and Medicaid were created in 1965. As political scientist Amber Knight explains, Medicaid in particular has played a key role in deinstitutionalization: It pays for more than half of total expenditures on home- and community-based services for people with disabilities.[35] States' desires to save money also helped shut down large disability institutions, especially once states could shift some costs of disability care onto federal programs like Medicaid. Meanwhile, popular support for institutionalization diminished, in part as a result of exposés of terrible living conditions in these facilities. One exposé concerned Willowbrook, a state "school" for children with IDD in Staten Island, which New York senator Robert Kennedy described after an unannounced visit in 1965 as a "snake pit" where thousands of residents were "living in filth and dirt, their clothing in rags, in rooms less comfortable and cheerful than the cages in which we put animals in a zoo."[36] The 1967 documentary *Titicut Follies* revealed similarly shocking conditions at Bridgewater Hospital for the Criminally Insane.[37]

A forgotten force behind deinstitutionalization, Ben-Moshe argues, is the activism of people with disabilities and their allies. Exposés certainly led to public outcry, but that was more reformist than abolitionist in nature, she says, as abject depictions of disabled people risked deepening their marginalization. People with disabilities and their allies, meanwhile, advanced abolitionist ideas. They not only rejected institutionalization but also called for broader ideological change, seeking to "change how people with disabilities are perceived and treated."[38] Psychiatrist Thomas Szasz, for instance, argued that mental illness is a metaphor and psychiatry an unscientific belief system rather than a proper branch of medicine.[39] He described civil commitment as an immoral atrocity committed by psychiatry in conjunction with the "therapeutic state" and called for the abolition of psychiatry as a medical field.[40] In 1970, Szasz cofounded the American Association for the Abolition of Involuntary Mental Hospitalization (AAAIMH) together with law professor George Alexander and sociologist Erving Goffman, who had published his book *Asylums* in 1961. Based on ethnographic research in a mental hospital with more than seven thousand patients in Washington, DC, the book theorizes psychiatric hospitals as prison-like "total institutions" that control all aspects of residents' lives. The AAAIMH existed from 1970 to 1980, published a newsletter called *The Abolitionist,* and sought to provide legal support for people institutionalized against their will.[41] In addition, various (ex-)mental patients'/survivors' organizations emerged in the 1970s and '80s that Ben-Moshe says combined reformist and abolitionist impulses. Some embraced terms like "health care consumer" and fought for community mental health services, while others rejected such terminology for obscuring the coercive nature of psychiatric power and depicted community mental health as spreading that power dangerously throughout society.[42]

For Ben-Moshe, people with IDD labels who organized into self-advocacy groups were the "most vocal abolitionists."[43] The most influential abolitionist ideas, meanwhile, came from researchers like psychologist Wolf Wolfensberger who challenged the othering and segregation of disabled people by advocating theories of "normalization" or "social role valorization" (SRV). These theories hold that the living conditions and social roles of people with IDD should be as similar as possible as those of nondisabled peers, considering factors such as the organization of time into "normal" rhythms of work, leisure, and rest, and having one's choices and desires respected as often as possible. In time, the "subjugated knowledge" of normalization/SRV became accepted as scientific, which facilitated the closure of large residential IDD institutions. Indeed, Ben-Moshe argues that deinstitutionalization has been more successful in the realm of IDD than in the case of psychiatric disabilities, though it has received far less attention. Oftentimes, "those with I/DD fared better in their move into community living," Ben-Moshe writes, an outcome she ascribes in part to differing stereotypes. People with IDD are often imagined as innocent, while people with mental illness are thought of as dangerous.[44]

In both mental health and IDD, deinstitutionalization has been fraught, however. The antipsychiatry ideas of Szasz and others have been largely rejected as a "lunatic fringe," in favor of an understanding of mental illness as essentially brain disorders best treated by psychopharmaceuticals.[45] There is a widespread sense that the deinstitutionalization of psychiatric patients has failed because it has led to both increased houselessness and mass incarceration. Ben-Moshe rightly complicates this account. The closure of large mental hospitals preceded the prison boom by at least a decade, she reminds us, and mass incarceration affects predominantly men of color, whereas most people in large disability institutions were white women. Moreover, the growing shortage of affordable housing helps explain the rise in houselessness, which itself has disabling effects. Still, the American Psychiatric Association (APA) recently published a report on "the psychiatric bed crisis," and some mental health professionals call for a return to the asylum.[46] In the realm of IDD, meanwhile, the success of normalization/SRV theory has created problems of its own. As these ideas became hegemonic, they inaugurated new forms of constraint on disabled people, now disciplined into "normal" behaviors.[47] The radical othering of people warehoused in state institutions gave way to segregation in privately run group homes and workshops, Ben-Moshe says, where "all life's activities, including eating, hygiene, sexuality, and intimacy, are policed and surveilled constantly." Nonconformity is still seen as a problem to be solved with (re)institutionalization, rather than as a manifestation of difference that should be valued and celebrated.[48] What does all this mean for abolition?

Deinstitutionalization and/as Abolition: Ben-Moshe's Analysis as Paranoid Critique

Decarcerating Disability is a groundbreaking work. It is the first and, for now, only book-length analysis of deinstitutionalization from an abolitionist perspective. The book invites both prison abolitionists and critical disability theorists to reckon with the significance and promise of this historical event. Disability is not always considered in prison abolitionism, and mental illness and intellectual and developmental disabilities have historically been marginalized in disability studies, which initially centered experiences of physical disability.[49] The field has also long centered white people in the Global North, for whom disability pride and legal protection from discrimination could be sufficient remedies. From these perspectives, neither state psychiatric hospitals nor mass incarceration seem pressing concerns for disability theory or justice. Ben-Moshe is one of a growing number of critical disability theorists, including those aligned with crip-of-color, Mad, and disability justice frameworks, who seek to go beyond liberal rights claims, pride, and inclusion. These authors seek to affirm the value of disabled people's lives and perspectives and at the same time challenge the debilitating effects of poverty, racism, and warfare that slowly wear down populations.[50] From these perspectives, disability justice requires not just the elimination of stigma or greater access to existing institutions, but a more far-reaching overhaul of the global economic, social, and political order. Ben-Moshe affirms this radical agenda and folds it into an expansive abolitionism, already on display in the volume she edited with Allison Carey and Chris Chapman in 2014, *Disability Incarcerated: Imprisonment and Disability in the United States and Canada.*

Ben-Moshe's abolitionist approach challenges analyses that turn to deinstitutionalization for lessons in prison reform. In a 2011 article, Bernard Harcourt, for instance, argues that just as new psychiatric drugs supported deinstitutionalization in the 1960s, mass incarceration in jails and prisons could be reduced by providing more and better psychiatric care.[51] Many incarcerated people have mental health challenges, and Harcourt argues that prison and jail populations could be shrunk by moving people with severe mental illness out of, or diverting them from, the criminal legal system. Instead, they would enter psychiatric institutions or GPS-monitored home confinement. He also cautiously proposes increasing incentives to take medication for aggressive behavior, among other proposals for federal leadership and campaigns to shift public perceptions of criminalized people. Second, Harcourt suggests that just as the creation of Medicaid incentivized states to close large disability institutions by reimbursing at least some outpatient mental health treatment, federal leadership is key in reducing mass incarceration. The federal government, he says, should give states "an economic and fiscal incentive to move convicts out of state prisons and into non-custodial programs."[52] Third, learning from the role exposés played in deinstitutionalization, Harcourt suggests we must try to "shift the public perception" of both the prison system and the people confined there, building support for decarceration by exposing the often bad and sometimes terrible prison conditions and rehumanizing the "convicts" forced to live in them.

Where Harcourt sees increased psychiatric medication and "non-custodial programs" as vehicles of decarceration, Ben-Moshe sees the substitution of one form of unfreedom for another. She wishes to abolish incarceration as such, understanding sites of incarceration to include "prisons, nursing homes, psychiatric hospitals, residential facilities for those with intellectual and other disabilities, and, at times, our own homes (or their lack)."[53] In fact, for Ben-Moshe, incarceration can even operate without constraining freedom of movement. Following Mad scholar-activist Erick Fabris, she theorizes forced psychiatric medication as a kind of "chemical incarceration."[54] Her attentiveness to the many forms of warehousing, segregation, and confinement is a great strength and could inform a more radical politics than that offered in Harcourt's article. Such a politics could seek to address the root causes of incarceration in both its punitive and therapeutic guises to interrupt the cycle in which different policies and institutions produce similar effects of inequality and unfreedom. Since Ben-Moshe's analysis suggests that racial capitalism and neoliberalism are among the root causes of incarceration, a radical crip abolitionist politics would advance redistributive and anti-capitalist visions and demands.

It does not follow, however, that a radical abolitionist politics could or should reject making difficult trade-offs or affirming ideas or policies that could backfire or generate problems and exclusions of their own. Harcourt acknowledges that each of his proposals comes with limitations and dangers, most centrally the risk that people released or diverted from jails and prisons will merely end up in other institutions, a phenomenon known as "transinstitutionalization," but he suggests there is no alternative. "Given our previous experience with deinstitutionalization, there is no reason to believe that it will be possible to reduce prison populations without getting our hands dirty," he says.[55] Keeping our hands clean might *seem* like a possibility for Ben-Moshe's abolitionism because she rejects the specific reforms that Harcourt endorses and describes as "Faustian bargains." In fact, *Decarcerating Disability* does not just reject Harcourt's policy proposals; it turns away from political questions of power and strategy and focuses instead on eradicating "carceral logics."[56] This "politics of purity" leaves abolitionists in an impasse, I argue, because it avoids making the kinds of redistributive demands that Ben-Moshe's own analysis suggests are needed. Its political limitations, I now suggest, can be traced back to the paranoid abolitionism of Michel Foucault.

A Paranoid Critique

In chapter 1, I theorized Foucault's abolitionism as "paranoid" in Eve Kosofsky Sedgwick's sense of the term. I discussed how Sedgwick uses the term "paranoid reading" to describe a mode of critique focused on exposing hidden oppression to generate change.[57] Marked by suspicion and oriented toward negative affect, paranoid critique seeks to unmask nefarious forces and anticipate their (re)occurrence. It offers a "strong" theory that can explain many phenomena, but such a large explanatory reach also makes paranoid thinking vulnerable to circular reasoning. It can find oppression everywhere because everything can be explained as an instance of oppression. By the same token, paranoid analyses tend to be so focused on diagnosing oppression that they overlook exceptions or variations to the rule they seek to expose. All in all, paranoid thinking is highly attuned to systematic oppression and committed to ending it, yet its ability to effect change is limited, Sedgwick suggests, by undue faith in the transformative power of exposing or denaturalizing oppression and disdain for "reparative" measures that "merely" make life more livable. I argued that Foucault's abolitionism can generate resignation because it illuminates the pervasiveness of carceral power but cannot offer a vision of what abolition is for. Ben-Moshe herself finds Foucault's work to fall short on theorizing resistance. She notes that *Decarcerating Disability* "strives to expand [Foucauldian] genealogy beyond analysis of instruments of power to the topography of their resistance" by focusing on disabled people's contributions to deinstitutionalization.[58] Yet Ben-Moshe's analysis, I argue, shares much with Foucault's paranoid critique, and her commitment to illuminate and enable anticarceral resistance is not enough to break out of the impasse generated by the paranoid position.

Like Foucault, Ben-Moshe offers an expansive understanding of carceral power, what Sedgwick calls a *strong theory.* Ben-Moshe claims Foucault as an important influence, which makes sense: He is a key thinker of the connections between prisons and asylums, and between medical and legal power. Before cofounding the activist Prisons Information Group (GIP) in the early 1970s, Foucault had critically examined the treatment of "madness" in modern societies, a scholarly analysis that was taken up by emergent antipsychiatry movements.[59] The GIP focused its energies on prisons but it also declared psychiatry and "the hospital system" to be intolerable.[60] And Foucault's *Discipline and Punish* shows that punishment in the age of the prison obtains a new meaning as "cure" for criminal deviance. Unlike public torture, which sought to terrorize onlookers through the spectacular destruction of the convict's body, prisons employ technologies such as isolation and forced labor to transform the convicted person's "soul." As nineteenth-century judges aimed to impose sentences that fit not only the offense but also the offender, psychiatric expertise gained an important role in criminal trials, entwining judicial and medical power over people deemed "abnormal."[61] Deviation from norms, Foucault writes, came to be understood as a sign of "the multiple danger of disorder, crime and madness."[62] Conversely, prisons, asylums, and clinics all set out to cure deviance or at least contain it. Because these are "the sites of incarceration pervasive in the contemporary lives of those racialized and pathologized," Ben-Moshe writes, they are "the main sites of carceral enclosure discussed" in *Decarcerating Disability*.[63] To challenge them, she sometimes critiques "corrections," a term that encompasses both rehabilitative punishment and medical interventions to cure deviance.[64]

Ben-Moshe's strong theory is more explicitly critical of capitalism than Foucault's, however, and more attentive to race, gender, sexuality, and settler-colonialism. Ben-Moshe draws on the Marxist abolitionism of Angela Davis and the activist group Critical Resistance (CR) to analyze prisons and psychiatric hospitals as part of an "institutional-industrial" or "carceral-industrial complex." The terms, used interchangeably, are adaptations of "prison industrial complex" (PIC), advanced by Davis and CR to think about state punishment structurally, as a practice driven by the interests of economic and political elites rather than as a rational response to individual criminal acts.[65] These elites may wish to protect public safety, but they may also use punishment to increase profits, grow markets, limit political dissent, get (re)elected, or manage capitalist crises. This structural analysis implies that prison abolition requires first and foremost disrupting these instrumental investments in punitive practices; developing alternative mechanisms to deal with serious harm is part but not all of abolition. With the term *carceral-industrial complex*, Ben-Moshe expands this analysis from punitive to therapeutic confinement, implying that the latter is also driven by forces that do not only or straightforwardly seek to provide care to those who need it. Like Davis, she focuses on capitalist profit motives: disabled people are a valuable resource to "a growing private industry of nursing homes, boarding homes, for-profit psychiatric hospitals, and group homes," for instance.[66] These private industries have expanded in the wake of deinstitutionalization, and they benefit from state subsidies for people with disabilities that continue to privilege institutionalized care over home care.[67]

Decarcerating Disability further draws on the work of Nirmala Erevelles and other critical disability scholars of color to connect disability and incarceration to racism. Ben-Moshe uses the term "race-ability" to think about race and disability as "mutually constitutive" oppressions, for instance, and "criminal racial pathologization" to describe the oppressive othering of Black people. These broad terms and definitions allow her to bring together seemingly varied phenomena such as the criminalization of Blackness (practices that facilitate the punishment and imprisonment of Black people, especially Black men, based on the perception that they are dangerous); assimilationist settler-colonial policies, such as the forced transfer of Indigenous children to residential schools to "kill the Indian and save the man"; and the pathologization of mind/body differences, which justify the subjection of disabled people to paternalist power and their confinement in designated residential facilities.

To resist carcerality and advance abolition, Ben-Moshe holds *faith in exposure,* another characteristic of paranoid critique. As was previously mentioned, she is skeptical about the tactic of exposing conditions of confinement to the broader public. Exposés of severe neglect, overcrowding, and other maltreatment and abuse in mental hospitals played a role in deinstitutionalization, she says, but they tended to encourage reform, not abolition. She places faith, however, in genealogy, the Foucauldian method of "exposing what appears as self-evident in the present and tracing the various ways these contingencies were constructed in the past."[68] Where exposés showed that conditions of confinement violated widely accepted standards of humane treatment, thus exposing a gap between normative expectations and empirical realities, genealogy unsettles the very notion of humane treatment. It denaturalizes what seems self-evident or necessary but does not offer prescriptions, which resonates with the paranoid belief that exposure to unsuspected oppression will bring about an unspecified change. "Psychiatrization, for example, is not natural or God given," Ben-Moshe says; "it is a specific discourse arising in a particular historical moment that had come to be seen as ahistorical and inevitable. Imprisonment as a form of punishment is also a contingency, as is punishment as a result of crime or wrongdoing." Ben-Moshe does not articulate alternatives to psychiatry, prisons, and punishment but rather embraces disorientation and uncertainty. She theorizes abolition as a "*dis-epistemology,* [a] letting go of attachment to certain ways of knowing," and sometimes describes abolition as a "counterhegemonic" epistemology that "oppos[es] the status quo and taken-for-granted assumptions" and envisions "a world in which carceral and segregated locales are viewed as senseless and commonsenseless."[69]

Ben-Moshe's belief in the transformative potential of disorientation and uncertainty exists alongside a negative assessment of most efforts at change.

Efforts to improve conditions inside jails, prisons, and disability-related institutions "perpetuate the myth that the system is broken and therefore in need of improvement" while it actually "performs based on its espoused rationales (segregation, confinement, incapacitation)."[70] Put differently, reform efforts perpetuate the mystification of carceral enclosures as benevolent or benign and paper over their violence. Even deinstitutionalization, which Ben-Moshe supports, gave way to a "deinstitutional industrial complex" and created new markets and profit opportunities in the form of state-subsidized nursing homes, group homes, and day habitation centers.[71] Echoing Foucault's concern that seeming alternatives to the prison could spread carceral technologies throughout the social body, Ben-Moshe writes that psychiatric care clinics in the community could "increase surveillance on those psychiatrized."[72] We already saw that for Ben-Moshe, court-mandated psychiatric medication amounts to "chemical incarceration" even if the people in question have freedom of movement.

Sedgwick might see here signs of the *anticipatory* nature of paranoid thinking, which tries above all never to be taken by surprise. "No time could be too early for one's having-already-known, for its having-already-been-inevitable, that something bad would happen. And no loss could be too far in the future to need to be preemptively discounted," Sedgwick writes.[73] *Decarcerating Disability* is full of examples of changes that seem progressive or even radical but are revealed to be mere variations on the same oppressive structures. Sometimes, they even make things worse. "For example, demands for inclusion of people with disabilities in employment or education do not critique or change the system of exploitative racial capitalism or the settler ableist system of education but only expand it to fit more people," Ben-Moshe writes. "This expansion is what abolitionists often term as reform measures, which increase the scope of harm."[74] Because Ben-Moshe defines segregation as a key feature of carcerality, it would seem that inclusion is anticarceral, but that is only sometimes the case.[75] For Ben-Moshe, inclusion most often means inclusion in an institution or structure that is still carceral, a superficial transformation she associates with liberalism and reformism. Note that her example describes inclusion and reform not just as superficial and inconsequential but as actively harmful.[76] She coins the term "Dis Inc." to connect the *incarceration* and *incorporation* of disability, suggesting that the forced confinement and the social, cultural, and economic incorporation of "minority difference" are different, but equally troubling forms of oppression that serve capitalist imperatives.[77] As she puts it elsewhere, *Decarcerating Disability* "aim[s] to show not just the (economic, cultural, political) price of exclusion but that of inclusion."[78]

Ben-Moshe's hopefulness about deinstitutionalization and inclusion is thus tempered by a range of *negative affects,* another characteristic of paranoid thinking. The desire to abolish the institutional-industrial complex and the various structural forces that undergird it, such as "the settler racial heteropatriarchal ableist nation-state," exists alongside the suspicion and anticipation that efforts at change are likely to be recaptured by dominant forces.[79] Ben-Moshe breaks with the suspicion and anticipation of paranoid thinking when she argues that disability and madness offer valuable perspectives on the world, forms of knowledge she calls "cripistemologies."[80] This is one of the reparative moments in *Decarcerating Disability,* even if it doesn't specify the content of the perspectives being offered. In a similar vein, and like the French Prisons Information Group (GIP) discussed in the previous chapter, *Decarcerating Disability* affirms not just the knowledge but also the resistance efforts of incarcerated people, and one of the aims of the book is to uncover "suppressed histories of resistance and oppression" from people with intellectual and psychiatric disabilities. This uncovering and valuing of resistance efforts could be read as paranoid faith in exposure, but we could also read into it solidarity and support. Perhaps the most significant break with paranoid thinking is found in *Building Pedagogical Curb Cuts,* a book coedited by Ben-Moshe that focuses on ways to make educational institutions more accessible to students and scholars with disabilities.

In its dominant manifestations, however, the abolitionism developed in *Decarcerating Disability* fits the characteristics of paranoid critique. As I now suggest, it produces a politics of purity that turns us away from political struggles to build power and make demands on the state.

A Politics of Purity

Paranoid critique is highly attuned to the ways seemingly emancipatory policies or practices might reproduce oppression. Perhaps the most poignant example from *Decarcerating Disability* is Ben-Moshe's discussion of Wolfensberger's "social role valorization" (SRV) or "normalization" model. SRV began as "subjugated" professional knowledge: It opposed the warehousing and othering of people with IDD and argued that their lives should be as "normal" as possible. This approach furthered deinstitutionalization, but it also entailed the micromanagement of people's behaviors, now in smaller residential settings, to align them with (white, middle class, heterosexual understandings of) "autonomy," "independence," and "citizenship." "Through checklists and increased technocratic surveillance, normalization was solidified as a policy and a way of policing difference," Ben-Moshe observes.[81] The example shows the value of a theoretical framework that is attuned to the multiple faces of power and suspicious of dominant understandings of freedom and autonomy. These are among the great and enduring strengths of Foucauldian thinking.[82]

At the same time, in its anticipation that efforts at change will be recaptured, paranoid critique can undercut efforts to secure political wins. As Sedgwick says, half-jokingly, "I'm a lot less worried about being pathologized by my therapist than about my vanishing mental health coverage—and that's given the great good luck of having health insurance at all. Since the beginning of the tax revolt, the government . . . has been positively rushing to divest itself of answerability for care to its charges, with no other institutions proposing to fill the gap."[83] To readers of *Decarcerating Disability,* Sedgwick's remark can seem flippant, making light of the dangers of pathologization and therapeutic power. The quote asks us to consider, though, what greater vigilance would and would not accomplish. Paranoid critique, Sedgwick suggests, is ill-equipped to challenge neoliberal divestment and demand that the state provide funding and other resources for care. Her claim is borne out by Ben-Moshe's analysis, which sees neoliberal divestment as a reason deinstitutionalization failed yet stops short of making redistributive demands.

As Ben-Moshe knows better than anyone, abolition cannot be only a negative project of elimination. Getting people out of institutions is just the start. It must be accompanied by the creation of new infrastructures to support the formerly confined, along with new conceptions of democratic citizenship that include them. This is precisely what failed to happen in the case of deinstitutionalization, as *Decarcerating Disability* shows. The book ascribes this failure largely to the ascent of neoliberalism. "Deinstitutionalization did not lead to homelessness and increased incarceration," Ben-Moshe writes, challenging dominant accounts of prisons as the new asylums. This account wrongly assumes that the same people or groups who were previously institutionalized were subsequently imprisoned, and that deinstitutionalization therefore caused mass incarceration. Ben-Moshe offers a different explanation that blames "racism and neoliberalism" for increasing both homelessness and imprisonment, "via privatization, budget cuts in all service/welfare sectors, and little to no funding for affordable and accessible housing and social services, while the budgets for corrections, policing, and punishment (of mostly poor people of color) skyrocketed."[84] We saw that psychiatric hospitalization peaked in 1955, and that President Kennedy threw his support behind community mental health care in the early 1960s. Neoliberal policies began to take hold by the end of that decade, with Nixon successfully campaigning on a law-and-order platform. Neoliberal ideologies of individual responsibility, free markets, and limited government support closing down state disability institutions—as governor of California, Reagan reportedly called institutions and psychiatric hospitals "the biggest hotel chain in the state"—but they are a far cry from the radical disability inclusion envisioned by abolitionists. People went from being confined by the state to being abandoned by it: a liberation of sorts, but not the freedom that disability activists had hoped for. As large institutions closed and their typically unionized staff was laid off, care work was shifted onto unpaid or underpaid women. The job of home health aide, mostly held by women of color, is one of the lowest paying occupations in the country, and nearly one in five home health aides lives below the federal poverty line.[85] In a painful irony, high rates of workplace injury mean that health aides are likely to become disabled themselves.[86]

Federalism proved to be another obstacle to building new infrastructures alongside deinstitutionalization. In the United States, political power is shared between the federal government and the states, and the latter have significant autonomy. As Ben-Moshe observes, federal policies facilitated the closure of many large disability institutions, which is why Harcourt sees strong federal leadership as key to reducing mass incarceration today. But in the case of deinstitutionalization, federal policies had uneven effects on the ground. Under Kennedy, the federal government provided temporary subsidies for community mental health centers (CMHCs) for instance, but half of the envisioned CMHCs were never built, the others were so heterogeneous that they were difficult to regulate federally, and "local concerns often translated into treatment for those with less serious mental illnesses," leaving behind those in need of the most intensive care.[87] Federalism is also one of the reasons why Medicaid has been a limited resource for many people with disabilities who wish to live independently. As Amber Knight explains, "Medicaid is structured as a federal-state partnership, and scholars have described it as a diffuse policy that takes very different forms in different places . . . states vary widely in their eligibility criteria and in the types, extent, and quality of services offered."[88] As a result, disabled people's ability to receive services and resources in the community depends a great deal on where they live, and many people with serious mental illness struggle to get the care and resources they need from a patchwork of programs and agencies.[89] High poverty rates among people with disabilities mean that such resources are often urgently needed. A recent study found that more than a quarter of adults with disabilities live in poverty, more than twice the rate of nondisabled adults.[90]

Ben-Moshe's account of deinstitutionalization could lead to abolitionist demands for guaranteed housing, healthcare, and income and to strategic thinking about how best to work the federal political system. Instead, the paranoid style of her critique leads Ben-Moshe toward knowledge practices and the self. "Abolition," Ben-Moshe writes, "is not about specific locales or even practices but about *ridding ourselves of logics,*" specifically "carceral logics."[91] The term "carceral logic" occurs only a few times in *Decarcerating Disability,* and it does not have one consistent definition, but it does important political work. Framing the object of abolition as a logic disconnects abolitionism from concrete political struggles and might even place it beyond their reach. Abolition is now about "ridding ourselves of [carceral] logics," an epistemic process of purification that is at odds with the "dirty hands" politics and Faustian bargains advocated by Harcourt. Where Harcourt argues that federal funds could persuade states to decarcerate, for instance, Ben-Moshe describes incarceration as "a logic of state coercion and segregation of difference."[92] On the one hand, the description is strikingly general and abstract. The "segregation of difference" subsumes many different scenarios, rationales, and legal processes potentially involved in incarceration—ranging from criminal to civil law, from punishment to care, and from mental health crises to intimate partner violence. At the same time, Ben-Moshe associates carceral logics specifically with *state* coercion, even though that describes only some of the instances she describes as incarceration: notably, when people are arrested, sentenced to jail or prison time, or hospitalized against their will, a practice known as civil commitment. As *Decarcerating Disability* shows, however, economic pressures and a lack of alternatives can be just as powerful as state coercion in forcing people with disabilities into segregated residential institutions. We are left with the sense that carceral logics can take many forms but are always inherently oppressive. There is no indication, meanwhile, what political struggles or wins could abolish them.

Toward a Politics of Care

Roadmaps and blueprints are overrated in radical politics, Foucault and Ben-Moshe both argue, and they have a point. Proposals for how to do things differently might be perfectly coherent and yet fail to gain traction as long as the status quo seems tolerable to us. Moreover, as realists they know that opposing forces have a vested interest in keeping things as they are. For Ben-Moshe, these include the institutional- and the deinstitutional industrial complex. Both thinkers also appreciate that in an important sense we do not know yet what is possible until we try it, and both try to cultivate an openness to the unknown. Uncertainty and experimentation are crucial to abolitionist politics, precisely because it is a realist political project rather than a rigid moral code. I have argued that an effective abolitionist politics must also offer an alternative vision of democracy, citizenship, and the state, however, as well as guidance on the practical struggles that could realize them. *Decarcerating Disability* recovers the role that activism played in deinstitutionalization, but its paranoid critique of carceral logics is more likely to inspire self-purification than collective political action.

Chapter 3 discusses a vision of abolition that affirms *both* the dismantling of systems of domination *and* the creation of new democratic institutions to realize equal citizenship. Angela Davis places prison abolition in a lineage of social movements that were "eventually more or less successful" at dismantling racist institutions, starting with chattel slavery, which was ended by the Civil War and Radical Reconstruction.[93] Davis hedges on these movements' success because they were not able to prevent the emergence of new forms of racism. Radical Reconstruction, for instance, was defeated by white supremacist and capitalist forces, and gave way to almost a century of Jim Crow segregation. Still, Davis affirms the value and significant victories of these antiracist movements and calls on us to continue them in the present and into the future. Rather than see them as futile or even as counterproductive as paranoid thinking might (just think of Foucauldian arguments about power taking more "insidious" forms over time that are less easily recognized as dangerous), Davis acknowledges the reality of such shapeshifting *and* affirms the importance of ongoing political struggle. Importantly, such struggle can be inspired and motivated by historical precedents. Contemporary abolitionists often speak of the importance of situating themselves and their political struggles in a longer timeline. Charlene Carruthers, scholar-activist and cofounder of Black Youth Project 100, for instance, connects her commitment to political struggle and her political joy to "'celebrating my lineage, the people that I come from. Me and momma, my grandmama, the 10,000 grandmothers at my back. And knowing that I'm not at this thing alone and I'm not the first to do it.'"[94]

What struggles and demands could expand democratic freedoms for people with disabilities and other historically oppressed groups? Ben-Moshe's critique of neoliberalism could entail support for a strong welfare state that resists privatization, regulates corporations, and guarantees housing, health care, and other life necessities to its residents—something like the democratic socialism affirmed by Davis. Amber Knight, for instance, argues that deinstitutionalization is unfinished and "requires a more substantial public investment in home and community-based services" than Medicaid and other existing programs have thus far delivered.[95] More specifically, Ben-Moshe's attentiveness to disability could translate into a politics of care committed to interdependency, disability justice, and liberatory access.[96] Feminist political theorists have long challenged the idea of the autonomous, independent, and implicitly male citizen and have sought to reconceive citizenship on the model of interdependency, acknowledging that all of us need care at least at some points in our lives.[97] As Joan Tronto argues, care and its just distribution are key democratic concerns, a reality that is obscured when care is feminized, devalued, and privatized.[98] Disability justice theorists and activists similarly insist on interdependence. In the words of Mariame Kaba, "the notion that we supposedly are not interdependent on each other can only exist in an ableist world. Because if you have any sort of disability, you desperately need a relationship with other people—you can't be on your own or you will die. You have to recognize the interdependence, or build interdependence. You don't have a choice."[99]

Mia Mingus suggests that making social movement spaces accessible to people with disabilities—what she calls creating "liberatory access"—is part of the work of political transformation. Liberatory access, she says, "demands that the responsibility for access shifts from being an individual responsibility to a collective responsibility." By collectively seeking to eliminate or diminish the obstacles that exclude people with disabilities and prevent their full participation, "access shifts from being silencing to freeing; from being isolating to connecting; from hidden and invisible to visible; from burdensome to valuable; from a resentful obligation to an opportunity; from shameful to powerful; from rigid to creative . . . In this way, [l]iberatory access both resists against the world we don't want and actively builds the world we *do want.*"[100] This both/and, I have argued, both tearing down and building up, both refusing and affirming, is crucial to abolitionist politics. The next chapter discusses the abolitionist thinker who has developed that insight most fully: Angela Davis.

3

Reconstructing the State?

Angela Davis's Pursuit of Abolition Democracy

> The attempt to make black men American citizens was in a certain sense all a failure, but a splendid failure.
>
> —W. E. B. Du Bois, *Black Reconstruction in America*

Angela Davis is probably the best-known advocate of prison abolition in the United States and around the world. For more than fifty years, the scholar-activist has publicly advocated prison abolition as part of a project to radically overhaul the American and global order. In writings and public appearances, Davis critiques the interlocking structures of racism, sexism, and capitalism, which she holds responsible for repressive "tough-on-crime" policies and for most harmful conduct. She grants that alternative responses to harm need to be developed, but these are not her main focus. For Davis, the rejection of how the United States punishes is an entry point into a broader refusal of the current order and a commitment to reshape it along democratic socialist lines. "When we call for prison abolition, we are not imagining the isolated dismantling of the facilities we call prisons and jails," Davis says. "The prison is deeply structured by economic, social, and political conditions that themselves will also have to be dismantled."[1] The punishment system, in her account, is both a symptom of broader injustices and a tool to maintain them, which is why exchanging one form of punishment for another is not enough. Instead, Davis seeks to encourage organized collective action in pursuit of broad structural change. No other figure has made the case for prison abolition for such a long time or with such public visibility.

Despite her fame, Davis's abolitionist politics are rarely examined in detail and often misunderstood. Davis is a philosopher who studied with Adorno and Marcuse and taught for many years in the History of Consciousness and Feminist Studies departments at the University of California, Santa Cruz, where she is now Distinguished Professor Emerita. Yet her scholarship occupies an uneasy place in the academy, in part because of its public and activist bent. None of Davis's books have been published by a university press and her writing style tends to be geared toward a general audience rather than a specialized academic one.[2] Indeed, Davis's theoretical work is embedded in a lifetime of political engagement and activism, starting with campaigns in the 1960s to free political prisoners.[3] Davis became a political prisoner herself in 1970 when she spent sixteen months behind bars on charges of which she was ultimately acquitted, an outcome fought for by a global campaign to "free Angela." During her incarceration, she wrote two influential essays on Black radical politics, one focused on political prisoners, the other on Black women's resistance to slavery.[4] Her later publications on prison abolition are similarly connected to activism. In 1997, she cofounded the abolitionist grassroots organization Critical Resistance (CR), which remains one of the most visible abolitionist groups in the United States. Davis's activism has made her a hero to some, a villain to others, but both responses have often come at the expense of critical intellectual engagement. As Neil Roberts observes, "To write about Angela Davis is to wrestle with the paradox of a figure known more for a particular aesthetic and period of incarceration than for the overall content of her formidable intellectual work."[5] In political theory, in-depth critical engagements with her work remain rare.[6] Meanwhile, some of Davis's closest interlocutors wrongly assume that she is fundamentally opposed to electoral politics, law, and the state.

This chapter offers a different interpretation of Davis's abolitionism. Davis, I suggest, advances an *agonistic abolitionist politics* that overcomes the limitations of the paranoid abolitionisms discussed in the previous chapters. Foucault and Ben-Moshe both offer strong critiques of incarceration, but they are so preoccupied with the risk that proposed alternatives will fall short or be recaptured that they cannot say what abolition is for. Instead, they hope that unsettling commonsense thinking will spark transformation, and they affirm incarcerated people's protests and resistance efforts. Where Foucault's abolitionism tends to generate a sense of resignation, that of Ben-Moshe leads to a politics of purity that aims to eliminate carcerality in all its forms. Davis, in contrast, combines a strong critique of incarceration and the wish to unsettle commonsense thinking with a positive vision of abolition as the pursuit of democratic socialism.[7] She insists on acting in and on the world, with care not only for the common good but also for the inevitable limitations of our tactics and unintended consequences of our actions. Where Ben-Moshe argues for eradicating "carceral logics" from abolitionist minds and projects, Davis counsels abolitionists to "work" the tensions and contradictions they will inevitably encounter, to the best of their abilities and for the sake of equal democratic citizenship. Though Davis does not describe her politics this way, these are characteristics of agonism, a realist political theory that sees contestation as a fundamental and permanent feature of democratic politics because politics inevitably produces remainders.[8] Agonism counters idealizations of popular unity, political consensus, and impartial justice because they obscure dissensus, disavow responsibility for it, and close down struggles for other democratic articulations. It sees the pursuit of political purity as impossible and self-defeating, and paranoid suspicion as insufficient because it stops short of building or supporting democratic power. What is needed is an approach that knows we will never get abolition "right" once and for all but that can use all available resources to fight for it, nonetheless.

Like Ben-Moshe, Davis grounds her abolitionism in a historical precedent. She reaches back not to deinstitutionalization, however, but to Radical Reconstruction.[9] From 1865 to 1877, the U.S. federal government used military, legislative, and financial power to support the "reconstruction" of Southern states away from Black enslavement. This effort included food assistance, the creation of schools and universities for Black people, the drawing up of labor contracts for Black workers, and some land redistribution, all overseen by the hastily drawn up and underfunded federal "Freedmen's Bureau." The federal government also used military force to push back on mounting white supremacist violence in the South, where states and terrorist groups like the Ku Klux Klan used violence and intimidation to stop Black people from exercising their rights, including Black men's right to vote affirmed by the Fifteenth Amendment of 1870. Davis draws on W. E. B. Du Bois to theorize Reconstruction as an effort to realize equal citizenship through far-reaching structural change. The abolition of slavery, Du Bois argues in *Black Reconstruction in America* (1935), requires both the absence of slavery and the presence of institutions to democratize access to education, housing, health care, income, and political decision-making. Ben-Moshe's example of abolition—deinstitutionalization—successfully closed large disability institutions but failed to transform the broader society, which liberated people from one form of unfreedom but left them vulnerable to other forms. During Reconstruction, in contrast, institutional changes resulted in impressive advances for the formerly enslaved. Black people's citizenship and right to due process and equal protection were enshrined in the Constitution, as was Black men's right to vote. Freedmen held office at local, state, and federal levels, including the U.S. House of Representatives, the U.S. Senate, and state supreme courts, and Black lawmakers helped create taxpayer-funded public education.[10]

Reconstruction was ultimately defeated by the forces of white reaction and capital, and the Freedmen's Bureau gave way to almost a century of Jim Crow segregation. Still, for Davis, Reconstruction provides a vision of abolition as the realization of equal democratic citizenship, achieved through institutions that meet people's basic needs and provide mechanisms for participation in collective self-governance. She calls this vision "abolition democracy," ascribing broader normative meaning to a term Du Bois used to describe the mid-nineteenth century constellation of forces that opposed slavery and advocated interracial democracy. For Du Bois, abolition democracy names "the liberal movement among both laborers and small capitalists" for whom "the only real object of the Civil War . . . was the abolition of slavery, and it was convinced that this could be thoroughly accomplished only if the emancipated Negroes became free citizens and voters."[11] Its support of private property and belief in the American Dream clashed with Black demands for redistribution, however, and it did not fully recognize the threat that capital posed to its democratic vision. For Davis, in contrast, abolition democracy cannot be realized under capitalism but requires democratic socialism. It describes an egalitarian, participatory vision of democracy beyond capitalism and the color line.

To those who claim that prison abolition is an impossible dream, the example of Reconstruction shows that far-reaching social, political, and economic change *has already happened.* The example helps make the case that prison abolitionists are realists, whose democratic aspirations are grounded in political realities past and present. Of course, from a paranoid perspective, Davis's vision of abolition democracy looks suspicious. Who is to say that schools, clinics, and other institutions won't reproduce troubling power relations under the guise of realizing equal citizenship? After all, Foucault shows that schools do not simply liberate minds but also instill disciplinary norms, and Ben-Moshe demonstrates that modern medicine has been complicit in the marginalization and segregation of people with disabilities. Others have shown how government initiatives to "empower" citizens both enable and constrain them, and Saidiya Hartman offers a darker reading of Reconstruction that foregrounds the new kinds of subjection produced under the guise of freedom.[12] Most critiques of Davis's abolitionism express concern not about normalizing power or subjectivation, however, but rather about the state. For anarchist abolitionists William C. Anderson and Dean Spade, the state is inherently carceral and must be abolished along with police and prisons. From their perspective, Reconstruction looks like reformism and its failure evidences the state's irredeemable violence and anti-Blackness.[13] These authors find abolitionist examples in forms of collective action outside of and often against the state: mutual aid, autonomous "communes," confrontations with police and other forms of "armed self-defense."[14] For Spade, abolitionists who believe that sustained collective action may turn the carceral state into a life-supporting one are stuck in "fantasies . . . that prevent us from addressing [the state's] harms."[15]

Is it a *fantasy* to believe that the racist, carceral state could be transformed into a democratic, life-supporting one, as Spade argues? Or is this a *hope* that abolitionists rightly foster to sustain the kind of organizing and activism that could bring new realities into being? An agonistic abolitionism, I argue, is less certain than Anderson and Spade that the state is irredeemable and that voluntary communities are the only or best instantiations of democracy. It recognizes the violence and limitations of existing state institutions, but refuses to give up on democratic governance or public goods.[16] It also follows Craig and Ruth Wilson Gilmore in pluralizing and historicizing the state, now understood as a dynamic constellation of capacities whose exercise is determined by political struggle.[17] What possibilities open up for abolitionism when we trust neither the state nor communities to be inclined toward democracy, but also refuse to cede either to a carceral politics? This is what Davis's agonistic abolitionism allows us to consider.

I begin by discussing how Davis develops her agonistic abolitionism over time, as she adapts her earlier revolutionary politics to the punitive, post-revolutionary era of the 1990s and 2000s and critically engages Foucault's work. Second, I turn to a central feature of Davis's agonistic abolitionism: her focus on the relationship between slavery and prisons, and eventually between prison abolition and Radical Reconstruction. Finally, I discuss both the promise and challenges of thinking prison abolition through the lens of Reconstruction.

The Shifting Contours of Radical Politics

In her own telling, Angela Davis first became critical of prisons in the 1960s through her involvement in campaigns to free South African freedom fighter Nelson Mandela, Black Panthers Huey Newton and Ericka Huggins, and Puerto Rican nationalist Lolita Lebrón.[18] Like others on the Left, she understood all four to be political prisoners, accused of crimes but guilty only of organized resistance to racist oppression. Her involvement in these campaigns, in turn, was part of her growing engagement with antiracist and anticapitalist organizing. Born in 1944, Davis grew up in a segregated neighborhood in Birmingham, Alabama, that was frequently targeted by white terrorists. The attacks included the bombing of a church by the KKK that killed four Black girls, some of whom Davis knew. After attending a progressive Quaker high school in New York, Davis enrolled at Brandeis University where she worked with Herbert Marcuse and spent a year studying abroad in Paris. "By the mid-1960s," Neil Roberts writes, "Davis' political thought was influenced by Marcuse's mentorship and the intellectual currents of Frankfurt School critical theory to which Marcuse was a contributor, the ethical dimensions of Hegelian and Marxist thought, black social movements, and existential phenomenology."[19] Following her graduation, she spent two years in Frankfurt studying with Adorno, before moving to California to complete her PhD in philosophy with Marcuse at the University of California, San Diego.[20] In 1968, she joined the Communist Party and the Black Communist Che Lumumba Club, and she soon joined the Black Panther Party in Los Angeles.[21] In 1969, Davis began teaching in the philosophy department at UCLA, a job she went to court to keep when the Board of Regents tried repeatedly to fire her for her Communism.

It was not until Davis became a political prisoner herself that she published her first works calling for prison abolition. Between 1970 and 1972, Davis was detained for sixteen months while awaiting trial on charges including kidnapping and murder. The charges stemmed from Jonathan Jackson's armed takeover of a courtroom that left him, the two defendants, and the judge dead. Davis knew Jonathan from her involvement in another political prisoner campaign: She had helped create the defense committee for Jonathan's brother George Jackson and two other men accused of killing a prison guard in California's Soledad Prison.[22] According to government officials, Davis was accused of complicity in the courtroom takeover because of her personal connections to both Jonathan and George Jackson and because the guns Jonathan used in the event were registered in her name. Davis, though, maintained her innocence, explained that she owned guns for self-defense, and argued that she was targeted because she was a Black revolutionary communist, a message relayed by a powerful international solidarity campaign that soon took off.[23] In jail, Davis began working with activist intellectual Bettina Aptheker on an edited volume of mostly Black revolutionary writings from, about, and against prison, including texts she herself wrote while incarcerated.

If They Come in the Morning . . . Voices of Resistance was published in 1971 while Davis was still behind bars. In a coauthored preface, Davis and Aptheker write that they hope the book will help unite the Left for a collective struggle against fascistic state repression and ultimately for the revolutionary overthrow of capitalism. This struggle includes prison abolition, they say, because the state increasingly uses the judicial and prison system for political repression, as evidenced by the imprisonment of both political radicals (including Davis herself) and large numbers of poor Black and Brown people behind bars. Prison abolition is aligned with revolutionary transformation, not just of prisons and courts but of society as a whole.[24] The book includes Davis's essay "Political Prisoners, Prisons, and Black Liberation," written from jail, which theorizes punishment as a repressive state tactic to maintain a racist, capitalist order and places political prisoners at the forefront of revolutionary struggle. Political prisoners already wish to change the existing order—whatever crime they are accused or convicted of, Davis says, they are in fact incarcerated because of the threat they represent to the status quo—and other prisoners increasingly see themselves as "the victims of an oppressive politico-economic order, swiftly becoming conscious of the causes underlying their victimization."[25]

Davis's writings on prison abolition in this period are explicitly conceived as mobilizing tools meant to advance imminent revolutionary change. She sees both mass mobilization and visionary leadership as a necessary part of revolutionary transformation. Political leaders should provide not only a diagnosis of the present moment but also tactical and strategic guidance.

In a letter to imprisoned Black Panther Party member Ericka Huggins, Davis praises Huggins and Bobby Seale for their work "to illuminate the path toward concrete expression of our grievances and our demands for revolutionary change."[26] In a different text, she praises George Jackson's "extraordinary ability . . . to persuade his captive companions to embark on the correct path to liberation."[27] The vision of revolution is centralized and totalizing. Leaders, both incarcerated and nonincarcerated, will equip people with the theoretical and practical tools to overthrow capitalism and achieve "total liberation." This revolutionary abolitionism found a wide, international audience. Members of the French Prisons Information Group (GIP) visited Davis and Jackson behind bars, for instance, and the GIP dedicated a booklet to Jackson's assassination.[28]

The revolution Davis hoped for did not come to be. A counterinsurgency prevailed that, far from abolishing prisons, expanded policing and punishment to unprecedented levels.[29] "When I first became involved in antiprison activism during the late 1960s," Davis recalls in 2003, "I was astounded to learn that there were then close to two hundred thousand people in prison. Had anyone then told me that in three decades ten times as many people would be locked away in cages, I would have been absolutely incredulous."[30] Yet bipartisan support for "tough-on-crime" policies, including increased funding for police and new prison construction and corresponding cuts to welfare, as well as the enactment of harsh mandatory minimum sentences, "three strikes and you're out" laws, and limitations of parole and early release, led to a skyrocketing of the number of incarcerated people in the 1980s and '90s. As prison populations exploded, they became more racialized, to the point that by the mid-1990s, one in three young Black men was incarcerated, on probation, or on parole.[31] Davis argues that the dominant ideology of colorblindness helps mask the injustice and harm of racialized mass punishment, which is attributed to Black criminality and justified as a necessary protection of public safety.[32] There are not enough "broad, radical grassroots movements in poor black communities" to offer ideological counterweight to this criminalization of Black Americans, Davis observes in a 1997 essay, and there is "waning anticapitalist consciousness" in society at large.[33] The fall of the Berlin Wall and the collapse of the Soviet Union have led the United States to exchange the figure of the communist for that of the criminal as quintessential national enemy, she says, further justifying massive financial investments in the war on crime.[34]

In this political context, Davis uses prison abolition as an opportunity to revive an antiracist and anticapitalist democratic politics. While parts of the Left cling to lost dreams of socialist revolution, Davis develops abolitionist theories and practices that take on the extraordinary racial and class violence of mass incarceration and the liberal-democratic state responsible for it.[35] Having left the Communist Party in 1991, she cofounds the abolitionist group Critical Resistance (CR) in 1997. CR's first conference, "Critical Resistance: Beyond the Prison Industrial Complex," gathers several thousand activists, academics, and current and former prisoners in Berkeley the following year and helps energize prison abolitionist thinking and activism nationwide.[36] In a series of essays and books, Davis theorizes an abolitionist politics that is informed by Foucault's paranoid abolitionism but also overcomes its limitations. Specifically, Davis recognizes the value of disorientation and uncertainty but overcomes the negativity of paranoid critique with an agonistic politics that can articulate what abolition is *for*.

Davis's Agonistic Abolitionism

Davis is not commonly thought of as an agonistic abolitionist. Some see her as a reformist because the abolitionism she develops from the 1990s onward decenters armed insurrection.[37] This is also the period when Davis breaks with the Communist Party—after decades of membership and two runs for vice president on its ticket—and becomes firmly established in the academy, so it is easy to conclude that she has abandoned her revolutionary roots. Yet Davis's abolitionism, I argue, is better understood as a reconceptualization of radical change than its abandonment or betrayal. She has abandoned a vision of revolution as a dramatic event in which militants seize control of the means of production, but she remains committed to a radical overhaul of society and ultimately the global order. Like many Marxists and abolitionists, she now conceptualizes radical change as a long-term, incremental process.[38]

Others recognize Davis's politics as radical and abolitionist but assume this must mean that she rejects electoral politics, law, and the state. Quinn Lester, for instance, claims that Davis "alongside other abolitionists today does not view the state as an appropriate or even useful actor in th[e] process [of abolition]" and suggests she relies instead on "the self-organizing capacity of the people themselves to both destroy carceral power and build new liberatory institutions."[39] It is true that Davis values social movement organizing and sees it as the motor of progressive or radical change; in this sense she relies on "the self-organizing capacity of the people." This is not a rejection of the state or state institutions, however.[40] When asked whether she thinks "it is time for people to disengage completely from the main political parties and from this concept that our 'leaders' call 'representative democracy'" by "stopping voting and starting to create something from the bottom up that is new and organic," for instance, Davis responds in the negative. "I certainly don't think existing political parties can constitute our primary arenas of struggle, but I do think that the electoral arena can be used as a terrain on which to organize," she says.[41] Similarly, although Eduardo Mendieta writes in his introduction to *Abolition Democracy* that "DuBois [*sic*] represents for Davis an anti-capitalist, antistatist, antilaw perspective," Davis says in the book that "of course we [prison abolitionists] must call upon the law—both at the national and international level, but we should also recognize the limitations of law."[42] Both calling upon institutions, discourses, and practices and recognizing their limits: these are elements of Davis's agonistic abolitionist politics.

Davis's abolitionism is not only against the prison industrial complex but also for democratic self-governance and equal citizenship. She sees tensions and contradictions not as problems for abolitionism to overcome but rather, in agonistic and realist fashion, as central and inevitable features of political life. She knows that even the best democratic politics will generate its own problems and exclusions, but she does not conclude that politics is futile. Abolitionists must "work" contradictions, she says, implying that political action is a tactical and strategic doing based on existing realities. They must "passionately attend . . . to the needs of prisoners" by calling for better prison conditions, for instance, "and *at the same time* call for alternatives to sentencing altogether, no more prison construction, and abolitionist strategies that question the place of the prison in our future."[43] Calling for better prison conditions—better health care, more educational opportunities, etc.—might grow prison budgets and even enhance prisons' legitimacy in the eyes of the public, but it would support the survival of those incarcerated now. Conversely, supporting budget cuts to carceral facilities may allow abolitionists to keep their hands clean, but it may result in "leaner and meaner" but no less resilient jails and prisons.[44] In *Freedom Is a Constant Struggle,* Davis similarly advocates approaches that are flexible and that can "work the contradiction," for instance between opposing the military and still supporting gay rights within the institution.[45] There is no categorical distinction between reform and abolition, she says. Abolitionist political practice is situated, strategic, and imperfect.[46]

Working the tension, I suggest, means proceeding with caution, charting a path between naiveté and resignation. It involves asking, when considering potential demands to make or campaigns to organize, what will happen if we win, while acknowledging that we cannot fully control or foresee the effects of our actions.[47] This approach neither restricts abolitionist politics to electoral politics and state institutions nor defines abolitionism inherently in opposition to the state. It is messier than a politics of purity, but it is better equipped to win. Where Ben-Moshe strives for an abolitionism that would be free of "carceral logics," Davis endorses any initiative that attempts "to reverse the impact of the prison industrial complex on our world" and "advance the abolitionist agenda of decarceration," even if it is "associated" directly or indirectly "with the existing system of criminal justice."[48] Her agonistic approach incorporates elements of paranoid critique without being defined by it.[49] First, like Foucault and Ben-Moshe, Davis offers a "strong theory" that defines prisons expansively. She uses the term "prison industrial complex" (PIC) to depict punishment as an industry in which various actors—private corporations, politicians, media entities—have vested interests, including financial ones.[50] The term broadens analyses of prisons beyond the criminal legal system or issues of crime to "a set of symbiotic relationships among correctional communities, transnational corporations, media conglomerates, guards' unions, and legislative and court agendas."[51]

Second, Davis seeks to expose the problematic nature of imprisonment. Like Foucault and Ben-Moshe, she relies on genealogy to denaturalize prisons and generate disorientation and unsettlement, which she sees as politically productive.[52] Davis also suggests that the very idea of prison abolition can puncture the perceived self-evidence or necessity of prisons. "Raising the possibility of abolishing jails and prisons as the institutionalized and normalized means of addressing social problems in an era of migrating corporations, unemployment and homelessness, and collapsing public services," she says, "can hopefully help to interrupt the current law-and-order discourse that has such a grip on the collective imagination, facilitated as it is by deep and hidden influences of racism."[53] She adds that an abolitionist strategy is "designed to *force a rethinking* of the increasingly repressive role of the state during this era of late capitalism and to carve out a space for resistance."[54] Here, Davis converges with paranoid abolitionism's "faith in exposure," its belief that making oppression visible will incite radical thinking and experimentation.

Davis combines these paranoid elements, however, with a defense of democracy missing in Foucault and Ben-Moshe. Her strong critique and faith in exposure are not embedded in a framework that relentlessly anticipates the recapturing of political successes. Where paranoid critique seeks to stave off disappointment, Davis's abolitionism is motivated by hope for a better future and risks specific proposals to reach it. Her account of abolition democracy, informed by Radical Reconstruction, provides the fullest articulation of her normative vision.[55] If Reconstruction can seem like an abolitionist precedent to Davis, that is not only because her abolitionism is less paranoid than that of Foucault and Ben-Moshe, but also because her abolitionism, unlike Foucault's, inscribes prisons in the history of slavery and racial captivity.

Centering Slavery

In her 1998 essay "Racialized Punishment and Prison Abolition," Davis notes that *Discipline and Punish* fails to theorize the racial and gendered dimensions of punishment, a failure that distorts its genealogy of the prison. Foucault traces Western European and U.S. penitentiaries back to sixteenth-century European institutions of confinement like the Rasphuis in Amsterdam or the Maison de Force in Ghent, Davis observes, but he fails altogether to examine "the impact of the institution of slavery on U.S. systems of punishment."[56] Foucault's silence on slavery entails a silence on race and racism, Davis argues, not just in Foucault's work but in most prison abolitionism, especially but not only in Europe. After all, *Discipline and Punish* is "arguably the most influential text in contemporary studies of the prison system."[57] Davis sets out to correct the whiteness of prison studies and abolition by developing a history of American punishment attuned to race, class, and gender. She begins this work in "Racialized Punishment and Prison Abolition" and develops it more fully in the short book *Are Prisons Obsolete?* (2003). Against the Eurocentric whiteness of *Discipline and Punish*, Davis envisions a genealogy of U.S. punishment that would "accentuate the links between confinement, punishment, and race."[58] Where Foucault connects prisons to schools, workplaces, and clinics, and Liat Ben-Moshe expands on the carceral nature of disability institutions like mental hospitals and nursing homes,

Davis connects prisons to "at least four great systems of incarceration . . . : the reservation system, slavery, the mission system, and the internment camps of World War II."[59]

Davis's understanding of incarceration, like that of Foucault and Ben-Moshe, goes far beyond the criminal legal system. The internment of Japanese Americans resulted from an executive order after Japan's attack on Pearl Harbor, while Spanish missions in California, which forced Indigenous people into settlements called reductions, were operated by Catholic missionaries.[60] Racial chattel slavery was premised on private property rights in human beings and a transatlantic market in their trade, and to this day, tribal reservations are overseen by the U.S. Department of the Interior. Yet Davis argues these systems of incarceration share important features, both with each other and with jails and prisons. They all forcibly confine people, based on their ascribed identity or class position rather than on any act of wrongdoing, and they serve to assimilate, segregate, or exploit. Though criminal punishment purports to respond to specific acts of lawbreaking, Davis argues that in the United States it actually singles out poor people of color.[61] And though punishment purports to protect public safety, Davis argues that it also variously assimilates (under the guise of rehabilitation), segregates (especially in the case of supermax prisons with solitary confinement), and exploits (through un-paid or underpaid prison labor).

Davis focuses her analysis on the continuities between racial chattel slavery and state punishment past and present. She argues that slavery was never legally abolished, only displaced to the criminal legal system through a "loophole" in the Thirteenth Amendment, which declares: "Neither slavery nor involuntary servitude, except as punishment for crime whereof the party shall have been duly convicted, shall exist within the United States, or any place subject to their jurisdiction."[62] For Davis, the exception clause authorizes slavery's continued existence in the form of criminal punishment, an argument that has gained a wide audience through Ava DuVernay's 2016 documentary *13th*.[63] The precise role of the amendment is disputed, but criminal punishment undeniably became a tool to oppress and exploit the formerly enslaved.[64] After the Civil War, Southern states began instituting "Black Codes," which made Black people punishable for "offenses" such as being unemployed, unhoused, exercising freedom of movement, or otherwise being "idle and disorderly"—all considered forms of criminal vagrancy.[65] White people convicted of crimes were typically sent to prison, but Black people were often "leased out" to private entities such as former plantation owners or railroad companies to perform forced labor under brutal conditions. The convict lease system was "the spawn of slavery," W. E. B. Du Bois argued, as Southern criminal courts "sought to do by judicial decisions what the legislatures had formerly sought to do by specific law—namely, reduce the freedmen to serfdom."[66]

In her critical engagement with *Discipline and Punish,* Davis shows which aspects of Foucault's genealogy must be changed to account for these facets of American history. Where *Discipline and Punish* limits its discussion of the United States to mostly white penitentiaries in the Northeast (Walnut Street Jail and Eastern State Penitentiary in Pennsylvania, and Auburn Prison in New York), Davis discusses slave plantations and convict leasing in Alabama, Mississippi, and Arkansas. Where Foucault theorizes imprisonment as an effort to transform the "soul" of deviant citizens, Davis reminds the reader that until the Civil War, Black people were rarely incarcerated in penitentiaries because they were claimed to lack a soul and because, like white women, they were denied full citizenship and were more typically punished by individual men. Where Foucault posits a shift from the spectacular violence of public torture to the seemingly incorporeal power of surveillance and detention, Davis theorizes the transfer of physical violence and forced labor from slavery to the state punishment apparatus. Last, Davis expands Foucault's discussion of the "'self-evident' character of the prison" by noting that "within the US—and increasingly in postcolonial Europe—the disproportionate presence of people of color among incarcerated populations has also acquired a 'self-evident' character." This is not because these groups are thought to need transformation, she adds, but rather because "the prison's purpose is . . . to concentrate and eliminate politically dissident and racialized populations."[67] Unlike Foucault, Davis also highlights women's contributions to freedom struggles, considers how gender affects state punishment, and theorizes sexual violence as the product of gendered, racial, and class oppression.[68] Sexual violence, Davis argues, cannot be ended by more or more equitable criminal law enforcement, if that could even be obtained. Rather than a solution to sexual violence, jails and prisons are part of their cause, she says. Sexual violence is a common part of incarceration in the United States, both in the form of high rates of rape and sexual assault, and in the form of strip- and body cavity searches.[69]

Finally, Davis's attention to race and racism allows her to link the struggle against prisons explicitly to slavery abolition and take inspiration from Radical Reconstruction. *Are Prisons Obsolete?* places prison abolition in a lineage of abolitionist social movements that were "eventually more or less successful" at dismantling racist institutions—slavery, lynching, and segregation—that seemed normal and necessary to most.[70] The book theorizes prisons as repositories of practices that have been deemed unacceptable in the regular political order and that are all forced disproportionately on people of color: unfreedom and domination, forced and unpaid or barely paid labor, sexual assault. When Davis inscribes prison abolition in a historical lineage of antiracist social movements, then, she acknowledges the incompleteness of these previous victories. Each time, white supremacy persisted, which required new battles to be fought. Davis does not conclude that antiracist organizing is futile, however. Rather, she calls on people today to continue the unfinished work of previous generations. In *Abolition Democracy* (2005), she specifically turns to the example of Radical Reconstruction.

Visions of Abolition

Davis's interpretation of Reconstruction is inspired by W. E. B. Du Bois's *Black Reconstruction in America,* which theorizes it in radical-utopian fashion as a workers' revolution led by enslaved people.[71] Black people freed themselves from slavery by going on a "general strike," abandoning plantations, and joining the Union army, Du Bois argues.[72] The army could not have won without the military contributions of the formerly enslaved, which he says also humanized Black people in the eyes of whites: "Nothing else made Negro citizenship conceivable, but the record of the Negro soldier as a fighter."[73] The military victory over the slaveholder class gave way to a "dictatorship of labor" represented by the Freedmen's Bureau. The revolution did not last: Du Bois writes that the effort to "make black men American citizens was in a certain sense all a failure, but a splendid failure." It was no less "splendid" for having failed, or, more precisely, for having been defeated by a "counter-revolution of property." Black people took on a "great and just cause; fighting the battle of the oppressed and despised humanity of every race and color," and working hard to secure access to education and other basic needs.[74] Du Bois describes the Reconstruction period as "a brief moment in the sun" for Black people before they "moved back again toward slavery" in the form of bonded labor, convict leasing, and Jim Crow segregation.[75]

Davis discusses Du Bois and Reconstruction at greatest length in *Abolition Democracy* (2005), a collection of interviews with philosopher Eduardo Mendieta. Her discussion revolves around the insufficiency of negative freedom—freedom from external restraint—for slavery abolition. The formerly enslaved, Davis writes, needed much more than legal emancipation or negative freedom. They needed "the economic means for their subsistence. They also needed access to educational institutions and needed to claim voting and other political rights, a process that had begun, but remained incomplete, during the short period of radical reconstruction that ended in 1877. Du Bois thus argues that a host of democratic institutions are needed to fully achieve abolition—thus abolition democracy."[76] For Davis, abolition democracy describes a political and economic order that provides education and health care, economic resources, and opportunities to participate in political decision-making to all, including Black people and other racialized groups.[77] Radical Reconstruction began this process, but it "remained incomplete," which allowed aspects of slavery to linger. The incomplete abolition of slavery is felt most acutely "not only . . . by black prisoners," Davis writes, "but [also] by poor Latino, Native American, Asians and white prisoners" and is evidenced by the growing reliance on prisons as "a receptacle for people who are deemed the detritus of society."[78]

Davis thus theorizes the twentieth- and twenty-first-century prison industrial complex as "a result of the *failure* to enact abolition democracy."[79] The ongoing social, economic, and political marginalization of Black Americans facilitated their mass incarceration more than a century after Reconstruction. Racist ideologies link Blackness and criminality and treat Black people as disposable.[80] Conversely, prison abolition would not only reduce reliance on prisons and jails but it would further seek to realize the kinds of political and economic changes that Reconstruction began but did not finish. "Prison abolition is a way of talking about the pitfalls of the particular version of democracy represented by US capitalism," Davis writes.[81] Like Foucault and Ben-Moshe, she sees prison abolition as requiring broad structural change far beyond jails and prisons, but only Davis provides a sketch of the kind of society that prison abolitionists seek to create. As I will now discuss, Davis's alignment of prison abolition with the establishment of democratic socialism, understood as a continuation of Radical Reconstruction, both solves problems for abolitionism and creates difficulties of its own.

A New Reconstruction? The Complexity of Abolition

On the one hand, Davis's turn to Reconstruction solves the problem of abolition's negativity, which the previous chapters showed can lead to resignation or to a politics of purity. For Davis, prison abolition is both a fight *against* prisons and a struggle *for* institutions to meet people's needs. "Abolitionist advocacy," Davis says, "can and should occur in relation to demands for quality education, for antiracist job strategies, for free healthcare, and within other progressive movements."[82] The positive vision of prison abolition, combined with its inscription in a long and impressive history of Black freedom struggles, seems better equipped to support long-term social movement building than the paranoid abolitionisms of Foucault and Ben-Moshe. Davis sees broad popular organizing and mobilization as the motor of progressive and radical political change, and she insists that this work is long, sometimes tedious, and requires patience and persistence. "Organizing is not synonymous with mobilizing," she writes. What is needed is not just intermittent public demonstrations in the streets but also the creation and maintenance of communities in struggle.[83] "Sometimes we have to do the work even though we don't yet see a glimmer on the horizon that it's actually going to be possible." Even then, it is important to persist. Organizing then becomes a preparation or rehearsal for moments or conjunctures when political interventions might be possible.[84] A positive vision of what prison abolition is for, I suggest, can help motivate and sustain organizing work, especially when immediate victories are hard to come by. At the same time, precisely because Davis presents a positive vision, the contested meaning of abolition and the complexity of abolitionist politics become more readily apparent. I will discuss three areas of abolitionist debate related to Davis's account. My aim is not to settle these debates but to help us see the issues and disagreements at hand more clearly.

First, exactly how does contemporary imprisonment relate to slavery, and abolition democracy to prison abolition? I have argued that the example of Reconstruction allows Davis to overcome the limitations of paranoid abolitionisms by offering a tangible example of radical change to be inspired by. It helps make abolition thinkable and can embolden political actors by framing their task as continuations or emulations of past struggles and accomplishments rather than as total innovation.[85] Still, as my discussion has shown, Davis also draws more direct connections between slavery and imprisonment, suggesting causal links (because Reconstruction failed, mass incarceration was possible) as well as structural similarities (slave plantations and prisons are both forms of racialized confinement and exploitation). Some abolitionists have expressed concern that descriptions of prisons as the "new slavery" offer misleading understandings of the present. These include the myth that private companies exploit incarcerated people's labor at a large scale and that prison privatization is a driving force behind mass incarceration, when in fact the vast majority of jails and prisons are publicly run and only a fraction of incarcerated people perform labor for the private sector.[86] Craig and Ruth Wilson Gilmore have argued that a narrow focus on corporate profit motives obscures the *political* drivers of mass incarceration, such as the state's use of punishment to shore up its waning legitimacy, eroded by free-market, antistate ideologies.[87]

Abolitionists also disagree about the role of confinement and coercion in a democracy. Davis invokes the term "abolition democracy" to give positive content to her abolitionism, but other theorists of the concept do not challenge imprisonment or punishment as such. Du Bois critiques the criminalization of Black people, for instance, but he also holds that people with "depraved natures" should be "firmly but humanely" punished with the aim of correcting them, ideally through forced labor.[88] Among other reforms, he recommends the establishment of juvenile reformatories to separate young criminals from adults,[89] a measure that contemporary prison abolitionists would likely reject as reformism that ultimately strengthens the penal system. Similarly, political theorist Joel Olson, who offers the most in-depth political theory exploration of abolition democracy to date, argues that realizing abolition democracy today requires ensuring that everyone's basic needs are met and abolishing "explicit and normalized white advantages in housing, education, employment, asset accumulation, health, criminal justice, and politics." This abolition is necessary, he says, "both because such preferences are morally wrong and because struggles against them point toward greater democratic possibilities."[90] He mentions racial inequalities in criminal justice but does not prioritize them over other racial disparities, nor does he privilege punishment when theorizing the racialized harms of the American state or critique prisons as intolerable state violence.

These divergent interpretations raise the difficult question of what forms of coercion are permissible in a robust abolition democracy, and which are beyond the pale. It is a sign of Davis's realism that her abolitionism does not require the complete elimination of confinement. In her 1971 essay on political prisoners, she advocates "abolish[ing] the prison system *in its present form,*" namely as a tool of the state to suppress political dissent and maintain racial and class hierarchies.[91] Decades later, in *Are Prisons Obsolete?,* she describes prison abolition as a project to "crowd out the prison so that it would inhabit *increasingly smaller areas* of our social and psychic landscape."[92] Elsewhere, she argues that an abolition democracy would have less need for punishment because there would be less lawbreaking and harm linked to oppression and marginalization, and less need to deflect attention from such social problems.[93] A robust democracy would also be less willing to condemn people to civil or social death or otherwise treat them as disposable, she suggests.[94] For instances where people "assault the rights and bodies of others," Davis proposes "a justice system based on reparation and reconciliation rather than retribution and vengeance."[95] This nuanced critique places Davis in the company of Joy James, who writes that "what is reasonably contested is not the responsibility and need to contain people to prevent them from harming themselves or others" but rather "containment fashioned as enslavement and policing and imprisonment shaped by racial and economic status."[96] Ben-Moshe, in contrast, rejects confinement even for "the dangerous few."[97]

Second, Davis's invocation of Reconstruction confronts abolitionists with the democratic remainders of that example. As Saidiya Hartman shows, Reconstruction ended chattel slavery but also inaugurated new forms of Black subjection. These included the burdening of freedmen with debt: the symbolic debt of gratitude for the "gift" of emancipation, and the financial debt of exploitative sharecropping arrangements falsely framed as economic freedom.[98] When the Freedmen's Bureau negotiated contracts for agricultural labor, moreover, it drew them up in a way that imposed or reinforced a patriarchal family structure, in which the male head of household controls his wife and children.[99] Furthermore, Black people were denied the promised "forty acres and a mule," control over land that would allow for economic independence, while white people benefited from the massive dispossession of Indigenous lands authorized by the Homestead Act of 1862 and the Southern Homestead Act of 1866. Keri Leigh Merritt describes these Acts as "unquestionably the most extensive, radical, redistributive governmental policy in US history," one that "excluded African-Americans not in letter, but in practice" and generated white wealth through Indigenous dispossession and elimination.[100]

Not only did full abolition democracy remain unrealized during the brief period of Reconstruction, then, but the very project of realizing equal democratic citizenship in the United States exists in significant tension with struggles for Indigenous sovereignty.[101] As Kevin Bruyneel observes, the American Left tends to remember Reconstruction as a story about race and class, in which a multiracial working-class coalition was defeated by capitalist white supremacy. Working-class whites ultimately chose racial solidarity with white capitalists and the "wages of whiteness" (white people's superior social standing) over class solidarity with Black people, the story goes, thus betraying abolition democracy. What is missing or undertheorized in such accounts, Bruyneel argues, is that abolition democracy was defeated not simply by capitalist white supremacy but by white *settler* capitalism. Black people's "movement back toward slavery," he observes, "was caused in significant part by their dispossession from land and the prospect of owning land," which was violently seized from Indigenous people for the benefit of whites.[102]

What would it mean to draw not only prison abolitionist but also decolonial lessons from Reconstruction? Such an effort would fit with the abolitionisms of Davis as well as Ben-Moshe, who both critique settler-colonialism. Davis often critiques the Israeli occupation as a contemporary example of settler-colonialism and argues that prison abolitionism must include transnational solidarity with Palestinians.[103] Regarding Reconstruction, Bruyneel suggests that a decolonial abolitionist approach must theorize land outside of the reductive settler capitalist frame that treats it as private property to be exploited, bought, or sold. This means attending to Indigenous peoples' "ontologically central relationality to the lands and the human and nonhuman life residing in and through it," he says, and demanding that the U.S. government respect its treaties with tribes.[104] It means attending, also, to the many meanings that land held for Black people during Reconstruction and to all that was lost when Black people were dispossessed from their homeplaces. The dispossession of Indigenous peoples and Black people is not the same, and Bruyneel acknowledges "tensions and incompatible objectives" between Black and Indigenous politics.[105] Still, "a blended abolitionist and decolonizing approach could turn the meaning of [the Reconstruction] era into something new and germinal for contemporary theorizing of solidarity, coinhabitation, governance, and resistance," he says. "This approach requires rigorous attention to the ways in which the disavowal of Indigenous people and settler colonialism undermines not only the effort to attend to important structural components of the US political context but also the attempt to excavate and analyze the deeper roots of white supremacy, anti-Blackness, heteropatriarchy, and capitalist domination."[106]

Third, the example of Reconstruction brings to a head abolitionist disagreement about the role of the state in abolition. Reconstruction followed five years of Civil War, a conflict so deadly that it killed an estimated 2.5 percent of the U.S. population.[107] And the Reconstruction efforts were backed up by the military force of the federal government, which Du Bois argues was necessary in the face of violent white resistance to Black equality by repressive local governments and terrorist groups like the Klan. As Quinn Lester puts it, "Du Bois's abolition democracy . . . was one where the predominant problem was the inability for black freedmen to organize and fully control the apparatus of the state to fight white supremacist violence."[108] In Du Bois's words, "force alone could dislodge the planters and allied capitalists and firmly fasten labor government in the South."[109] Yet in 1877 the federal government withdrew its troops from the South and Reconstruction collapsed. The experiment to make the formerly enslaved free citizens and laborers gave way to a white democracy based on state-sanctioned racial segregation, discrimination, and enduring settler-colonialism. As Lester rightly observes, "Du Bois' story brings to the fore—both for abolitionists in the 19th century and today—the question of state violence and abolition's relationship to state sovereignty as such."[110] Abolitionists, it turns out, are deeply divided on the issue.

On the one hand, there is broad agreement that the struggle for prison abolition may include violent conflict. In the 1970s, Davis saw armed conflict as part of revolution. The "black masses," she wrote from jail, "are growing conscious of their responsibility to defend [political prisoners] and ultimately to bring about total liberation through armed revolution, if it must come to this."[111] In the 1990s, she critiques the "quintessentially masculinist" conception of revolutionary practice that conflates power with "power over the means of violence," but she stops short of rejecting violent resistance outright.[112] Abolitionist thinker and activist Mariame Kaba, meanwhile, raises the question of war in a 2019 interview. "I think about war a lot," she says. "I think about it in the context of abolition, knowing full well that there could have not been an abolition to challenge slavery without the civil war . . . So, I'm thinking a lot about how we're going to organize ourselves in this moment, in our oppressive proto-fascist moment, and I'm thinking about if we're going to need war again in order to actually facilitate the next phase of the long abolitionist phase. Kind of the third Reconstruction that some people are talking about."[113] William C. Anderson similarly reflects that "escalated conflict and perhaps another full-scale war are real possibilities" and argues that "armed self-defense should become more of a serious consideration."[114]

Abolitionists disagree, however, about how violence relates to the state. Where Du Bois and, in my reading, Davis depict violence as a tool of the state that must sometimes be used to protect Black freedom and interracial democracy from white supremacist forces, anarchist abolitionists reject this vision. For Dean Spade, "police, prisons, borders, and militaries are co-constitutive with the state form" and police and prison abolition must include the abolition of the state. He disputes the idea that the state could equalize power relations within a polity. The state does not stop but merely regulates domination by "owners, bosses, and landlords," he says, at best limiting extreme abuses while strictly curtailing popular resistance. "Even communist and socialist countries have been organized to facilitate . . . domination and extraction for elite interests," he adds.[115] William C. Anderson similarly advocates an anarchist abolitionism in *The Nation on No Map*. Black people have never been full citizens of the United States, Anderson argues, and they have suffered both violence and abandonment at its hands. Their position of "statelessness" is an injustice but one with radical potential. It could be the first step in "collective detachment" from the United States in particular and from the state form as such. Such detachment could enable revolutionary abolitionism, based on the demand for autonomy and advanced through community-based action to support collective survival.[116] "People are creating mutual aid groups, planting gardens, caring for one another, and sharing funds to support each other's needs. We can begin to organize these efforts to form an economy of interconnected communities and efforts to counteract the neglect and violence of the state," Anderson writes.[117] Rather than take Reconstruction as an example, then, these authors turn to mutual aid and collective self-defense: grassroots institutions based on voluntary participation and without claim to a monopoly on legitimate violence.

For these anarchist abolitionists, it is simply not realistic to expect that state power could support Black liberation, meet marginalized people's needs, or expand and deepen democratic self-governance. Like Davis, they are political realists, but they offer different accounts of reality and assessments of what is possible. For Anderson, ancestors who saw the right to vote as an "unrealistic means of achieving liberation" confirm the need for Black anarchism today.[118] Similarly, Spade argues that "fantasies of [the state] becoming caring prevent us from addressing its harms." "People fear chaos, violence, and mayhem without it," he adds, "yet *we know* that it produces rather than prevents or addresses violence, and that shared practices of care and collective self-determination can better meet our needs than systems based in extraction and domination."[119] Invoking efforts to hold the state accountable, appeal to it, or claim its power, Saidiya Hartman says, "*We know better.* There is too much history, too much blood to imagine that the apparatus of terror and violence might avail itself for our liberation or lend itself to uses other than policing and extraction, militarism and death."[120]

Who is right? Is it a fantasy to believe that the state might come to support what Davis calls abolition democracy? Or is it a fantasy to believe that we might realize such far-reaching radical change without enlisting the state apparatus? The question is hard to answer because both visions are so far removed from current realities, and both anarchist and democratic socialist abolitionisms involve a kind of hopefulness that what seems realistic or impossible now could drastically shift. As Kaba puts it, "hope is persevering against the evidence and then watching the evidence change."[121] Still, the historical evidence of Reconstruction warrants more hopefulness for the state than some anarchist abolitionists allow. When Anderson cites Du Bois's dictum "The slave went free; stood a brief moment in the sun; then moved back again toward slavery," he reads in it only the continuities of Black unfreedom. "From the nonevent of emancipation to the afterlife of slavery, Black America has been required to consistently think outside of the state because the state has consistently been our oppressor," he writes.[122] Davis, I have argued, acknowledges the continuities of slavery but also highlights its interruption: the "brief moment in the sun," which was not simply an escape from the state but rather the temporary and incomplete experience of equal citizenship. She offers an abolitionist politics that is at once hopeful and suspicious, both of the state and of the so-called community. The next chapter applies this agonistic approach to the abolitionist debate where the role of the state seems most fraught: How should abolitionists respond to sexual violence?

4

What About the Rapists?

Abolition Feminism, Community Accountability, and the Question of the State

> The reliance on the criminal justice system has taken power away from women's ability to organize collectively and has invested this power within the state.
>
> —Critical Resistance and INCITE! Women of Color Against Violence, *Statement on Gender Violence and the Prison Industrial Complex*

> I am proposing that all of the folks that have been disappointed by systems work together to create alternative systems. I am proposing that we organize.
>
> —Rebecca Farr, member of Communities Against Rape and Abuse (CARA)

In the past few decades, feminists of color have been at the forefront of efforts to render justice and accountability outside the criminal legal system. Organizations such as Communities Against Rape and Abuse (CARA) and Generation FIVE, and activists including Mariame Kaba, Leah Lakshmi Piepzna-Samarasinha, and Mimi Kim, have developed grassroots responses to violence, particularly to sexual and gender violence. They have critiqued the criminal legal system for failing survivors and sometimes even punishing their self-defense.[1] Importantly, they have gone beyond critique and developed guidelines and processes for what to do instead, taking on cases ranging from child sexual abuse to partner abuse in activist communities.[2] As one CARA member puts it, feminist abolitionists are inviting "all of the folks that have been disappointed by systems [to] work together to create alternative systems."[3] All combine feminist opposition to sexual and gender violence with abolitionist opposition to the violence of state punishment. Through and alongside grassroots initiatives, which are sometimes recorded and analyzed in online handbooks, zines, anthologies, and scholarly publications, "abolition feminists" have developed new conceptions of safety, justice, and accountability.[4]

Abolition feminists' determination to translate critiques of criminal punishment into efforts to "create alternative systems" aligns them with the agonistic abolitionism discussed in the previous chapter. Where paranoid abolitionisms are so suspicious of the status quo and proposed alternatives that they struggle to articulate what abolition is *for,* agonistic abolitionism combines ongoing questioning and critique with efforts to construct democratic alternatives. As Angela Davis argues, prison abolition requires both the dismantling of the prison industrial complex and the creation of new institutions to meet people's basic needs and support their political participation. Inspired by W. E. B. Du Bois's analysis of Radical Reconstruction, Davis envisions the transformation of the punitive and racist liberal-capitalist order into a socialist "abolition democracy." For Davis and likeminded abolitionists, opposition to current state institutions is accompanied by support for new political forms. Legal scholar Allegra McLeod, for instance, argues that abolition democracy is advanced through "revitalized local democratic politics," in which communities "actively redirect their own state and local governments" and engage in "collective institution-building political work."[5] For Ruth Wilson Gilmore, abolitionists must undo the contemporary "anti-state state" that derives its legitimacy solely from its policing, punishment, and military functions, and (re)direct state funding and resources toward life-supporting goals, such as housing, health care, and education. These and other basic needs—economic security, food security, strong relationships—are at the heart of how abolitionists envision a safe and just society.[6]

When it comes to rendering justice in the aftermath of serious harm, however, very few contemporary U.S. abolitionists support a role for the state. Most abolition feminists advocate "community accountability" or "transformative justice" mechanisms in which self-organized communities work to repair harm and transform its enabling conditions through political organizing.[7] As Mimi Kim observes, these initiatives have mostly emerged in radical social movement spaces outside both state institutions and nonprofit organizations,[8] and they are often imagined to be fundamentally at odds with state and legal processes. adrienne maree brown, for instance, describes transformative justice as "the work of addressing harm at the root, outside the mechanisms of the state, so that we can grow into right relationship with each other," adding that "most of us have no intention of ever mimicking state processes of navigating justice."[9] Abolition feminist activist Shira Hassan goes further and argues that transformative justice cannot be institutionalized and must be an improvised response to harm.[10] Even Davis uses antistatist language when discussing abolition feminism. She denounces "feminisms that call for the criminalization and incarceration of those who engage in gender violence," which she says "do the work of the state."[11] Her use of the singular in this phrase—*the* work of *the* state—forecloses abolitionist or other radical uses of state capacities by reducing the state to the punitive function that Davis and other abolitionists rightly reject. This conflation of the state with its criminal legal system happens in other influential abolitionist writings as well. Mariame Kaba's book *We Do This 'til We Free Us* groups her critiques of the criminal legal system and the police under the heading "The State Can't Give Us Transformative Justice."[12] The state may not *give* us justice, but what might we be able to *claim* or *take* from the state in this domain? Are state justice mechanisms inherently disempowering or unjust, or could they be remade and used for abolitionist and democratic ends? And could it be that abolition feminist justice initiatives model, not simply the power of "community" in opposition to the state, but alternative ways of wielding the power to govern?

This chapter explores these questions by looking closely at prison abolitionists' efforts to do right by survivors of sexual violence as well as by the people who harmed them. The influential 2001 Statement on Gender Violence and the Prison Industrial Complex, coauthored by INCITE! Women of Color Against Violence (now INCITE!) and the abolitionist organization Critical Resistance (CR), has inspired numerous abolition feminists to pursue "community-based responses to violence that do not rely on the criminal justice system AND which have mechanisms that ensure safety and accountability for survivors of sexual and domestic violence."[13] I will analyze one such response in detail: the community accountability efforts of CARA, a radical feminist organization led by women of color that has developed guidelines for responding to rape and abuse. I will argue that CARA and other abolition feminists are right to view the state with extreme suspicion when it comes to responding to sexual and gendered harm. Not only is the racialized, classed, and settler-colonial violence of mass incarceration the main impetus for the resurgence of prison abolition in the United States, but modern criminal legal systems have significant antidemocratic effects. They demobilize citizens and justify paternalist protection while treating some individuals and groups as threats that must be excluded from the polity.[14] Moreover, criminal legal systems are ill-equipped to handle rape and other forms of sexual violence, harms that are both serious and infuriatingly common, especially in the lives of Indigenous women and women of color. By some estimates, fewer than 1 percent of rapes and attempted rapes end in a felony conviction for the aggressor, and in those cases, the experience of a criminal trial might have been harrowing for victims.[15] In the face of these realities, abolition feminist initiatives like CARA enact the kind of citizenship needed in an abolition democracy. They take stock of an intolerable reality—widespread sexual violence that the criminal legal system says it takes seriously but only rarely takes on—and refuse to accept it. They take collective action, asserting their right and ability to help shape our shared world. And as CARA's example demonstrates, they collectively develop guidelines for their efforts at community accountability and transformative justice, which shows an effort to take collective action responsibly.

At the same time, it is important to recognize that these practices too have limitations and dangers and generate remainders of their own. CARA is highly attuned to this reality, but it risks being obscured by the opposition, common in abolition feminist discourse, of the community to the state and of accountability and repair to punishment. Here, Foucault's paranoid critique is a helpful resource. His suspicion of power is not limited to the state or to violent coercion but extends to seemingly benign and nonviolent efforts to regulate conduct in and by groups. Legal scholar RA Duff further argues that restorative justice involves retributive punishment, which suggests that abolition feminists' community accountability and transformative justice efforts are in some continuity with, and not only in opposition to, punishment as practiced by the state. From an agonistic perspective, such continuities are not a reason to reject community justice efforts, but I suggest they should lead us to reconsider the role of the state. Because abolition feminists not only generate collective power but also wield significant and potentially punitive power over others, we need institutional forms that both build and preserve this power and limit it.

The chapter proceeds in three parts. I begin with the features of the existing criminal legal systems that have prompted abolition feminists to "create alternative systems": their concentrated violence toward race- and class-subjugated communities and their broader antidemocratic effects. Next, I theorize abolition feminist efforts as enactments of the kind of citizenship needed in an abolition democracy, before arguing that abolition feminists' systems have more in common with state punishment than is commonly acknowledged. I conclude by arguing that these commonalities—wielding punitive power over others, and seeking to reform wrongdoers—do not diminish the value of abolition feminist efforts, but do alert us to their dangers, and urge us to reconsider a role for state institutions and the law.[16]

The Injustices and Harms of the Criminal Legal System

Abolition feminists' suspicion of the state is grounded, first and foremost, in the extreme harms of U.S. mass incarceration. It was the recognition of these harms that sparked the resurgence of prison abolition in the late 1990s, which was quickly followed by collaborations between prison abolitionists and radical antiviolence feminists.[17] These feminists, grounded in traditions of Black, Indigenous, and Women of Color feminism, theorized racialized mass incarceration and the broader carceral state as threats to the safety and freedom of women of color.[18] The organization INCITE!, for instance, declared that its inaugural conference, held in 2000 at the University of California-Santa Cruz, aimed to:

> (1) develop analyses and strategies around ending violence that place women of color at the center; (2) to address violence against women of color in all its forms, including attacks on immigrants' rights and Indian treaty rights, the proliferation of prisons, militarism, attacks on the reproductive rights of women of color, medical experimentation on communities of color, homophobia/heterosexism, and hate crimes against queer women of color, economic neo-colonialism, and institutional racism, and (3) to encourage the antiviolence movement to reinsert political organizing.[19]

Like earlier radical Women of Color feminist initiatives such as the Combahee River Collective, INCITE! centers women of color and pursues their liberation from multiple forms of oppression.[20] This includes ending interpersonal violence, but the group centers structural and institutional violence and oppression. It includes criminal punishment under that umbrella. The "proliferation of prisons" is described as violence against women of color, who constitute a relatively small part of the total prison population but whose incarceration rates were, and are, rapidly growing.[21] INCITE's explicit inclusion of Indigenous, immigrant, and queer women further extends its structural critique beyond sexism, racism, and the carceral state to include colonialism and settler-colonialism, nativism, and compulsory heterosexuality. Because violence is framed as both an individual and a structural problem, antiviolence work must involve political interventions. The feminist antiviolence movement is critiqued for having been "sabotaged by a mainstream social service-oriented agenda" that is led by professionals rather than by women of color survivors and whose dependence on state funding discourages radical political organizing.[22]

This intersectional critique of violence is more fully developed in "Gender Violence and the Prison Industrial Complex," a joint statement issued in 2001 by INCITE! and the abolitionist organization Critical Resistance (CR). "We call on social justice movements to develop strategies and analysis that address both state AND interpersonal violence, particularly violence against women," the statement begins. Prisons and police brutality are theorized as state violence, and the criminal justice system as a whole is described as "an institution of violence, domination, and control" that "has increased the level of violence in society." Modeling critical self-reflection as a part of collaborative organizing, the statement first critiques the feminist antiviolence movement for centering state punishment, and then critiques the antiprison movement for focusing narrowly on men of color and for failing to address sexual and domestic violence.[23] "It is critical that we develop responses to gender violence that do not depend on a sexist, racist, classist, and homophobic criminal justice system," the statement declares. Yet alternatives to incarceration developed by antiprison activists, the statement says, have "generally failed to provide sufficient mechanisms for safety and accountability" for survivors and have often relied on "a romanticized notion of communities." "While prison abolitionists have correctly pointed out that rapists and serial murderers comprise a small number of the prison population, we have not answered the question of how these cases should be addressed. The inability to answer the question is interpreted by many antiviolence activists as a lack of concern for the safety of women." The statement then challenges social justice movements to develop "community-based responses to violence that do not rely on the criminal justice system AND which have mechanisms that ensure safety and accountability for survivors of sexual and domestic violence." The task of building feminist-abolitionist justice mechanisms is daunting, but the statement insists that taking it on could be generative. "The reliance on the criminal justice system has taken power away from women's ability to organize collectively and has invested this power within the state," the statement reads. "We seek to build movements that not only end violence, but that create a society based on radical freedom, mutual accountability, and passionate reciprocity."

Abolition feminists' claim that the purported protection offered by the criminal legal system and the military actually amounts to violent aggression resonates with realist analyses of the state. "Apologists for particular governments and for government in general commonly argue . . . that they offer protection from local and external violence," Charles Tilly observes, but "since the repressive and extractive activities of governments often constitute the largest current threats to the livelihoods of their own citizens, many governments operate in essentially the same ways as racketeers."[24] In criminal protection rackets, racketeers force people to pay for protection from violence that the racketeers threaten to inflict. Tilly argues that the difference between criminal racketeers and state governments is one of degree, not of kind. It depends on how real the threat is, to what extent it is produced by the self-described protector, and at what price it is provided. States argue, of course, that their threats and use of violence are legitimate, unlike the criminality of mobsters and other racketeers, but this claim to legitimacy, Tilly says, largely rests on their near monopoly on force: "A tendency to monopolize the means of violence makes a government's claim to provide protection . . . more credible and more difficult to resist."[25] Prison abolitionists add that the legitimacy of state violence is reproduced and reasserted by criminalizing the resistance, self-defense, and survival activities of Black people and other marginalized groups and depicting them as dangerous threats.[26]

The so-called protection of the carceral state, then, is experienced very differently by different groups. Its costs are borne mostly by the most marginalized citizens and residents, who are policed, incarcerated, and disenfranchised at the highest rates, while its rewards are reaped by those for whom punishment and policing provide opportunities for employment, profit, and political campaigning. The development of the carceral state, Ruth Wilson Gilmore observes, has hollowed state legitimacy to the "aggression agencies" of prisons, police, criminal courts, and the military and eroded the legitimacy of state action for other purposes.[27] The expansion of punishment has gone hand in hand with the "organized abandonment" of or "strategic divestment" from Black neighborhoods, for instance, which are "characterized by high rates of unemployment, low rates of home ownership, and inadequate health and human services to meet the needs of disadvantaged families."[28] Black women in these neighborhoods are "most vulnerable to male violence in all its forms," Beth Richie observes. The carceral state has also criminalized immigration and vastly expanded the detention of undocumented immigrants. Formally, immigrant detention centers are not prisons. Immigrant detention is governed by civil law and framed as a prelude to deportation rather than punishment for a crime, but in practice both forms of confinement look very similar.[29]

In the domain of sexual and gender violence, the state's claim to offer protection through punishment is especially weak, and weakest for multiply marginalized women. This is the case despite increasingly punitive policies against sexual and gender violence, which were often passed with feminist support. The federal Violence Against Women Act (VAWA), for instance, part of the 1994 Crime Bill, created the Office on Violence Against Women in the Department of Justice and earmarked $1.6 billion to investigate and prosecute rape and other violent crimes against women. It also incentivized states to pass "mandatory arrest laws," which require police officers to make an arrest if they find probable cause of intimate partner violence.[30] VAWA further encouraged states to establish sex offender registries, an effort that was expanded by Megan's Law in 1996. The professionalization and mainstreaming of the feminist antiviolence movement, denounced early on by radical feminists of color and later by INCITE!, took place in this context. Grassroots rape crisis centers, for instance, or shelters for survivors of intimate partner violence, were gradually folded into the state's punitive governance. Most volunteer-led organizations became professional nonprofits dependent on state funding, and that state funding became increasingly contingent on carceral "solutions" to sexual and intimate partner violence: mandated reporting, filing criminal charges, testifying in court.[31]

These punitive policies have not ended sexual or gender violence, which remain rampant. A study by the National Institute of Justice estimates that one in six women in the United States experience rape in their lifetime—a rate that increases to one in five for women of color and one in three for Native women.[32] In the vast majority of cases, the attacker is someone familiar to the victim. Most survivors do not report their rape to the police, and most reports do not lead to prosecution or conviction.[33] Sex workers report that sexual coercion by police officers is common, and police officers have higher rates of intimate partner violence than other groups.[34] American jails and prisons are rife with sexual violence and heterosexist gender norms, which troubles their status as a "solution" to sexual violence, especially considering that most incarcerated people are eventually released. As the INCITE! and CR statement puts it, prisons "also inflict violence on the growing numbers of women behind bars" in the form of "slashing, suicide, the proliferation of HIV, strip searches, medical neglect and rape." Mandatory arrest laws, meanwhile, counteract the state's long-standing permission of patriarchal violence in the private sphere, but they have also increased arrest rates for men and for women, who are sometimes seen as the sole aggressor and sometimes arrested along with their partner.[35] Queer and gender-nonconforming women of color are especially likely to be perceived as aggressors and criminalized, indicating that deserving victims still tend to be imagined as white, straight, cisgender, and middle class.[36] A recent meta-analysis finds that "arrest for domestic violence [is] ineffective in limiting repeat offending," while other research suggests that these policies may lead to higher rates of intimate partner homicides.[37] INCITE! and CR's observation that "women who seek redress in the criminal justice system feel disempowered and alienated" is affirmed by a recent survey of callers of The National Domestic Violence Hotline, which found that callers who had contacted the police (82 percent of respondents) tended to feel that the police interaction made them less safe (39 percent) rather than safer (20 percent).[38] Despite these negative outcomes, most respondents (62 percent) said they would call the police again, mostly because they felt law enforcement was their only option.[39]

Abolition feminists' claim that the criminal legal system disempowers survivors and the broader public is also affirmed by earlier abolitionist scholarship on criminal law. In the 1977 essay "Conflicts as Property," abolitionist sociologist Nils Christie famously argues that the modern state disempowers citizens by claiming the exclusive right to resolve conflicts. Rather than let citizens sort out conflicts locally, states put in place criminal proceedings where legal professionals—prosecutors, lawyers, and judges—handle them in highly bureaucratized ways that are far removed from people's everyday lives. States claim that this approach is necessary to protect victims and prevent vendettas, but their "conflict theft," as Christie calls it, has significant political costs. First, like INCITE! and CR, Christie argues that the criminal legal system harms victims. His concern is not that criminal legal proceedings retraumatize victims by forcing them to recount the assault and face cross-examination that seeks to undermine their credibility, as feminists sometimes argue. For Christie, it is *disempowerment* that is victimizing. He characterizes victims' marginalization in criminal proceedings as a kind of victimization by the state. Their disempowerment takes the form of a lack of direct participation in, and a lack of control over, criminal legal processes. The victim, Christie says, is represented by the public prosecutor and reduced to the "triggerer-off of the whole thing."[40]

Like the joint statement, Christie argues that the criminal legal system also does collective harm. The state's conflict theft, he says, deepens citizens' passivity and disengagement and deprives communities of opportunities at norm clarification. "Conflict might kill, but too little of them might paralyse," he warns. Conflicts are dangerous, but being deprived of them presents its own dangers, if not to individuals then to communities and ultimately to democratic citizenship. For Christie, this is because conflicts "represent a *potential for activity, for participation*" that is in dangerously short supply in modern societies.[41] Citizens are more likely to feel isolated and disempowered, paralyzed as Christie puts it, than capable of participating in the shared governance of our collective life. "Modern criminal control systems," he says, "represent one of the many cases of lost opportunities for involving citizens in tasks that are of immediate importance to them."[42] Sorting out how a conflict should be handled, determining what norm has been violated and what repair is called for, can *bring people together* in a process that, beyond the specific incident in question, brings into play the norms considered important. It is an opportunity "for a continuous discussion of what represents the law of the land," which from the perspective of democratic theory could enliven the sense that citizens in a democracy are both subjects to and authors of the law.[43] Criminal legal proceedings are less suited to such norm clarification, Christie argues, because legal argumentation follows its own rules that are far removed from everyday life. "Many among us have, as laymen, experienced the sad moments of truth when our lawyers tell us that our best arguments in our fight against our neighbour are without any legal relevance whatsoever and that we for God's sake ought to keep quiet about them in court," he remarks. "Instead they pick out arguments we might find irrelevant or even wrong to use."[44]

Feminist political theorist Iris Marion Young offers specifically feminist reasons to see the criminal legal system as a threat to democratic citizenship. Writing in 2003, Young describes the United States as an authoritarian security state that disempowers its citizens by posing as a "masculine protector."[45] When the security state tells citizens to accept warfare, state secrecy, and discretionary power as the price to pay for safety, Young argues, it mobilizes a familial patriarchal logic in which women and children accept their subordination to husbands and fathers in exchange for protection from external threats. This logic, with its dramatic and often violent battle between "good" and "bad" men, is so familiar as to seem common sense, but it is corrosive of political equality. Young focuses on the so-called war on terrorism, but her analysis could easily be extended to the punitive neoliberal state responsible for mass incarceration, which abolitionists sometimes describe as a kind of domestic warfare.[46] Tough-on-crime discourses and policies are all about "good guys with guns" saving us from the criminal "bad guys," which intensifies fear of crime along with a sense of dependence on masculine protectors. If the latter turn out to be sexual aggressors, it might seem there is simply nothing we can do.

Together, Christie and Young help us see abolition feminists' experiments with grassroots accountability and justice mechanisms as important democratic interventions. Such political mobilizations and assertions of collective power are all the more needed given the pervasiveness of sexual and gender violence and the harm inflicted by the state's institutions that purport to protect us from it: police, criminal courts, and prisons. In the years since the joint statement by INCITE! and CR, new grassroots antiviolence efforts have taken off, animated by the statement's Women of Color feminist and abolitionist values. INCITE! became a network of chapters and affiliated organizations and stimulated new thinking and writing through additional conferences and the publications of two anthologies, *Color of Violence* (2006) and *The Revolution Will Not Be Funded* (2007).[47] What is now called "abolition feminism" is a vibrant social movement advanced through multiple organizations, initiatives, and publications and changing over time.[48] I will now discuss one specific initiative in depth, the "community accountability" efforts of CARA as described and analyzed by the group's members.[49] I show that CARA enacts agonistic democratic citizenship, and I suggest that the limitations and risks of its approach invite us to reconsider the potential role of the state and law in abolition feminism.

Democracy in Action: Communities Against Rape and Abuse

Communities Against Rape and Abuse (CARA) emerged in 1999 when the feminist antiviolence organization Seattle Rape Relief (SRR) closed its doors. According to former SRR volunteer and founding CARA member Alisa Bierria, SRR was founded "in 1972 by women who had organized a Speak Out on Rape at the University of Washington campus, [and] began as a volunteer organization with explicitly feminist politics."[50] Over the ensuing decades, SRR professionalized and became a registered nonprofit with paid staff, seventy volunteers, a board of directors, and a $500,000 budget. When a budget shortfall precipitated the sudden closure of SRR in 1999, Bierria and other volunteers spoke out against the direction SRR and the broader feminist antiviolence movement had taken since the 1970s. Growing professionalization, they argued, "means less critique of institutions that perpetuate sexual violence, no connection between anti-oppression theory and violence against women theory, less outreach to marginalized survivors (sex workers, prisoners, etc.), no community based fundraising initiatives, thinking about survivors as 'clients' rather than people, and perhaps, most importantly, little to no organizational accountability to the community, specifically survivors."[51] Bierria and other former volunteers used the collapse of SRR as an opportunity to found a new organization that would approach sexual violence from a radical intersectional feminist perspective grounded in community organizing. In the following years, CARA started practicing "community accountability" around sexual violence, an approach described and theorized in the essay "Taking Risks: Implementing Grassroots Community Accountability Strategies," coauthored by CARA members Alisa Bierria, Onion Carrillo, Eboni Colbert, Xandra Ibarra, Theryn Kigvamasud'Vashti, and Shale Maulana and published in INCITE!'s first anthology.[52]

CARA, I argue, enacts agonistic abolitionism by responding to a remainder of what currently passes for justice: the lack of collective response to most instances of sexual harm. This state of affairs is widely known, but it rarely undermines the sense that the criminal legal system mostly works and should retain its monopoly on handling crime. In fact, people often invoke rape to insist on the need for criminal courts and prisons that are so unlikely and so ill-equipped to handle this kind of harm. CARA, in contrast, refuses to accept the status quo as a "good enough" approximation of justice. But rather than seek to reform the criminal legal system so that it sends more perpetrators to prison, as "carceral feminists" are said to do,[53] or hope that generating intolerance of the system will mobilize people politically in unspecified ways, as paranoid abolitionism might, CARA sets out to "create alternative systems."[54] Through collective experimentation and reflection, they develop a different perspective on justice and its processes, pursuing community accountability instead of criminal punishment. In so doing, CARA resists the criminal legal system's disempowering effects on democratic citizens who become more and more dependent, deskilled, isolated, and ultimately disinterested in political affairs. Instead, they take the risk of collective action and assert their right and ability to participate in shaping our shared world. Their development of guidelines for their and others' community accountability work, moreover, shows an effort to exercise power responsibly. It is also an attempt to encourage and enable others to learn or relearn the skills of collective conflict resolution.

The essay "Taking Risks" describes ten general principles of community accountability work, followed by three sample scenarios based on CARA's interventions. The ten principles, the authors say, emerged from their efforts practicing community accountability, and both the principles and the scenarios are offered with the aim of helping build a broader revolutionary movement.[55]

1. Recognize the humanity of everyone involved.
2. Prioritize the self-determination of the survivor.
3. Identify a simultaneous plan for safety and support for the survivor as well as others in the community.
4. Carefully consider the potential consequences of your strategy.
5. Organize collectively.
6. Make sure everyone in the accountability-seeking group is on the same page with their political analysis of sexual violence.
7. Be clear and specific about what your group wants from the aggressor in terms of accountability.
8. Let the aggressor know your analysis and your demands.
9. Consider help from the aggressor's friends, family, and people close to her.
10. Prepare to be engaged in the process for the long haul.[56]

Throughout the text, the authors emphasize the need for flexibility and risk-taking in a process that is "hard and messy" as well as "vital, deeply liberatory, meaningful, and geared toward movement building."[57] This description of community accountability work resonates with Christie's description of the enlivening, activating, and connecting nature of direct participation in conflicts. CARA and Christie also share a suspicion of the criminal legal system and professionals: CARA starts by rejecting the notion that sexual violence is "a hyperdelicate issue that can only be addressed by trained professionals such as law enforcement or medical staff."[58] By claiming the authority to respond to sexual violence, the group breaks with dependence on both masculine protectors and therapeutic experts and moves beyond the suspicion, unsettlement, and critique of paranoid abolitionisms. Specifically, CARA claims the authority to know what causes sexual violence and what might end it, to determine what should happen in individual cases, and to put those judgments into action, imposing them on unwilling aggressors if need be.[59]

First, CARA claims general epistemic authority on the topic of sexual violence when it defends a "feminist, politicized understanding of rape" as a type of oppression embedded in a broader rape culture that must be dismantled. If an accountability-seeking group doesn't already have a shared "political analysis of sexual violence," it must develop one, CARA cautions (principle six), and the group posits feminist, antiracist, and pro-queer commitments as a fundamental requirement.[60] The group's insistence that sexual violence should be understood as a structural phenomenon leads it to value discussions about sexual violence and the development of group norms that counter it, beyond efforts to hold individual aggressors accountable.[61] In fact, as a grassroots organization, the group is much more successful at the former efforts than the latter—a point to which I will return. Second, CARA asserts the authority to know what a just response to individual cases of sexual violence looks like. Or rather, it authorizes survivors and those around them to determine the meaning of "accountability" in specific cases. In order to prioritize the self-determination of the survivor (principle two), "it is critical to take into account the survivor's vision for when, why, where, and how the abuser will be held accountable," CARA states.[62] Ultimately, the accountability group must be "clear and specific about what [it] wants from the aggressor" (principle seven) and communicate its analysis and demands with them (principle eight). Making specific demands helps create opportunities for redemption and restoration, and wards off the risk that the survivor and others linger in vengeful rage.[63]

Third, CARA claims the authority to impose its demands on others. "Organizers must be grounded in the potential of their own collective power, confident about their specific demands as well as the fact that they are entitled to make demands, and then use their influence to compel the aggressor to follow through with their demands," the group writes.[64] There is a claiming of collective power here, including power over others—the *right to compel* aggressors to take specific actions—even as CARA's own scenarios reveal the limitations of social "influence" or "credibility" as means of compulsion.[65] In the first scenario, involving a Black organizer named Dan who repeatedly sexually harasses Black women at an antiracist youth organization he helps lead, CARA members try for multiple years to intervene through meetings with Dan and other members of his organization. In the process, several additional women accuse Dan of harassment, and the youth organization discusses sexual harassment and institutional sexism, but CARA notes that "Dan still has not been accountable for his behavior. That is to say, he has not admitted that what he did was wrong or taken steps to reconcile with the people who he targeted."[66] Accountability is also not attained in CARA's second scenario, in which two white women accuse Lou, a white employee at a popular music club, of sexual assault. Though this example involves a broader range of tactics, not just meetings but also public shaming and a boycott of Lou's place of employment, it is not enough to enforce the accountability demands: that Lou publicly apologize, pursue counseling, and "inform future partners and friends that they have a problem and ask for their support in the healing process." The group demands that "if the perpetrator moves to a new community," moreover, "they must continue to comply with the community guidelines set forth above."[67] Only in CARA's third scenario, in which a young activist with CARA is sexually assaulted by a leader of a Chicano activist organization to which she belongs, are the accountability demands met, in large part because the organization is responsive to the survivor's account.[68]

By CARA's own criteria, then, the group's accountability efforts have a mixed record of success. Aggressors rarely comply with the demands made, but in all three scenarios, victims of sexual assault receive support from people around them, aggressors face condemnation of their actions, and groups discuss sexual violence or engage in educational trainings on the topic. Christie might see in these proceedings examples of the "norm clarification" and community building that conflicts can lead to when they are left in the hands of those directly involved. Like CARA, Christie prioritizes collective deliberations about what harm was inflicted and how it could be repaired—practices at which CARA largely succeeds—over sanctioning offenders. In this sense, CARA accomplishes what the criminal legal system is constitutively ill-equipped to do: involve communities in a process aimed at examining and potentially changing broader cultural norms. Christie might also stress the development of the habits and skills of conflict management that have been eroded by the increased anonymity of social life and the state's conflict theft. CARA itself claims such skill building as a valuable outcome. Whatever the outcome of a particular community accountability process, CARA writes, "you may find that you are more prepared and skilled to facilitate a process of holding others in your community or circle of friends accountable in the future."[69]

Young might further see in CARA's acknowledgment of its failures a valuable democratic counter to the security state's spurious promise of (masculine) protection. "Democratic citizenship should first involve admitting that no state can make any of us completely safe and that leaders who promise that are themselves suspect," she writes.[70] Abolitionists go further and insist that struggles for justice and accountability require long-term organizing for structural changes that would prevent and diminish violence. As Mariame Kaba writes, "only building power among those most marginalized in society holds the possibility of radical transformation. And that's an *endless quest for justice*."[71] If victims or their allies feel dissatisfied with the lack of accountability for a particular aggressor, that dissatisfaction could inspire them to take on such long-term organizing work. This happens in CARA's second example. When a group fails in its efforts to hold an aggressor accountable, they ultimately "switch . . . tactics and focus . . . more on community-building, education, and prevention" of sexual violence.[72] Abolition feminist Andrea Smith similarly theorizes the creation of progressive communities as an integral part of abolitionist justice efforts. Only long-term organizing work, she argues, can create the conditions under which sexual violence is both less likely to occur and more likely to be met with a robust community accountability response.[73]

CARA's example shows what collective action can accomplish in cases where the criminal legal system simply shrugs its shoulders at a lack of evidence. The group models responsiveness to reports of sexual violence, courage in its claiming of power, and responsibility in how it wields that power, evidenced by the collectively developed guidelines that begin with the injunction to "remember the humanity of everyone involved." I will now argue that CARA's description of its approach as "a practice of liberation" that does not depend on institutions, however, obscures the nature and the dangers of the power exercised in community accountability work.

Rethinking Community Accountability

CARA relies on collective action by some members of a community to hold others accountable for inflicting sexual harm. As a *process,* this reliance on the self-directed action of individuals and groups is very different from the bureaucratic and professionalized criminal legal apparatus of the state. The latter mobilizes a rigid set of rules and protections that ideally apply equally to anyone in a given territory. Despite prosecutors' considerable discretionary power in leveling criminal charges, there is a normative expectation that similar sanctions are imposed in similar cases. This homogeneity is understood to be key to equal citizenship, and it can be legally enforced, for instance under the Constitutional principle of "equal protection of the laws."[74] Community accountability, in contrast, does not reference a fixed or written body of rules, and is practiced by people who know each other. There is no established process, and accounts of sexual violence are given great weight. Where criminal legal processes require that guilt is proven beyond reasonable doubt ("preponderance of the evidence" is the standard in civil law), CARA "develop[s] a process of engagement with a person's story of being violated, rather than thinking of the process as a fact-finding mission with an end goal of determining the Objective Truth of What Really Happened." "We critically engage the story to come up with our best assessment of its most important elements," the group says, "and then develop a plan to address the situation based on solid political values and organizing principles."[75] As we saw, the survivor's demands largely determine the specific accountability measures sought, which can vary significantly from case to case. This variability is not seen in liberal terms as a threat to democratic equality, but rather as democratic and pluralist responsiveness to the particularities of specific people and cases.

When we consider the *kinds of power* exercised, however, some continuities with state punishment come to light. These continuities are not reasons to reject community accountability work, but they complicate the mapping of oppression and liberation onto the state and the community, respectively. CARA, for instance, proposes such a mapping when it writes: "Instead of depending on institutions to support us—institutions that will often respond oppressively if they respond at all—community accountability work helps us to develop a practice of liberation in our personal lives, our community lives, and our political lives."[76] Complicating these oppositions allows us to see the potential risks and limitations of community accountability work in addition to their democratic promise and power. It also invites us to consider the potential promises of state institutions and law for abolition democracy, and not only their antidemocratic roles and effects. As I argued in chapter 3, an agonistic abolitionism is at once hopeful and suspicious, both of the state and of the community. There is something to be learned, then, from the suspicion of paranoid abolitionism, even if such suspicion on its own tends to discourage or curtail political action.

What power or powers are at work when community members hold people accountable for sexual harm? CARA explicitly mobilizes social pressure, including public shaming, as a means toward the end of accountability, which typically involves personal reform. CARA rejects the idea that sexual violence can only be handled by medical or law enforcement professionals, and it treats such violence as a political issue rooted in male domination, heterosexism, and rape culture. It follows from this analysis that sexual violence can only be ended through structural change, accomplished through collective action.[77] Still, when it comes to holding individual people accountable, the group affirms survivors' demands that the aggressor pursue therapy. The demand is made in two of the three scenarios described in the essay. It is also the first example of accountability offered by CARA. "Does accountability mean counseling for the aggressor? An admission of guilt? A public or private apology? Or is it specific behavior changes? Here are some examples: You can organize in our community, but you cannot be alone with young people. You can come to our parties, but you will not be allowed to drink. You can attend our church, but you must check in with a specific group of people every week so that they can determine your progress in your reform."[78] These examples showcase CARA's trust in individuals and groups to determine what accountability means *for them,* and the group explains its reluctance to offer "a one-size-fits-all community accountability model" as a recognition of and respect for pluralism.[79]

Compared to the coercive power wielded by the American state's criminal legal system—years and lifetimes of caging, disenfranchisement, stigmatization, and discrimination—these demands are beacons of reasonableness, pragmatism, and restraint. There is no sign of vengefulness or cruelty, the demands are measured and focused on preventing further harm, and CARA even has the strength to set its sights higher than the individual aggressors it deals with. When confrontations, shaming, and boycotts fail to persuade aggressors to admit wrongdoing or enter therapy, CARA does not turn to physical force. Instead, it lets aggressors be and turns to areas where it can be effective: violence prevention and other community organizing work. This could be an acknowledgment of the long timeline of change that abolitionists envision, a sense that abolition is a "horizon" rather than an (imminent) event.[80] It could also be a further sign of CARA's realism: an implicit acknowledgment that victims of sexual violence rarely achieve the accountability they hope for, beyond a relatively toothless condemnation of the aggressor's actions, even with radical feminist collectives like CARA on their side. In any case, CARA sets an impressive example of feminist collective action that deserves to be emulated. Still, a realist perspective urges us also to consider what could go wrong in this kind of endeavor, and what its unintended consequences might be.

From a Foucauldian perspective, CARA's accountability efforts show similarities with carceral punishment. In this light, demands for counseling and mandatory check-ins about personal "reform" look like efforts at rehabilitation or "re-socialization," which Foucault describes as carceral.[81] His suspicion is based on the role that rehabilitation has played in justifying imprisonment. The seemingly humane and benevolent aim of transforming people for the better has in practice facilitated the pathologization of people convicted of crimes as abnormal and dangerous. For Foucault, the rehabilitative ideal does not simply promote the reintegration of people with criminal convictions, but also their long-term stigmatization, surveillance, and exclusion.[82] He is similarly skeptical of therapy as a more subtle and efficient type of social control compared to caging people in prison cells. In the mid-1970s, he speculates that generalized discontent with the prison stems, in part, from the need for "more sophisticated and flexible means for relaying the control of illegalities, and this is the method of control through knowledge [*le savoir*]: psychology, psycho-pathology, social psychology, psychiatry," and so on.[83]

Foucault's concerns about therapeutic power find some validation in CARA's essay. The group authorizes long-term surveillance of people deemed aggressors, for instance, as evidenced by the example of the weekly "check in" with a church group to determine "your progress in your reform" and the advice to include the aggressor's family and friends (principle nine) to "ensure . . . long-term follow through with the accountability plan. Friends can check in with him to make sure he is attending counseling, for example."[84] At the same time, Foucault's suspicion of abolitionist alternatives can easily foster inaction and resignation, I have argued, and abolition feminists have good reason to pursue at least some personal change. "To create safer environments, people and circumstances must be transformed," Kaba writes, and how could we *not* want rapists and abusers to better themselves?[85] Still, the continuities between community accountability and rehabilitative punishment alert us to potential risks of these grassroots efforts. Scholars have commented on the promise of groups like CARA to "create new possibilities for thought and action by transforming and expanding the shared epistemic resources that constitute our social imaginaries."[86] For Brady Heiner and Sarah Tyson, community accountability groups create space to reckon with existing epistemologies and "begin to think, imagine, and feel what those future political and epistemological systems might be like."[87] Foucault helps us see that by leaving the meaning of accountability almost entirely up to communities, CARA creates room not only for experimental departures from established understandings of justice but also for the spread of carceral practices and assumptions beyond the formal criminal legal system. The pursuit of rehabilitation, moreover, is notoriously boundless. Suspicion is not easily alleviated, and some people may be deemed "incurable."

Christie adds the further concern that a "treatment perspective" is one-sided and obscures conflict. "The basic model of healers is not one of opposing parties," he observes, "but one where one party has to be helped in the direction of one generally accepted goal—the preservation or restoration of health." His claim is not that "both sides" to every conflict should be given equal normative weight, or that society shouldn't have rules that forbid rape and abuse. Rather, he cautions against the assumption that we all agree about the norms and values of our life in common, or about how they apply to specific conflicts. It is difficult to be in conflict with someone about the norms and values of our collective life when we think of that person as needing treatment or cure, Christie suggests.[88] Abolition feminists resist such a "treatment perspective" when they theorize sexual violence as a product of heterosexism, but they risk endorsing it when they advocate counseling for sexual aggressors (as happened in two of CARA's three scenarios), describe abuse as requiring "professional support," or characterize supremacy as "a numbing and narrowing disease."[89] Christie's skepticism about "compulsory treatments" is in tension with most abolition feminism but finds support in abolitionisms grounded in critical disability and crip theory, explored in chapter 2.

If community accountability is, at least in part, an effort to resocialize and rehabilitate people who inflict unjust harm, is it a practice of punishment? Many abolition feminists deny that it is. Community accountability and transformative justice are commonly opposed to both "carceral" and "punitive" approaches to harm, which are denounced as forms of state violence. It is true that none of the accountability measures discussed by CARA are purely retributive. They don't inflict harm for its own sake but aim, rather, to foster positive transformation and help strengthen communities. Legal scholar RA Duff, however, argues that responses to crime that aim at restoration are not alternatives to punishment but rather alternative forms of punishment.[90] This is because they hold specific people accountable for wrongfully inflicting harm and expect them to show remorse and to take on the burdensome task of compensation and repair. The assignment of culpability and the demand that wrongdoers experience some hardship in the process of repairing the harm caused, Duff argues, show that restorative justice involves retributive punishment. The infliction of hardship is not an end in itself, but it is an inevitable part of restoration, repair, and reconciliation, especially when someone has been found to have inflicted serious harm. "Repentance is of its nature painful," Duff says, "the repentant wrongdoer cares, or has come to care, for those whom she wronged, for the values she violated; she must therefore be pained by that wrong and that violation."[91] Moreover, "if I am to show you (and myself) that I really do repent my wrongdoing, by offering a more than merely verbal apology, the reparation I undertake must be something burdensome—something that symbolizes the burden of moral injury that I laid on my victims and would now like (if only I could) to take on myself; the burden of wrongdoing that I laid on myself; and the burden of remorse that I now feel."[92] CARA seeks to do much more than hold individuals accountable, such as inciting collective organizing to transform violent and unjust structures and conditions. But it also exercises collective power to get aggressors to take responsibility for their actions and better themselves.

From Duff's perspective, this means that they are involved in the work of punishment.

If community accountability work is riskier than it initially seemed, could state institutions and the law contain more abolitionist promise in facilitating collective responses to harm than is commonly recognized? Modern state punishment systems, as INCITE!, CR, and Christie point out, have disempowered citizens while violently othering people convicted of crimes, a development taken to extremes by the U.S. carceral state. Could there be other political and legal institutions that preserve the kind of collective power generated by CARA and also offer protections from it? Exploring this question means moving beyond blanket rejections of "the state," which obscure the historical variability of state formations and inadvertently affirm "a larger anti-political trend . . . that frames states and institutions of government as endemically violent and coercive rather than as instruments to be wielded by the people in whose name they govern."[93] As Jane Gordon observes, "surely 'states' include neofascist varieties, political institutions that expand human freedom and the conditions and actors that enabled them to do so, and everything in between. If so, the question is not whether we are for or against states but about the *kinds of* political institutions we need and deserve and how they are tirelessly constructed."[94] Developing new political institutions that could embody and advance abolition democracy requires the kind of courageous collective action and experimentation modeled by CARA. It might find a useful resource, I will now suggest, in an earlier body of abolitionist legal scholarship.

Nils Christie's notion of "conflict theft" is often referenced in abolitionist literature on restorative or transformative justice, but his proposal for an alternative court system, developed in the same essay, is rarely discussed. This nonengagement is part of a broader silence in contemporary U.S. abolitionism about the European school of abolitionist legal thinking of which Christie was a part, a tradition that includes Louk Hulsman and Herman Bianchi. This silence might be due, in part, to Angela Davis's early dismissal of these and other "major theorists of prison abolition" in a 1997 essay.[95] As Davis, in the 1990s, started "retrieving, retheorizing, and reactivating the radical abolitionist strategy first proposed in . . . the sixties and seventies," she found some promise in Foucault but very little in these legal thinkers, whose abolitionism she says means "peacemaking" but not the overhaul of structural racism.[96] It is true that these authors do not theorize race beyond the observation that criminalization targets already marginalized groups, and focus their efforts on creating alternative conflict resolution mechanisms.[97] They all reject criminal law and criminal courts, and oppose imprisonment under most circumstances, but they believe that the law and legal institutions might support democratic self-governance and accept a role for coercion in justice mechanisms. Contemporary U.S. abolitionists like Davis aim at much farther-reaching radical change and have good reason to be far more suspicious of the state than these earlier authors, all white male scholars and scholar-activists in law and criminology who wrote from positions of considerable social power and authority. They did so, moreover, in countries with smaller and less repressive penal systems, such as the Netherlands and Norway.

Still, as this chapter has made clear, contemporary prison abolition includes practices for responding to harm, which exert significant and arguably punitive power over others. What insights about organizing such power might these earlier authors have to contribute? Christie and CARA agree that when citizens handle their own conflicts directly, they build important political skills as well as stronger communities.[98] But where CARA's accountability processes are entirely community-based and do not have recourse to law, Christie envisions a court system that is victim- and lay-oriented but that is nonetheless a state institution governed by law. The courts would provide a public venue where communities could discuss specific conflicts, focusing on what harm was done to the victim(s) and how such harm could be repaired, especially by the offender but also potentially by others. The law would play a role in the first stage of the process, the determination of specific lawbreaking by a specific person or group, but after that, Christie envisions that the participants would have a great degree of freedom in determining what is relevant in the case and what repair is called for. Next, a judge could potentially inflict punishment. Christie does not reject punishment altogether, but rather theorizes it as "that suffering which the judge found necessary to apply *in addition to* those unintended constructive sufferings the offender would go through in his restitutive actions *vis-à-vis* the victim," thereby affirming Duff's claim that restorative justice involves suffering.[99] Christie deems punishment a necessary possibility because in some cases, "neighborhoods might find it intolerable that nothing happened" beyond repair to the victim.[100] Fourth and last, the participants would consider "service to the offender." If the court proceedings exposed that the offender has unmet needs, it should try to have them met, "not to prevent further crime," Christie says, "but because needs ought to be met."[101] In sum, Christie's proposal focuses largely on efforts of repair according to principles of civil law but retains an element of criminal punishment.

From an abolition feminist perspective, Christie's proposal raises significant difficulties but also contains some promise. The law would regulate and potentially limit what actions warrant community intervention: Christie suggests that the lay- and community-oriented court would gather only if a person was determined to have broken the law. This leaves unresolved what proof would be required—an especially sticky issue in cases of sexual violence.[102] Christie's proposal also deliberately leaves room for the infliction of punishment by a judge, which contemporary abolitionists would likely see as a betrayal of abolitionism. I have questioned, however, whether punishment and community accountability are so neatly opposed, and Christie's distinction between punishment and "service to the offender" has the benefit of limiting paternalistic or therapeutic forms of power that abolition feminists sometimes endorse or enable. Where CARA sees important benefits to community accountability processes even if they rarely manage to impose demands on rapists and abusers, Christie imagines a court process authorized to impose such demands but whose real value lies elsewhere. "I am not suggesting these ideas out of any particular interest in the treatment or improvement of criminals," he says. "I would have suggested these arrangements even if it was absolutely certain they had no effects on recidivism, maybe even if they had a negative effect. I would have done that because of the other, more general gains. And let me also add—it is not much to lose. As we all know today, at least nearly all, we have not been able to invent any cure for crime . . . We might as well react to crime according to what closely involved parties find is just and in accordance with general values in society."[103]

In any case, these kinds of courts could be a backup in case more informal, community-based efforts are impossible or fail. That is how administrative and civil law already work, Herman Bianchi points out, and it is the approach he advocates. "Although the abolitionists are in favour of handling disputes out of court wherever possible, we would still need a judiciary," Bianchi writes. "For if it ever happens that negotiations get out of hand [or never get started, I would add], and one of the parties is in danger of being victimized, he should have the right of appeal to a court. That too is justice."[104]

Democratic citizens need democratic institutions, and vice versa. Even the best institutional design to pursue justice and accountability after harm is powerless if it is not taken up, claimed, defended, and adapted in ways that align with abolition democratic values.[105] There is no escaping the chicken-or-egg problem that "good laws" (and institutions) are needed to make "good citizens," while good citizens are needed to make good laws. We may imagine that this is a problem of founding that happens only at the beginning of political regimes, but as Bonnie Honig reminds us, the "paradox of politics" actually recurs daily, as democratic orders are continuously made and remade. From this perspective, the question of institutional design cannot be separated from what kinds of skills, habits, and dispositions people bring to it. The paradox of politics also reminds us of the dynamic nature of political orders. Citizens' collective efforts can eventually become official state institutions, just as states can delegate tasks and responsibilities to civil society. The latter has been part of the development of the neoliberal carceral state, which abandoned those who depended on the state's social welfare provision to the market and the voluntary, nonprofit sector. As Gilmore observes, the voluntary sector has become a "shadow state" that provides "direct social services previously provided by wholly public New Deal/Great Society agencies."[106] The pursuit of abolition democracy could push in the opposite direction. Community accountability and other contemporary abolition feminist initiatives could be the seeds for future public goods, "centrally organized to benefit everyone who is eligible."[107]

A great strength of abolition feminism has been its willingness to experiment with new mechanisms of accountability and justice. Such collective action requires courage, and it models the pursuit of radical change through the combination of critique and collective experimentation that Foucault called for but that his paranoid abolitionism struggles to support. I singled out CARA's theory and practice of community accountability in this chapter, but other examples of abolitionist justice work abound.[108] If I eventually turned to older, more traditionally scholarly proposals for abolitionist uses of courts and the law, it was not to privilege scholarly knowledge production over that of activists or to propose a blueprint, but rather to help expand current abolitionist thinking and practice beyond what I see as an overly restrictive opposition to the state and the law. When these are dismissed as carceral, I have argued, the limitations and risks of community justice practices are obscured and opportunities for abolitionist appropriations, redirections, or invention of state and legal institutions get lost. These kinds of efforts entail political risks, such as a widening of the carceral net, but dismissing them out of hand also comes at a cost: It could limit abolitionists' ability to make the change they envision durable and widespread. As I have stressed throughout this book, the challenges and paradoxes that abolitionists face are neither new nor unique but common to other radical movements and ultimately to democratic politics.

5

The Power of New Rights

Extreme Heat, the Right to Comfort, and the Emergence of Abolition Democracy

> We know what democracy means not by immersing ourselves in the Constitution's language but by imagining what it would mean for black people to be treated like free and equal human beings.
>
> —Dorothy Roberts, "Abolition Constitutionalism"

> A right is nothing unless it comes to life in the defense which occasions its invocation.
>
> —Michel Foucault

How might prison abolitionists make use of law? The previous chapter discussed a possible role for civil law in abolitionist responses to sexual and gender violence. I now argue that rights claims have a role in the abolitionist project. They could help articulate what it is *for* beyond everything it opposes, questions, and seeks to destroy. Because even "natural" or "human" rights depend on political organizations to protect and realize them, rights claims also invite further thinking about the kinds of institutions and political forms needed for abolition democracy.[1] Where the previous chapter discussed a possible limiting or constraining role for state institutions, rights claims attune us to more positive, enabling functions of the state and the law.

Abolitionists have good reason to be suspicious of rights, however. This book theorizes prison abolition as a realist political theory and project, and critical race theorist Derrick Bell argues that it is *unrealistic* in a deeply racist society like the United States to expect that "abstract legal rights" will advance Black people's freedom struggles.[2] The law and the courts are "instruments for preserving the status quo" that only "periodically and unpredictably" support oppressed people, he says. Most of the time, "abstract principles lead to legal results that harm blacks and perpetuate their inferior status."[3] When racial equality is interpreted formalistically, for instance, affirmative action policies that support applicants of color can look racist and unconstitutional. This is how the Supreme Court ruled in *Regents of the University of California v. Bakke* (1978), Bell points out, when it struck down a quota system used in medical school admissions that reserved seats for Black applicants. It is also how the court ruled in 2023 in *Students for Fair Admissions v. Harvard/UNC,* when it banned race-conscious admissions policies in higher education altogether.[4] Bell rejects such formalistic legal reasoning and argues that courts should instead take a realist approach to jurisprudence, which is responsive to actually existing inequalities, open to flexible reasoning, and attuned to the empirical effects of legal rulings. He does not think it likely that they will, however, and he counsels Black people "to acknowledge the permanence of our subordinate status."[5] Acknowledge is not the same as accept: Bell predicts that the abandonment of civil rights litigation could free up energy for antiracist defiance, which he sees as an intrinsically valuable affirmation of Black people's humanity even if racism is never overcome.[6] Still, Bell curtails hope for radical change and does not discuss how rights claims could be mobilized to support Black freedom struggles.

Does realism require giving up on racial equality as a goal and rights claims as a tactic in that struggle? Or are there ways to use rights claims strategically in pursuit of radical change without placing undue faith in law or the courts? I have argued that prison abolition fits in the realist political theory tradition but also challenges that tradition's conservative bent. Abolitionism, like Bell's racial realism, takes "a hard-eyed view of racism" and other oppressive empirical realities, but it is more hopeful about prospects for radical change.[7] Where Bell sees a cycle of hope for equal citizenship followed by disappointment at persistent racism, a cycle that breeds despair, abolitionists' reckoning with the many forces that support existing inequalities and oppression makes room for a different kind of hope. Abolitionist hopefulness expects less from existing institutions but more from collective action and organizing, and it staves off despair by seeing radical change as a process that unfolds on multiple scales and timelines. Abolitionists agree with Bell that radical change will not be initiated by existing institutions and would not be the fulfillment of their original mission or intent, but they see abolitionist practice as more than an effort to "make life bearable in a society where blacks are a permanent, subordinate class."[8] A community bail fund, for instance, might depict freeing someone from pretrial detention as a step in abolishing the prison industrial complex, and abolitionist thinkers routinely insist that a society without prisons is possible, even as they anticipate that it will take decades or lifetimes to accomplish. A core question explored in this book is how such radical change might be realized incrementally and whether and how state institutions and the law might be enlisted in its realization. I have argued for an agonistic abolitionism that approaches both state institutions and communities with suspicion: as neither inherently good and desirable nor as irredeemably bad and antidemocratic, but rather as potentially both. Such suspicion is a realist alternative to romanticizing and idealizing narratives that oversimplify political life and obscure the violence, exclusions, and inequalities of existing arrangements.[9] The challenge is how to prevent realist suspicion from devolving into paranoid critique that fosters resignation or the pursuit of purity, and retain the ability to take constructive action that "works the tensions" of abolitionist politics.[10]

This chapter suggests that emerging rights claims, the practice of claiming rights that are not yet recognized as legitimate, could advance an agonistic abolitionism. Like "nonreformist reforms," emerging rights claims work both within and against existing liberal-democratic political orders. Their proponents act as if they already inhabit the world they seek to bring into being, which gives their actions a proleptic character.[11] My argument is indebted to Bonnie Honig and abolitionist philosopher Lisa Guenther as well as to the legal thinking of Dorothy Roberts, who recommends that prison abolitionists "strategically use an abolitionist reading of the Constitution to defend their radical vision and implement steps toward achieving it."[12] What Roberts calls "abolition constitutionalism" is not motivated by naive trust in the wisdom of the Framers or in the democratic nature of constitutional law, but rather by the strategic value of *claiming* the Constitution's legal and symbolic authority for the abolitionist project rather than cede it to the white state and its punishment practices.[13] For Roberts, equal citizenship sets the standard of justice, and the Constitution is a means to realize that end. "We know what democracy means not by immersing ourselves in the Constitution's language," she says, "but by imagining what it would mean for black people to be treated like free and equal human beings. The purpose of constitutional fidelity is to insist that constitutional interpretations abide by this higher standard of justice."[14] The constitutional fidelity invoked by Roberts is also a kind of prolepsis: It insists that the Constitution means now what it would mean once racism is abolished.

What kinds of rights do equal citizens in an abolition democracy need and deserve? I supplement abolitionist claims for familiar, fundamental rights such as housing, education, health care, and political participation with a proposal for a *right to comfort.* This emergent rights claim originates in the context of Texas prisoners' demands for air-conditioning to cope with extreme heat, an increasingly common phenomenon on our warming planet. Debates about whether or not incarcerated people deserve air-conditioning tend to revolve narrowly around determining acceptable levels of prisoner suffering. The right to comfort is a tactical intervention in these debates. It challenges both the moralization of suffering and the reduction of health to mere survival, while gesturing toward a more expansive conception of human life that values pleasure and play. But the right to comfort need not remain limited to prison conditions. It could yet be taken up in other contexts to generate new visions of abolition democracy. A right to comfort could be claimed by friends and family members of incarcerated people who want to be able to hug their loved one during visits. It could also apply to people outside prisons who are trapped in extreme heat, including agricultural and construction workers and residents of "shade deserts": neighborhoods devoid of tree cover or other protection from sun exposure. The right to comfort might seem ridiculous, but as Honig reminds us, "the new is always laughable."[15] The outlandishness of this new right could prove productive, moreover. What would need to change to realize the right to comfort for all vulnerable groups?

I begin by tracking the ambivalent relationship to rights of Foucault, Olson, and Michelle Alexander, before turning to emerging rights claims in the context of extreme heat in Texas prisons.

With and Against Rights: Abolitionist Ambivalence

All realist abolitionists discussed in this book are suspicious of rights. Their concerns are familiar and widely shared in radical political theory: that rights discourse encourages a liberal individualist rather than a democratic socialist politics; that rights claims entail legal tinkering rather than substantive change; and that a focus on legal change empowers experts to wage courtroom battles at the expense of broad social movement organizing.[16] In light of these concerns, some radical feminist and disability/crip approaches have moved away from the language of rights and toward the language of reproductive or disability justice.[17] At the same time, abolitionists also make use of rights. They do so to advocate for people who are currently incarcerated or under other forms of correctional control, and also to invoke the characteristics of abolition democracy and differentiate their vision from the current neoliberal order. This critical, ambivalent relationship to rights recognizes that the political meaning of rights is not preordained and that their power might be harnessed at opportune moments.

Even Foucault made rights claims, mostly in the late 1970s and early 1980s, but already in the context of his work with the activist Prisons Information Group (GIP). He did so despite his propensity for paranoid thinking and despite his critiques of liberalism and universal human rights.[18] His concerns are well known: In short, Foucault rejects the idea of a fixed human nature as well as liberal or moral understandings of rights as bulwarks against power and politics. These accounts misleadingly depict power as primarily negative and external, Foucault suggests, a force of constraint on the actions and desires of subjects who are otherwise autonomous or sovereign, when subjects are actually constantly exposed to historically specific power relations that shape their bodies and selves. As he writes in *Discipline and Punish,* "the *real,* corporal disciplines constituted the foundation of the *formal,* juridical liberties" of the Enlightenment.[19] The oppositions presented here, between disciplines and liberties, the embodied and the juridical, the real and the formal, imply that rights obscure our concrete circumstances and constraints.

At the same time, Foucault and the GIP included rights claims in their toolkit. The GIP's founding manifesto, for instance, asserts that "we have the *right to know*" the realities of prisons: "who goes there, how and why they go there, what happens there."[20] To actualize this right, the GIP illicitly distributed an "intolerance survey" about prison conditions to incarcerated people in twenty prisons, an effort another GIP member described as "a way of declaring [detainees'] rights and affirming our will to advance them."[21] The GIP did not prioritize winning any particular right for prisoners, but neither did the group disparage claim-making or rights discourse as insufficiently radical or political. To the contrary, the GIP affirmed the importance of countering the rightlessness of incarcerated people, whose subjection to near boundless discretionary power the group named and challenged. After an uprising in the prison in Toul in December 1971, Foucault wrote in a press release: "Lists of demands were circulated. These began with the essential demands, those most difficult to obtain (e.g., transfer of the warden, chief of the guard, etc.), and they moved to the more detailed ones (shower temperatures, meals, etc.); but these are not merely details or rather every detail is essential when one struggles to obtain, against a boundless arbitrariness, a minimum of juridical status; when one struggles to have *the right to demand*."[22]

Like Ben Golder, I see Foucault's simultaneous critique and use of rights as a sign of his ambivalent relationship to rights, not as evidence of theoretical incoherence or latent liberalism. Such ambivalence is appropriate, Golder argues, since rights claims both contest some practices and affirm others and therefore have both stabilizing and destabilizing effects. Foucault became increasingly interested in rights as "potentially useful, tactical instruments in political struggle," Golder says, but he remained attuned to the risk that they uphold essentialist views of the human subject, negative views of power, or otherwise close off opportunities for resistance.[23] Foucault opposed the death penalty, for instance, but he did not do so on the grounds that it violates the right to life, which could make imprisonment seem unproblematic.[24] And he was aware that the political efficacy of rights claims depends in large part on political mobilization. It is significant that the GIP's rights claims, of the public's right to know and prisoners' right to make demands, justify unauthorized collective action to change existing realities of the prison system (the illicit intolerance survey, the prison uprising). The rights in question are not the final goal of the struggle, as if prisons would be tolerable if only we knew more about them or incarcerated people had greater leeway to make demands. Rather, they are steps along the way that might facilitate or incite further action and further change.

If rights claims begin as tactical interventions, they might travel beyond the particular context and juncture in which they are first made and take on broader significance. As Foucault observes, "liberties and their safeguards . . . are made often out of occasion, surprise or detour. It is then that they must be seized and made valid for all."[25] He makes this observation in an essay critiquing the French government's extradition to Germany of Klaus Croissant, the lawyer of the radical left Red Army Faction. Croissant was accused of colluding with his clients, deemed terrorists by the West-German government, but Foucault takes this case as an opportunity to defend the broader "*right to have a lawyer* who speaks for you, with you, and allows you to be heard and to retain your life, your identity, and the force of your refusal."[26] The right to such legal defense and representation is especially important because incarcerated people are inherently disadvantaged vis-à-vis the legal authorities, he says. Foucault theorizes the right to a legal defense as part of what he calls the *rights of the governed,* which also include a right to asylum for those dissidents and radicals who cannot tolerate (and may not be tolerated by) their current government.[27] These rights invoked by Foucault—the right to know, to make demands, to political asylum and legal representation—affirm and enable resistance efforts by limiting the power of the criminal legal system over the accused and the incarcerated, and by offering citizens an avenue to escape their governments. At the same time, they say little of substance about the kind of society pursued by Foucault, a silence that I theorized in chapter 1 as part of Foucault's "paranoid" style of abolitionism.

Joel Olson and Angela Davis, in contrast, use substantive rights and freedoms to describe abolition democracy. Both critique liberalism for extending formal rights and equality while letting racialized, classed, and gendered material inequalities flourish in civil society. In *The Abolition of White Democracy,* Olson argues that the United States has historically been a racial democracy in which institutions privilege whites and subordinate nonwhites.[28] The establishment of formal racial equality after the Civil War obscured but did not end this racial subordination, Olson observes, and he critiques liberalism for limiting understandings of equality to political rights and equal opportunity.[29] Under white liberal democracy, understandings of freedom are similarly constrained, he argues: Freedom is understood not as an activity but as a position of superiority over an inferior group, and as a result, "'negative' rights that protect one's status and property become more important than 'positive' liberties such as substantive participation in politics or the right to the prerequisites for such participation (nutrition, shelter, health care, education, sufficient leisure time)."[30] In fact, white democracy is "miserly," he says, and suspicious of social programs that provide such prerequisites.[31] Olson draws on the Black Radical Tradition to define democracy not in liberal terms but rather "in the most radical manner—as the ability of all persons to have a meaningful say in those affairs that affect their daily life—without worrying whether it is 'realistic.'"[32] Too often, Olson argues, democratic theorists limit themselves to "a chastened conception of democracy that appears resigned to liberalism" and offer only modest reforms.[33] The Black Radical Tradition, he argues, can help restore the "radical-utopian element in democratic theory and practice," where utopianism does not mean "the hopelessly unrealistic" but rather "political visions that go beyond the boundaries of conventional political thinking."[34] For Olson, abolition democracy offers such a political vision: of a democratic order that grants its members not just the formal right to but also the material resources needed for political participation. Davis similarly associates abolition democracy with "*substantive* as well as *formal* rights," including "the right to be free of violence, the right to employment, housing, healthcare, and quality education."[35] Democracy should not be limited to the "formality" of voting, she says.[36] Instead, she supports an understanding of democracy that includes "economic, racial, gender, and sexual justice and equality."[37]

Michelle Alexander, meanwhile, sees *human* rights claims as a tactic to overcome the limitations of formal equality and realize equal citizenship. Alexander occupies an ambiguous place in prison abolitionism: Her 2010 bestseller, *The New Jim Crow,* does not cite abolitionist writings or use abolitionist language, and its analysis of mass incarceration has been critiqued as too narrow.[38] Nonetheless, *The New Jim Crow* shares many characteristics with realist abolitionism. The book does not simply call for reforms but rather treats racialized mass incarceration as symptomatic of deeper injustices that must be addressed: racial divisions that serve capitalism and are perpetuated by unequal citizenship in a white democracy.[39] Equal civil rights have not been able to end this "racial caste" system, Alexander says, in part because they provide little protection against violence and rightlessness produced through criminalization. "Racial violence has been rationalized, legitimated, and channeled through our criminal justice system," she says. Violence that was once expressed as individual cruelty (slave masters) or collective terrorism (the KKK) is now "expressed as police brutality, solitary confinement, and the discriminatory and arbitrary imposition of the death penalty."[40] Alexander discusses at length how the courts have given legal sanction to the various stages and elements of the prison boom, from police authority to practice racial profiling and conduct searches without meaningful consent, to extremely harsh sentences, prosecutorial discretion, felon disenfranchisement, and the levying of fees.

Equal civil rights have failed to prevent or stop this assault on Black freedom, but Alexander hopes that a social movement centered on *human rights* could inaugurate equal citizenship. She invokes Dr. Martin Luther King, Jr., who in 1967 advocated a shift from civil to human rights and called a human rights movement potentially "revolutionary."[41] A human rights approach would offer "a positive vision of what we can strive *for,*" Alexander says: "a society in which all human beings of all races are treated with dignity, and have the right to food, shelter, health care, education, and security" as well as the right to work.[42] Alexander's appeal to human rights is also a rejection of affirmative action, and of dominant civil rights organizations that have focused their energies on defending this strategy in court.[43] Affirmative action has given some Black people greater access to colleges and universities as well as to public service jobs, Alexander says, but it has not helped most of the Black community, which by many measures is equally bad or even worse off than in the 1960s. The policy has functioned as a racial bribe, she argues: something that makes Black people feel better without resulting in adequate material change, all this "in exchange for the abandonment of a more radical movement that promised to alter the nation's economic and social structure."[44] A social movement for human rights, she argues, could uplift poor people of all races and help cultivate interracial class solidarity.

Foucault, Olson, Davis, and Alexander all share Bell's suspicion of abstract legal rights, but they nonetheless include rights claims and discourse in their abolitionism. Foucault most often invokes rights claims that facilitate resistance to governmental and especially penal power, while the other three use rights claims to advance a positive vision of what lies beyond white democracy and racial caste: mechanisms to counter normalized white advantage, meet the basic needs of all, and facilitate widespread political participation. These are important and necessary demands in a society where many cannot or struggle to afford adequate food, housing, medical care, and education, and where the most minimal form of political participation, voting, is undermined by felon disenfranchisement, restrictive voter ID laws, and extreme gerrymandering.[45] Realizing abolitionists' rights claims would likely diminish many harmful behaviors that are currently criminalized and punished and also make the public less punitive.[46] Yet there is also something odd about centering these familiar rights in a movement committed to the radical transformation of the world. Almost all the rights invoked by Olson, Davis, and Alexander are already acknowledged in the Universal Declaration of Human Rights, even if they have been only partially and unevenly realized.[47] As previous chapters have shown, abolitionists tend to value and embrace uncertainty, variously understood as problematization (Foucault), dis-epistemology (Ben-Moshe), or the unfinished (Mathiesen). I have argued for the need to combine such unsettlement with an affirmative politics that constructs democratic alternatives to the carceral state, but this agonistic approach maintains a role for uncertainty and the questioning of common sense. Could appeals to well-established human rights paradoxically *limit* the abolitionist project by making it too intelligible within existing frameworks? Of course, as Foucault points out, every rights claim is two-sided as it both unsettles and affirms. The question is how best to work that tension and advance a positive abolitionist project while resisting capture into reformism.[48] Emerging rights claims, I argue, could be one way to work this tension.

Abolition Democracy and Emergent Rights Claims

Emergent rights are rights claims that are not yet recognized as legitimate. As such, they are easily ridiculed or dismissed, but they may go on to win significant support. In fact, as Bonnie Honig points out, once rights are well established, we tend to assume that it had to be so. We come to see the new right as already contained in the old, and we ascribe the new right's credibility or success not to the hard work of political actors but to the inherent progression of the law. We take on a retrospective gaze that obscures the precariousness of rights, their dependence on popular support and their openness to contestation, especially when they are first articulated. "In the moment," Honig reminds us, "emergent rights-claims are experienced as fragile, contingent, and paradoxical. They presuppose and claim already to inhabit a world not yet built."[49] If many Americans now see the abolition of slavery as a logical unfolding of the Declaration of Independence, for instance, it actually took centuries of enslaved people's individual and collective resistance and decades of organizing and agitation by the abolitionist movement to convince Northerners that democracy and slavery are contradictory. Nineteenth-century abolitionists' calls for the immediate liberation of enslaved people and their admission into full citizenship were opposed, for instance, not only by supporters of slavery but also by "moderate" abolitionists such as Kentucky Senator Clay and President Lincoln, who urged respect for white people's property rights and supported the emigration of the formerly enslaved to Africa.[50]

The abolition of slavery was not the only unlikely demand that would go on to become reality. Many nineteenth-century slavery abolitionists also supported other causes that seemed ridiculous at the time and have since become common sense, such as women's rights, or gained significant support, such as vegetarianism.[51] For Olson, these examples show that an abolitionist politics makes space "for new forms of democratic participation and new political ideals."[52] The contemporary prison abolitionist thinkers discussed in this book certainly challenge a broad range of hierarchies and exclusions, from the warehousing of elderly and disabled people to the state's monopoly on handling serious interpersonal harm and the denial or curtailment of Indigenous sovereignty. As I will discuss, some also object to the caging of animals and advocate veganism on abolitionist grounds.

It is in the spirit of these and other expansive abolitionist and democratic claims that I propose that incarcerated people have a *right to comfort.* The idea will likely strike most people as ridiculous if not outright offensive. It may seem inappropriate to consider comfort when incarcerated people are still routinely denied basic necessities for survival, such as adequate food, medical care, and protection from interpersonal violence. These necessities are also lacking in the broader society, but incarcerated people are in state "custody," which means correctional authorities have an explicit legal duty to provide for their basic needs. A right to comfort may seem inappropriate, too, from the perspective that punishment should entail deprivation and suffering. Here, comfort seems evidence of the "coddling" that leftists are prone to, especially of "criminals," the most undeserving group of all. From an abolitionist perspective, meanwhile, the right to comfort could be dismissed as reformist: It could seem to imply a naive faith that prisons can be transformed into humane institutions, forgetting prisons' real function as machines to disappear and contain society's "undesirables," and why demand comfortable prisons anyway when we need to eliminate prisons altogether? I consider these views to develop a different perspective on the right to comfort as an agonistic abolitionist intervention. The immediate context for this rights claim is the extreme heat that is becoming more and more common, and incarcerated people's demands for air-conditioning in the face of temperatures that are causing suffering, injury, and death.

Extreme Heat and the Right to Comfort

Extreme summer temperatures are quickly becoming the norm, and many jails and prisons are poorly equipped to withstand it. They are often built from materials that trap rather than deflect the heat. When carceral authorities refuse to install air-conditioning or other forms of mechanical cooling, incarcerated people are effectively trapped in stifling conditions from which they cannot escape. The situation is especially grave in Texas, which has the largest state prison system in the country, is one of the hottest states on average, and refuses to cool most of its state prisons, particularly the areas where prisoners sleep and work.[53] The state requires county jails to keep indoor temperatures between 65 and 85 degrees Fahrenheit (18–29°C), but it has no such requirement for state prisons, where the heat index can reach highs of 130 degrees Fahrenheit (54°C).[54] These temperatures are deadly: In a typical year, the heat kills fourteen incarcerated people in the state, and in 2023, the year of a record-breaking heat wave, the Texas Tribune found that forty-one people died in unair-conditioned Texas prisons.[55] When entrapment in extreme heat doesn't kill, it often causes health problems and significant suffering. Prisoners in Texas describe getting only two to three hours of sleep at night and how during the day, the heat is "basically cooking" them alive. They liken the prison to an oven.[56] Nathaniel Code, incarcerated on death row in Louisiana, similarly describes "feel[ing] like I'm on fire or something."[57] To endure the heat, detainees try to avoid all activity. Keith Cole, incarcerated in Texas, tells a reporter that "a lot of times it gets so hot in our dorms that we have to strip down to our boxers, and we'll just lay on the floor because it's a little bit cooler on the floor than it is trying to sit up on our bunks."[58]

To make the case for air-conditioners, prisoners and their supporters have emphasized the health risks of exposure to extreme heat. Health concerns are at the center of a 2016 class-action lawsuit by Cole and others incarcerated at the Wallace Pack Unit in Texas, a "chronic care" facility that houses men who are chronically ill, disabled, or elderly.[59] At the time, Cole, who is Black, was sixty-one years old and had been diagnosed with diabetes, hypertension, and chronic cardiovascular disease. The class-action lawsuit argues that the high prison temperatures violate both the Eighth Amendment's prohibition on "cruel and unusual punishment" and the Americans with Disabilities Act (ADA), because detainees with "heat-sensitive" medical conditions "experience symptoms of heat-related illness more frequently or more intensely than able-bodied prisoners . . . [and] are also at greater risk of heat-related illness, including heat exhaustion, heat cramps, and heat stroke." Because many psychotropic medications reduce the body's heat tolerance, heat-sensitive disabilities include both physical conditions such as hypertension, asthma, and diabetes and mental illnesses such as schizophrenia and depression. Of the twenty incarcerated men known to have died from hyperthermia in Texas between 1998 and 2012, likely a gross undercount, nineteen were prescribed medications that reduce the body's heat tolerance. As Cole put it, "My age, with the medical conditions that I have, the medications that I'm on, extreme heat can kill me . . . So, it's not a comfort issue with me. It has nothing to do with that. This is a serious medical issue."[60] A spokesperson of the American Civil Liberties Union (ACLU) expressed the same view on extreme heat in prison: "This is not a comfort or luxury issue," he said, "but an issue of life and death."[61]

The health-based strategy has had some success in the courtroom. Arguments about heat-related illness and death have persuaded some judges and jurors that high prison temperatures "pose an unreasonable risk of serious harm" to incarcerated people—the current legal standard for cruel and unusual punishment.[62] Prisoner lawsuits contain testimony by medical experts about the severity of heat-related illnesses, their prevalence among incarcerated people, and the risk of death. Medical expertise not only helps establish harm as "serious," but it also provides quantitative data (such as actual and predicted morbidity and mortality rates) to help adjudicate what constitutes "unreasonable risk." Health-based critiques of the heat therefore appeal to the biopolitical logics of modern state power, which manages the biological existence of the population: birth rates, average life expectancy, the prevalence of disease, and so forth. As Foucault observes, modern states have never cared for all lives equally, instead making a "cut" between those whose lives are fostered and others who are exposed to death.[63] Arguments about incarcerated people's right to health both appeal to the state's duty to "make live" and contest its willingness to let people in prison—overwhelmingly men of color—die. In so doing, these arguments cut through the abstraction and legalism of rights that so frustrates realists from Bell to Davis. The accounts of heat spasms and hyperthermia that populate these lawsuits make clear that the rights at issue belong not to abstract legal subjects but to embodied human beings with a vital need to preserve their core temperatures around 98.6 degrees (37°C).

The focus of bodily health also resonates with abolitionist understandings of racism as a structural, material phenomenon with life-and-death stakes, rather than as a matter of individual prejudice or legal inequality. The realist thinkers discussed earlier in this chapter all look to racial disparities in wealth, income, health, educational attainment, and unemployment as evidence of persistent racism.[64] Among abolitionist thinkers, Ruth Wilson Gilmore is especially attuned to the life-and-death stakes of racism. In Gilmore's influential formulation, racism means "the state-sanctioned or extralegal production and exploitation of group-differentiated vulnerability to premature death."[65] The definition leaves open on what grounds a group is singled out, highlighting simply its artificially shortened life span. Gilmore cautions against the assumption that racism is inherently linked to phenotypical markers or biology. We might yet see the formation of a "convict race," she says, that would include the hundreds of thousands of white people behind bars.[66] After all, there is ample evidence that incarceration is a form of state-sanctioned production of vulnerability to premature death. The GIP already denounced suicides by incarcerated people as a product of imprisonment, not as deaths that just happen to take place in jails and prisons.[67] One study found that a year spent in a New York state prison diminishes life expectancy by two years; if a person has experienced solitary confinement, their risk of premature death after release is even higher.[68]

At the same time, health-based objections to extreme heat also have two significant limitations. First, they fail to engage the public's ambivalence about the suffering of incarcerated people. Support for "humane" punishment coexists with the expectation and desire that punishment entails suffering. In the 1981 ruling *Rhodes v. Chapman,* the Supreme Court decided that "the Constitution does not mandate comfortable prisons," and many feel strongly that punishment requires discomfort. "To the extent that prison conditions are 'restrictive and even harsh,'" Justice Powell wrote in the 1981 ruling, "they are part of the penalty that criminal offenders pay for their offenses against society."[69] Adjudicating the issue of air-conditioners thus typically becomes a balancing act between competing logics, as exemplified by this statement by a Deputy Sheriff about jail temperatures, issued from an air-conditioned office in Louisiana. "We don't want to make it real comfortable for [detainees] because we don't want them to come back," he said, suggesting that punishment only has a deterrent effect if it involves physical discomfort, and that people might choose comfortable incarceration over life on the outside. "We try to get it and keep it at a level that it's comfortable enough that they can *survive.*"[70] The desire to keep prisons uncomfortably hot but not lethally so splits the prison population into those who are most vulnerable and those who are not. Incarcerated people with diagnosed "heat-sensitive" health conditions may get air-conditioning; everyone else has to make do with personal fans and ice water. This is what happened with Cole's class-action lawsuit. The case ended in a settlement, overseen by U.S. District Judge Keith Ellison in 2018, that obliges the state to provide air-conditioning at the Wallace Pack unit and begin a process to ensure that detainees with medical sensitivities to the heat will be placed in air-conditioned facilities. The judge was "ecstatic" about this outcome and proclaimed it meant "a new day in Texas prison history," but it did not change the living conditions of most incarcerated people, and Cole refused to sign the settlement.[71] In the following years, the Texas legislature has refused to expand air-conditioning beyond detainees with medical sensitivities to the heat. In 2023, the state House allocated $545 million to air-condition all Texas prisons by 2031, but the Senate struck it from the budget, despite a budget surplus of more than $30 billion.[72]

The limited and fraught outcome of Cole's class-action lawsuit is typical of litigation for better prison conditions in the United States. As Lisa Guenther shows, American courts have time and again set minimum standards for prison conditions that have quickly become the norm, a "'just measure of deprivation'" inscribed in the law.[73] In this way, legal challenges to prison conditions have led to some improvements, but they have also entrenched a bare-bones definition of humane treatment that sanctions significant suffering. According to Eighth Amendment jurisprudence, prisoners must be provided with the minimum required for survival—adequate food, clothing, shelter, and medical care—but they may also legally be subjected to extreme isolation and overcrowding.[74] As Colin Dayan has analyzed, a series of Supreme Court decisions since the 1980s have "gradually eviscerated" constitutional protections against cruel and unusual punishment, paving the way for the torture memos under President George W. Bush, which "extended the limits of permissible pain" far beyond what had thus far been allowed.[75] Because Cole's case ended in a settlement, it does not constitute a legally binding precedent, but it too provides partial relief from the most egregious kinds of harm while allowing most of its manifestations to continue.

The second limitation of the right to health is that it leaves intact reductive definitions of human needs and humane treatment as mere survival. It names the infliction of heat-related illness and death as wrongs, but leaves open what would need to be present to protect people's health. Gilmore's critique of racism similarly condemns vulnerability to premature death, understood politically and structurally as something that is either produced or tolerated by the state for entire groups, not as a simple biological fact of individual bodies. Gilmore depicts such unequal vulnerability to premature death as an injustice that should be abolished, but this does not yet tell us about the kinds of *life* that abolitionists seek to enable for all. How might we articulate and demand a richer conception of life than the mere survival that prisons claim—and fail—to protect? Are there ways to affirm prisoners' protests against the extreme heat that are more disruptive to the logics undergirding the prison as an institution than the right to health and more illuminating of the kind of world abolitionists seek to create?

As unlikely as it sounds, considering prisoners' *right to be comfortable* could be an abolitionist alternative to the right to health. It advances an agonistic abolitionism that both problematizes common sense—the reduction of humane treatment to mere survival, desires for prisoners' suffering—and gestures toward an alternative way of thinking about what prisoners and others deserve. Rarely taken up by prison abolitionists, comfort implies satisfaction or pleasure taken in one's immediate surroundings. As I will discuss, it might even entail a right to leisure, touch, and shade. In these ways, comfort raises the bar for acceptable prison conditions, while shifting the focus from threats to life (addressed by the right to health) to exposure to suffering. Of course, a right to comfort does not make sense by established categories and logics. It is an emergent rights claim that does not comport well with the Supreme Court decision that the U.S. Constitution "does not mandate comfortable prisons" and it is at odds with common desires to see prisoners suffer.[76] We can see why Keith Cole and his lawyers work hard to insist that they are *not* asking for comfort: In today's courtrooms, and in much of public opinion, only threats to life stand a chance of being recognized as legitimate concerns about prison conditions. Moreover, a right to comfort runs counter to the heroic, militant forms of resistance privileged by some radical theorists. For Achille Mbembe and Banu Bargu, death fasts and other forms of martyrdom, especially in a prison context, exemplify radical resistance to the state.[77] From their perspective, demands for comfort seem reformist: merely a demand to have prisoners' bodies taken care of a little better but not a fundamental challenge to the power over life operative in prisons and in society at large. To theorists for whom death-making is a core function of the state in general, not just of contemporary, biopolitical state formations, claiming a right to comfort looks similarly misguided.[78]

Still, there are good reasons to take a right to comfort seriously as part of prison abolition. Such a right is easily ridiculed or dismissed, but as Honig has shown, emergent rights claims often appear laughable when they are first articulated. And while the claim to comfort goes against what Cole said he was fighting for, prison protests often include demands for changes that would improve prison conditions but that are neither necessary for survival nor instrumental to the achievement of other (nominal) goals of the prison such as rehabilitation. Considering a right to comfort could attune us to such demands and the opportunities for solidarity with incarcerated people they represent. Foucault and other members of the GIP observed the importance of prisoner demands for "basic comforts" such as better food, heated dormitories, and transistor radios in 1970s France, and Lisa Guenther has made similar observations in the contemporary United States.[79] She notes that when detainees in California waged a series of collective hunger strikes between 2011 and 2013, their five core demands included not only an end to indefinite solitary confinement, readily legible as a serious political demand opposing suffering that amounts to torture, but also access to art paper, colored pens, wall calendars, and sweat suits.[80] Protesters advanced their claims through hunger strikes, a protest tactic that endangers the body's health, but we should not assume too quickly that it was self-destruction in particular that made these protests subversive. The protesters insisted that they did not want to die—theirs was a hunger strike, not a death fast—and Guenther invites us to attend to the claims to comfort as radical demands. "Political movements that diminish or deny the vital importance of warmth, nourishment, and pencil crayons," she writes, "cannot claim to be radical, even if they embrace a pure, ideal form of prison abolition."[81]

For Guenther, demands for comfort are radical because they highlight our "creaturely" nature that connects humans to other animals. In this way, comfort opens up a posthumanist conception of politics that challenges the hierarchical opposition of humans to animals.[82] She frames the California protesters' demand for small pleasures not as a human rights claim but as a *creaturely* demand that would benefit humans and other animals alike.[83] Prisons harm people in similar ways to how factory farms harm nonhuman animals, she argues: by depriving them of their creaturely need to exist in a network of meaningful relations to others that allows for both connection and withdrawal.[84] When we describe the harm of prisons as dehumanization, we overlook the harm that they do to humans as social animals, and we overlook similar harms inflicted on animals in other settings. Guenther also considers *comfort* as a creaturely need undermined by incarceration. A meaningful experience of (human) political constructs such as justice, equality, or freedom, she suggests, requires that people have their creaturely needs met. Collective demands pertaining to bodily needs or pleasures are no less political than rights claims couched in the register of justice. The right to comfort, then, is not only provocative and unsettling compared to the familiar rights claims advanced by abolitionists; it also challenges their focus on *human* rights and pushes us to consider the well-being of animals. Some prison abolitionists already hold commitments to animal well-being (though they rarely theorize them as part of their abolitionism), and the objection to the caging of human beings invites questioning of other forms of confinement.[85] Does any living being belong in a cage?

Taking creaturely comforts seriously not only connects human beings to other animals but also offers a new conception of human existence. When the California protesters collectively demanded small comforts and pleasures, they did not argue that art paper was necessary for their health or a cost-efficient mechanism to lower recidivism rates, nor did they agree that they deserved to suffer. Rather, they refused both the interpretation of humane treatment as mere survival and the moralization of suffering by insisting on the right to play, pleasure, and leisure—even in prison. In this way, they rejected the demand that people must be useful and productive, a demand that once justified the prison as a machine for creating productive citizens out of the indolent poor and that continues to marginalize incarcerated people as "useless" members of society. This is a demand that is left intact and could even be reinforced by Michelle Alexander's discussion of the human right to work. "Employment," she says, "satisfies a basic human need—the fundamental need to be self-sufficient, to contribute, to support one's family, and to add value to society at large. Finding a job allows a person to establish a positive role in the community, develop a healthy self-image, and keep a distance from negative influences and opportunities for illegal behavior."[86] The right to comfort questions this moralization of work and invites connections between prison abolition and radical movements to secure a universal basic income and inaugurate a "postwork society." As Kathi Weeks writes, the point is not that working is never valuable or pleasurable, but rather that "there might be a variety of ways to experience the pleasure that we may now find in work, as well as other pleasures that we may wish to discover, cultivate, and enjoy." Moreover, she reminds us, "the willingness to live for and through work renders subjects supremely functional for capitalist purposes," an insight that should trouble Alexander and other prison abolitionists attuned to the capitalist dimensions of mass incarceration.[87]

Using human rights discourse to demand art supplies, the California prisoners reclaimed uselessness and inefficiency as part of being human. In so doing, they unsettled both the biopolitical understanding of human beings as populations to be managed, and the moralizing conception of guilty subjects who deserve to suffer and of human beings who ought to make themselves useful. The right to comfort seeks to do the same. It objects to the racial dehumanization that is "a necessary factor in the acceptance that millions of people (sometimes including oneself) should spend part or all of their lives in cages" as well as to the deanimalization at work in prisons and other sites of confinement.[88] It is a strange and unlikely right that nonetheless affirms key abolitionist impulses: to radically reimagine and remake the world, to insist that no (human) being is disposable, and to demand the creation of living conditions that allow us not just to survive but to flourish.

I have theorized the right to comfort as an agonistic abolitionist intervention in debates about high prison temperatures, but it could yet gain broader significance. The right to comfort could be taken up by and on behalf of incarcerated people in ways that activate intolerance to prisoner suffering and affirm their deservingness of more than bare life. The right to comfort resonates, for instance, with the *right to hug* claimed by children of incarcerated people, who demand to visit their parents in person rather than see them on a video call.[89] In the past decade, many jails and prisons have signed contracts with private corporations to provide so-called video visitation.[90] The technology sometimes expands contact between incarcerated people and the outside world, but it has also come at the expense of opportunities for in-person contact. Traditional visits are free, but loved ones have to pay for video calls, and jails often ban in-person visits when they implement so-called video visitation.[91] The commission that jails and prisons receive on video calls is just one of the benefits that the technology offers them. "Video visitation" also allays concerns about contraband and allows for easy surveillance:

the calls are recorded and "routinely accessed by prosecutors and used against defendants in court."[92] That eliminating in-person visits might have little or no effect on contraband (which can also be brought in by employees or, in some cases, be manufactured on the inside), and might well increase violence (by increasing isolation and desperation), is not considered in these arguments.[93]

As in the case of high prison temperatures, the deprivation of human touch inflicts significant suffering that is produced by the prison itself.[94] It is a predictable outcome of the built environment that separates people from their loved ones, sometimes hundreds of miles away, and of policies that obstruct in-person contact. The suffering is widely accepted and even desired despite evidence that it increases rather than diminishes criminalizable behavior and although it reverberates far beyond the incarcerated person to their families and friends. Children of incarcerated people are especially harmed by limited access to their parent and prohibitions on touch, which can be enforced by video call technology but also by plexiglass barriers in visiting rooms, so-called window visits where people talk through telephones. This is why the Bill of Rights of children of incarcerated parents, a document produced by the San Francisco Children of Incarcerated Parents Partnership (SFCIPP), includes "the right to speak with, see *and touch* my parent."[95] At a minimum, SFCIPP says, detention facilities must "provide access to visiting rooms that are child-centered, non-intimidating and conducive to bonding."[96] Like the right to comfort, the right to hug insists on the importance of our creaturely needs and desires, in this case our need for physical connection and touch. It emphasizes our relational nature, our embeddedness in networks of care, and gestures to the importance of what Shatema Threadcraft theorizes as "intimate justice": the creation of a world where Black women and girls and all people have the resources to develop and exercise their sexual, reproductive, and caretaking capacities in freedom.[97] Incarceration undermines all these capacities.

The right to hug is one way in which the right to comfort might travel beyond jails and prisons, the *right to shade* is another. Jails and prisons are not the only places where people are trapped in the heat. Many cities, especially the neighborhoods where poor people and people of color live and work, function as "urban heat islands," "dense concentrations of pavement, buildings, and other surfaces that absorb and retain heat."[98] Heat waves have long been the deadliest weather events in the United States, far deadlier than hurricanes, tornadoes, and floods, but they are unspectacular and do not "produce mega-billion-dollar property damage and economic disruption," and are "thus of minimal concern to the insurance industry, the decisive shaper of federal and state natural disaster policy."[99] Another reason for their neglect is that the deadly effects of heat waves are concentrated among the most marginalized: people who live in urban heat islands rather than near parks, fountains, and tree-lined streets; people who must wait for the bus in full sun rather than those who drive their own cars or can afford to take a taxi; people who work outside rather than in air-conditioned buildings and especially those who work outside with few or any labor protections, such as agricultural workers. Air-conditioning can mitigate some but not all of these vulnerabilities, and it generates its own problems: It consumes a lot of energy and generates heat, so that "the energy utilized to produce one person's cooling becomes someone else's thermal garbage," as urban theorist Mike Davis puts it.[100] It follows, Davis says, that the real issue is not air-conditioning. It is shade.[101]

In abolitionist circles, Mike Davis is best known for coining the term *prison industrial complex,* but he also theorized a human right to shade.[102] "Environmental comfort," he says, is stratified by race and class, and a radical politics of shade must demand "massive inner-city landscaping and tree-planting, immediate air-conditioning of schools, daycare centers and workplaces, the recycling of vacant lots into 'tot parks' and community gardens, the shading of bus-stops, public drinking fountains, and so on."[103] Shade is not a luxury, writer Sam Bloch concurs, but rather "a civic resource" that ought to be made available to all. "In the shade, overheated bodies return to equilibrium. Blood circulation improves. People think clearly. They see better. In a physiological sense, they are themselves again."[104] A right to shade resonates with abolition democracy not only because it attends to our bodily well-being and comfort but also because it offers a vision of remaking the built environment: less asphalt and concrete, more lush tree canopies, green roofs, and awnings. Such a focus on urban planning helps connect Reconstruction to reconstruction and embeds the grand changes sought by abolitionists in our everyday lives and surroundings.[105] Making room for shade trees means making room for their roots and canopies, which potentially requires broadening sidewalks and moving powerlines underground. More specifically, taking shade seriously embeds abolitionism in *political struggles* over public space and urban planning, pitting the right to shade against property owners, real-estate developers, and police bent on eliminating opportunities for "shady" behavior. "The destruction of urban refuge was part of a long-term strategy to discourage gay cruising [and] drug use . . . in downtown Los Angeles," Bloch observes, and when police install surveillance cameras, tree canopy is often removed to increase visibility.[106] Efforts to redesign the workday could complement struggles for urban redesign. The siesta—a long break from activity during the hottest part of the day—might be where the right to comfort and the right to shade converge most fully. It means leisure and rest, and while it might be adopted as a practical way to cope with extreme heat, we might come to value the break from productivity it represents.

None of these outcomes are guaranteed. As Honig and Foucault both remind us, the success of rights claims and other political interventions depends on whether and how they are received, taken up, and defended. Any rights claim is vulnerable to being ridiculed, co-opted, or dismissed. The "right to work" advocated by Michelle Alexander to advance an antiracist politics, for instance, has been used by the Right to name legislation that undermines unions. So-called right-to-work laws, currently on the books in twenty-six states, forbid unions from charging nonmembers for representing them in collective bargaining.[107] A right to comfort is similarly claimed by conservatives, not on behalf of incarcerated people or animals, but on behalf of white people disturbed by confrontations with racism and other injustices. This is a reactionary politics of comfort, on display in the Florida bill that prohibits making people "feel discomfort, guilt, anguish, or any other form of psychological distress on account of his or her race, color, sex, or national origin" and in similar "anti-woke" legislation.[108] These prohibitions on causing discomfort obstruct the teaching of Black and Indigenous history, ethnic studies, and women and gender studies in an attempt to block the emancipatory—and potentially abolitionist—politics they inspire. Even the language of abolitionism has been taken up by the Right, to name radical opposition to abortion, contraception, and commercialized sex. These rival mobilizations do not mean that prison abolitionists should abandon the issue of comfort or the language of abolition. Quite the opposite: They show that these terms resonate and have the capacity to gain political traction. Whether their realization will advance equal citizenship and abolition democracy or entrench white advantage and punitive governance will depend on political struggle. If prison abolitionists are to win, it is best to enter the fight with the broadest possible array of tactics at our disposal and visions of success.

Conclusion

Prison Abolition Past and Future

Hope is a discipline.
—Mariame Kaba

Is there hope for abolition? From heightened nativism, authoritarianism, and fascism around the world to accelerating global warming, the scale and seriousness of crisis is daunting. Waiting for someone or something else to come to the rescue—a strongman, a billionaire, a technological or scientific breakthrough—might be the most comfortable posture to adopt. It allows us to believe that even though we are powerless, someone out there has the skills or resources or will that are needed to save us. All that is required from us is patience and obedience to stay in the savior's good graces. Even resignation offers some reassurance. For all the sadness and grief it inspires, it also absolves us from the responsibilities and burdens of action. In encouraging inaction, it makes it easier for the dreaded outcome to become reality. As Rebecca Solnit observes, "proclaiming someone's or something's defeat contributes to it."[1] Claiming that there is nothing we can do about climate change might seem like an expression of clear-eyed realism or even solidarity with those most impacted, but Solnit sees it as "a form of sabotage" that doesn't help anyone. "I doubt that anyone in desperate straits has ever taken comfort from the idea that somewhere far safer, people are bitter and despondent on their behalf," she says. What is needed in response to climate change is commitment and collective action, not resignation and despair. The same is true of militarized policing and mass incarceration, whether these are used against criminalized citizens, immigrants, or climate refugees.

This book has argued that being realist about prisons, punishment, and confinement does not require us to be resigned to them. The strongest abolitionist approaches, I have argued, both awaken us to the harms of prisons and carceral power, and encourage us to act toward a more democratic society: to make demands and build alternatives, accepting the risk of shortcomings and disappointment. An agonistic abolitionism is best equipped to inspire such collective action, I argued, because it helps us see not only the risk of failure but also the possibility of success. It recognizes the violence wrought by states and legitimated by law, but it also sees them as potential tools to be wielded to abolitionist ends rather than ceded to the forces of white supremacy and capital. Its hopefulness is not a naive optimism but rather a commitment, or as Mariame Kaba calls it, a discipline.[2] Rather than rest in false certainty that there is nothing to be done, it commits to doing what is possible.

For all its insistence on acting here and now, an agonistic abolitionism invites us to take a long view of history. Kaba, for instance, describes herself as "just a tiny, little part of a story that already has a huge antecedent and has something that is going to come after that, that I'm definitely not going to be even close to around for seeing the end of." Kaba is an internationally renowned theorist, activist, and organizer, one of the many abolitionists deserving of much more attention in this book than I have been able to give, but her remark should not be interpreted as false modesty. Rather, it is part of the temporal frame of agonistic abolitionism. Situating our lives and political struggles in a history that began long before us and will continue long afterward, she suggests, can embolden us to act. It takes some weight off our shoulders and gives us company, when the pressure to get our politics right or anticipate its failure or cooptation can prevent us from acting altogether. This happens, for instance, when abolitionists use what I have called, following Eve Sedgwick, paranoid critique. Angela Davis's turn to Radical Reconstruction, I have argued, is a powerful counter to such resignation. It not only offers an example of the kind of radical change abolitionists pursue but also situates contemporary prison abolition in a storied lineage of antiracist struggle. This kind of contextualization makes us both smaller and bigger. By helping us see how small we are, we gain appreciation for the significance of the actions that are in our power. "When you understand that you're really insignificant in the grand scheme of things," Kaba says, "then it's a freedom, in my opinion, to actually be able to do the work that's necessary as you see it and to contribute in the ways that you can see fit."

This book offers a long view on prison abolition by situating the work of Kaba, Davis, and other contemporary abolitionists in a history dating back to the 1960s and '70s. As Davis's own prison writings show, this was a period of revolutionary antiracist and anticapitalist struggle in which the U.S. criminal legal system served as a tool of counterinsurgency. While Davis's abolitionism was militantly anticapitalist, Foucault and the French Prisons Information Group (GIP) decentered class struggle in an abolitionism focused on exposing the many faces of carceral power. The work of Thomas Mathiesen and later that of Nils Christie and Louk Hulsman, meanwhile, reminds us that the Norwegian and Dutch prison systems, often considered exemplary, have been the target of abolitionist scholarship and activism. As Liat Ben-Moshe stresses, the 1960s and '70s were also a time of deinstitutionalization, when one form of disability-related incarceration was successfully challenged and brought to an end. Though they were grounded in specific places, none of these abolitionisms restricted their critiques or visions of change to the carceral systems of one country, and they were connected in transnational circuits of exchange. This book has unearthed some of these exchanges, mostly through the traces they have left in abolitionist texts and footnotes: the GIP's conversations with Black Power activists and its subsequent response to the assassination of George Jackson, Foucault's visit to Attica Prison, Davis's critique of European abolitionists like Hulsman for pursuing "peacemaking" divorced from structural changes to racial capitalism. My hope is that this historical sketch might help us think of prison abolition as a living transnational tradition that has persisted and contains resources to help us chart a path forward, even, or especially, now.

Acknowledgments

I could not have written this book without the support of many people who affirmed the project and helped me formulate and refine its questions and claims. I am grateful to Bonnie Honig for her steadfast mentorship as dissertation adviser and beyond. Her guidance and the example of her work helped me find my way in political theory. I am amazed at my good fortune of having been at the right place at the right time to become her student. I am also thankful to Lars Tønder and Penny Deutscher for supporting the dissertation that contained the seeds for this book. Lars showed me new ways to think about the politics of embodiment and affect, while Penny taught me most of what I know about Foucault and provided crucial support in the journey from PhD candidate to faculty member. For first welcoming me to the study of politics, I thank Banu Bargu, Andreas Kalyvas, and David Plotke, along with the vibrant graduate crew of New Schoolers. I met Lexi Neame at the start of graduate school and have benefited from her friendship and brilliance ever since.

Most of the research for this book was completed from my position at Trinity College. Isaac Kamola and Serena Laws welcomed me to Trinity and to their home. Isaac championed this project from the start and read a very early version of the manuscript along with Christina Heatherton, Jordan Camp, and Andrew Dilts. I thank Mary Dudas for organizing and inviting me into multiple writing groups and for building a political theory community over shared meals. I'm glad for the addition of Gabe Salgado to the department and excited about how we all might yet grow political theory at Trinity. Stefanie Chambers has been a supportive department chair, and I thank her, Mary Beth White, and my other colleagues for making the Political

Science Department such a positive environment: Dang Do, Mary Dudas, Belén Fernandez Milmanda, Andy Flibbert, Hernán Flom, Sidra Hamidi, Isaac Kamola, Boris Litvin, Reo Matsuzaki, Kevin McMahon, Gabe Salgado, and Abby Williamson. Thanks also to Nadja Eisenberg-Guyot, who offered tea, solidarity, and insight at just the right time.

By inviting me to teach with Trinity's Prison Education Project (TPEP) shortly after I arrived at Trinity, founding codirectors Sheila Fisher and Joe Lea helped me keep my scholarship on prison abolition connected to practical interventions. I thank Lucy Cane for introducing me to the visionary and determined people of the Prison + Neighborhood Arts/Education Project (PNAP) while we were still in Chicago and for coteaching at Stateville Prison with me. At Trinity, Joe Lea has been an unshakable codirector. A special thanks to him and our new codirector James Truman for steering the TPEP ship as I worked to meet the deadlines for this manuscript. Thanks, also, to the many students who explored the politics of punishment and abolition with me in my class "Prisons and Justice in America." I could not have dreamed that the class might inspire Luka, Anna, Jake, and Reese to create Students Against Mass Incarceration (SAMI). Their committed, pragmatic action is a gift and a source of hope. Nayantara and Jake further provided valuable research assistance on this book, and Helena helped prepare the manuscript for publication.

Beyond Trinity, I am thankful to Ali Aslam and Erin Pineda for welcoming me into the political theory community they created as conveners of the Pioneer Valley Political Theory Workshop, and to Jane Gordon, Adam Dahl, and others for bringing together theorists from UMass and UConn. Longer distance, a virtual writing group with Kirstine Taylor and Lisa Beard provided an invaluable space for exploring, revising, and honing ideas. I cannot thank them enough for the care, insight, and generosity with which they approach even the messiest draft. Lexi Neame has seen the project emerge from its beginnings. Her crisply articulated ideas and editing have been invaluable. This book is clearer and sharper thanks to her generous reading, patient feedback, and conversation. Robert Nichols provided crucial feedback on one of the chapters in progress as a discussant at APSA. A Postdoctoral Research Leave Fellowship from the American Association of University Women (AAUW) made all the difference by providing precious time to write.

Many people read and commented on parts of what would become the book, including Ali Aslam, Kate Bergren, Christopher Berk, Michiel Bot,

Lauren Caldwell, Adam Dahl, Laura Ephraim, Anna Fenton-Hathaway, Emre Gercek, Jack Gieseking, Laura Grattan, Bonnie Honig, Tamsin Jones, Alex Manevitz, Meg Mott, Lexi Neame, Robert Nichols, Sam Ng, Erin Pineda, Mike Stein, and Lena Zuckerwise. I have benefited tremendously from presenting work in progress at NYU's Global Liberal Studies Program, the Pioneer Valley Political Theory Workshop, the Political Theory Workshops of UConn and Cornell, Reed College, at UMass Boston, and at many conferences: APSA, APT, WPSA, LSA, ASA, SPEP, and NEPSA. I thank everyone who participated in these events for their questions, suggestions, and critiques. Special thanks to Ali Aslam, Jane Gordon, Andrés Henao Castro, Johann Jäckel, Lexi Neame, Erin Pineda, and Kevin Thompson. At the University of Minnesota Press, Pieter Martin was a fantastic editor to work with. I also thank Ali Aslam and the anonymous reviewer for their insightful and generative feedback on the manuscript, which strengthened it considerably. I thank Reed Floarea for the index.

A heartfelt thanks, finally, to my family and friends for supporting me through this process that sometimes seemed impossible. I am especially grateful to those far away for keeping me close: my parents Jack and Anneke as well as Leticia, Lexi, Caroline, Lisa, Lot, and Sophie. My friend Jack always believed in the book, even at moments when I didn't, and shared wisdom, practical advice, and many home-cooked meals. In characteristic generosity and enthusiasm, he also began promoting the book years before it was finished. Johann encouraged me to keep calm and go on a run, and Inger shared her experience with the writing and publishing process. My brother Philip offered support and conversation, while Devlin, Tamsin, and Carol kept me connected to the joys of fiction and being in nature. In perhaps my greatest stroke of luck yet, I met Erin, who teaches me every day about embracing the uncertainty and openness of creative process, life, and love.

Notes

Preface

1. See, for example, Hulsman, "The Abolitionist Case." The term "dark figure of crime" refers to crime that is unreported and missing from official crime statistics. As American criminologist and sociologist William Chambliss observes, "the most consistent finding of the NCVS [the National Criminal Victimization Survey, an annual survey by the federal Bureau of Justice Statistics of a random sample of U.S. residents] is that most crimes are not reported by the victim." Chambliss, "The Politics of Crime Statistics," 467.

2. The claim that abolitionism "promises a heaven-on-earth that will never come to pass" is made by Roger Lancaster in "How to End Mass Incarceration."

3. According to the Prison Policy Initiative report, "Mass Incarceration: The Whole Pie," Black Americans make up 14 percent of the U.S. population but account for 42 percent of prison and jail populations, while white people make up 58 percent of the U.S. population and only 36 percent of incarcerated people. American Indian or Alaska Native people and Latinx people make up 1 and 19 percent of the U.S. population, respectively, and 3 and 20 percent of prison and jail populations. A study of New York state prisons found that each year of imprisonment translated to a two-year decline in life expectancy. Patterson, "The Dose–Response of Time Served in Prison on Mortality." From 2001 to 2019, suicide rates increased in detention facilities, and suicide is the leading cause of death in jails. Bureau of Justice Statistics, "Suicide in Local Jails and State and Federal Prisons, 2000–2019." Children with an incarcerated parent experience higher rates of physical and mental health challenges. Rosalyn Lee, Xiangming Fan, and Feijun Luo, "The Impact of Parental Incarceration on the Physical and Mental Health of Young Adults." Finally, a recent study by the Department of Justice found that 43 percent of people released from state prisons were arrested within one year of their release, and 82 percent were arrested at least once during the ten years following their release. Bureau of Justice Statistics, *Recidivism of Prisoners Released in 24 States in 2008.*

4. I do not use the term *paranoia* as a clinical diagnosis. Rather, I draw on queer theorist Eve Kosofsky Sedgwick's concept of "paranoid reading," which describes an influential style of literary and political critique. I discuss the potential ableist implications of the term in chapter 2.

5. See https://p-nap.org/about-us.

6. See, for instance, the PNAP project The Long Term. https://p-nap.org/the-long-term.

Introduction

1. Locke, *Second Treatise of Government,* para. 8.

2. Davis, *Abolition Democracy.*

3. Realism as a political theory tradition is different from how realism is understood in International Relations, where it implies specific beliefs about the nature of states and the international system. This book focuses only on the political theory meaning of realism.

4. Rawls, *A Theory of Justice.*

5. Kant, "Perpetual Peace," cited in Galston, "Realism in Political Theory," 387.

6. This is how Bernard Williams characterizes political moralism in *In the Beginning Was the Deed,* 1. Hannah Arendt famously places Plato at the beginning of a "parting of the men of action and the men of thought" that continued into her lifetime. Arendt, *On Revolution,* 177.

7. Honig, *Political Theory and the Displacement of Politics,* 2. Similarly, Matt Sleat writes that "the now familiar realist charge against much contemporary political theory is that through inappropriate idealizations, abstraction, and moralization it presents a misleading, if not outright false, account of politics that sits at too great a distance from reality to offer us much that can help us comprehend or get any meaningful intellectual grasp of our political lives." Sleat, "Introduction," 3. See also Galston, "Realism in Political Theory."

8. I have been inspired by Susan Bickford and Elizabeth Markovits's paper "Clear Eyes, Full Hearts," presented at APSA in 2022.

9. The best-known realist thinker to advocate modus vivendi arrangements is Raymond Geuss.

10. Honig and Stears, "The New Realism," 180.

11. As Matt Sleat observes, there is a revival of realism in contemporary political theory, but political realism has deep historical roots. Sleat offers a partial list of thinkers in this tradition, including Thucydides, Augustine, Niccolò Machiavelli, Thomas Hobbes, Friedrich Nietzsche, Max Weber, and Carl Schmitt, adding that "several other thinkers have recently been subject to realist interpretations and hence may warrant inclusion in the canon also, including Herodotus, David Hume, Jeremy Bentham, Immanuel Kant, Vladimir Lenin, Mohandas Gandhi, Hannah Arendt, Leo Strauss, Michael Oakeshott, and Isaiah Berlin." It is this kind of expansive understanding of realism that I mean when I call prison abolition realist. An in-depth engagement with contemporary realist political theory is beyond the scope of this book. Sleat, "Introduction," 11.

12. Machiavelli, *The Prince*, 61.

13. I thank Ali Aslam for suggesting this example.

14. See, for instance, Lerman and Weaver, *Arresting Citizenship*, or Page and King, "Truth and Reconciliation."

15. On left-wing pessimism, see Brown, "Resisting Left Melancholy"; Harney and Moten, *The Undercommons;* and Wilderson, *Afropessimism.* The "racial realism" of critical race theorist Derrick Bell occupies an interesting place between realism and pessimism: Like contemporary U.S. prison abolitionists, he argues that it is unrealistic in a deeply racist society to expect the legal system—specifically, the legal principle of "equality"—to advance anti-racist struggles. At the same time, Bell's realism is more pessimistic than that of contemporary abolitionists: Racial realists must "acknowledge that our actions are not likely to lead to transcendent change," he writes, but the struggle against white domination is both valuable in itself and a way to "make life bearable in a society where blacks are a permanent, subordinate class." I return to his ideas in chapter 5. Bell, "Racial Realism," 378, 377.

16. Both Davis and Gilmore situate their abolitionism in the Black Radical Tradition, a term used by Cedric Robinson in *Black Marxism: The Making of the Black Radical Tradition* (1983) to describe the global legacy of Black people's struggles against racial capitalism. For Davis, contemporary prison abolition continues nineteenth-century struggles against chattel slavery and the experiment of Radical Reconstruction. See Johnson and Lubin, "Angela Davis." Despite prison abolitionism's rhetorical invocation of slavery abolitionism, not all abolitionist thinkers theorize race and racism, however. Michel Foucault, Thomas Mathiesen, Nils Christie, and Louk Hulsman, all influential white European abolitionists working in the second half of the twentieth century, do not center race in their critiques of prisons. I consider the promise and limitation of their approaches in later chapters.

17. Davis is a leading Black feminist scholar and recently coauthored *Abolition. Feminism. Now.* with Gina Dent, Erica Meiners, and Beth Richie. Gilmore notes the centrality of women in Black freedom struggles in "Fatal Couplings of Power and Difference."

18. For this kind of typology of abolitionism, see Carrier and Piché, "The State of Abolitionism."

19. In chapter 2, I discuss the concern that "paranoid thinking" as a concept reinforces ableism. Though the concept of paranoia might not be used in critical disability studies, it is experiencing a resurgence of sorts in political theory and is taken up by Noga Rotem and George Shulman.

20. On political impasse, see Shulman, "Fred Moten's Refusals and Consents."

21. Honig, *Political Theory and the Displacement of Politics.*

22. Honig, 205.

23. Abolitionist political theorists Joy James and Andrew Dilts are prominent exceptions. Many abolitionist scholars working in the United States hold appointments in interdisciplinary programs and departments, such as History of Consciousness (Angela Davis, Professor Emerita), Criminology, Law, and Justice (Beth Richie

and Liat Ben-Moshe), Criminology, Law, and Society (Sora Han), or Media and Cultural Studies (Dylan Rodríguez). Many also hold multiple appointments: Richie is also professor of Black Studies, and Erica Meiners holds appointments in both Education and in Women's, Gender, and Sexuality Studies. Moreover, abolitionist scholars often work at the cutting edge of their fields, which further complicates efforts to identify them with specific disciplines. It is more to give a sense of the breadth of abolitionist scholarship, and less to secure simple disciplinary identifications, then, that I offer this partial list, which further includes Ruth Wilson Gilmore (Geography), Lisa Guenther, Brady Heiner, Chloë Taylor, Sarah Tyson, and Perry Zurn (Philosophy), Sarah Haley and Jordan Camp (History), Christina Heatherton and Emily Thuma (American Studies), Dorothy Roberts (Sociology, Law), Allegra McLeod, Amna Akbar, and Dean Spade (Law), Andrea Smith (Native and Indigenous Studies), and Eric Stanley (Gender and Women's Studies). In recent years, abolitionist scholarship has been assembled in the new interdisciplinary fields of Critical Prison Studies and Critical Carceral Studies.

24. See Pineda, *Seeing Like an Activist.*

25. Sometimes, scholars include restorative justice in this list, describing it as a project to punish in order to repair harm. Prison abolitionists, however, tend to theorize repair as distinct from, and sometimes opposed to, punishment. Nils Christie, for instance, explicitly separates repair and punishment in his influential essay "Conflicts as Property." For a discussion of repair as justification for punishment, see Cavadino et al., *The Penal System* and RA Duff, "Restorative Punishment and Punitive Restoration."

26. Davis, *Are Prisons Obsolete?;* Foucault, *Discipline and Punish.*

27. Foucault, "Alternatives to the Prison." Republican political theorist Philip Pettit observes that prisons inherently entail domination, which he takes as an argument against their use. Pettit, "Republican Theory and Criminal Punishment."

28. Davis, "Racialized Punishment and Prison Abolition." Joy James develops a similar critique of *Discipline and Punish,* focused on the endurance of spectacular racialized violence in the United States, in "Erasing the Spectacle of Racialized State Violence." I thank Shatema Threadcraft for the insight that Foucault's elision of race in *Discipline and Punish* is facilitated by this narrow geographic focus on Pennsylvania and New York, home to Eastern State Penitentiary and Auburn State Prison, respectively.

29. Davis, "Racialized Punishment and Prison Abolition."

30. See Hartman, *Scenes of Subjection;* Alexander, *The New Jim Crow;* DuVernay, *13th.*

31. See Mauer and Huling, *Young Black Americans and the Criminal Justice System*; and Prison Policy Initiative, "Race and Ethnicity." The racism of the U.S. criminal legal system is so strong that while globally, women form but a small minority of prisoners, Black women in the United States are incarcerated at comparable rates to white men. See Crenshaw, "From Private Violence to Mass Incarceration." See also footnote 3 to the preface.

32. As Muhammad observes in *The Condemnation of Blackness,* crime statistics have long been weaponized to perpetuate anti-Black policies and beliefs.

33. Gottschalk, *Caught,* 127. See also Alexander, *The New Jim Crow.*

34. See Ghandnoosh and Barry, "One in Five."

35. Gottschalk discusses the racial disparities in officially recorded violent crime in *Caught,* as does Alexander in *The New Jim Crow.* On the history of redlining, see Taylor, *Race for Profit;* and Rothstein, *The Color of Law.* On Black women's heightened vulnerability to violence, see Threadcraft, "North American Necropolitics and Gender"; Richie, *Arrested Justice;* and Kaba, *We Do This 'til We Free Us.*

36. Gottschalk, *Caught,* 279.

37. See Vera Institute, "How the United States Punishes People for Being Poor"; and Wacquant, *Punishing the Poor.*

38. See Rabuy and Kopf, "Detaining the Poor." For a broader discussion of how the neoliberal state both abandons groups to poverty and deprivation and criminalizes and punishes them, see Gilmore and Gilmore, "Restating the Obvious."

39. Hulsman, "The Abolitionist Case."

40. Davis, "Racialized Punishment and Prison Abolition."

41. On the criminalization of queer and trans* people, see Richie, "Queering Antiprison Work"; Stanley and Smith, *Captive Genders*; and Spade, *Normal Life.*

42. See the initiative "Survived and Punished."

43. Half of women who are murdered in the United States each year are killed by an intimate partner or family member. Bureau of Justice Statistics, "Female Murder Victims and Victim-Offender Relationship."

44. See, for instance, MacKinnon, *Toward a Feminist Theory of the State;* and Threadcraft, "North American Necropolitics and Gender." Other domains of intimacy and shared space pose similar threats; think of the workplace or the military.

45. Young, "The Logic of Masculinist Protection."

46. INCITE! and Critical Resistance, "Statement on Gender Violence and the Prison Industrial Complex."

47. Davis's essay "The Myth of the Black Rapist" in *Women, Race & Class* debunks this pretext for lynching and argues that feminist antiviolence work must be antiracist to be effective.

48. Foucault's discussion with French Maoists about popular justice evokes historical examples ranging from people massacring prisoners in the early years of the French Revolution, to extrajudicial killings of alleged Nazi collaborators shortly after the end of the Second World War, to the "revolutionary tribunals" of the Communist Red Army. They do not discuss the public shaming and other violence of the Cultural Revolution, which had begun in 1966. Kneecapping was a common punitive technique of the Irish Republican Army (IRA). See also my discussion of Geo Maher's vision of police abolition, which substitutes local violence for organized state violence, in Terwiel, "The Revolutionary Politics of Abolition."

49. Kirkner et al., "A Qualitative Study."

50. See, for instance, Enns, *Incarceration Nation;* Beckett, *Making Crime Pay;* Murakawa, *The First Civil Right;* and Gilmore, *Golden Gulag.*

51. While official violent crime rates peaked in the early 1990s, prison populations peaked in 2008, almost two decades later. On recorded violent crime rates from 1960 to 2013, see Brennan Center for Justice, "America's Faulty Perception of Crime

Rates." On trends in incarceration, see Bureau of Justice Statistics, "Correctional Populations in the United States, 2013." On the weaponization of crime statistics to perpetuate anti-Blackness, see Muhammad, *The Condemnation of Blackness.*

52. See https://www.aclu.org/issues/smart-justice/mass-incarceration.

53. See The Sentencing Project, "Americans with Criminal Records"; Bureau of Justice Statistics, "Correctional Populations in the United States, 2019"; and Uggen et al., "Locked Out 2022."

54. Gottschalk, *Caught,* 2.

55. Richie, *Arrested Justice;* James, *Warfare in the American Homeland;* Gilmore and Gilmore, "Restating the Obvious." Political scientist Marie Gottschalk speaks of a "carceral state" in *Caught.*

56. Gilmore and Gilmore, "Restating the Obvious." The point is also made by sociologist Loïc Wacquant, an early theorist and critic of contemporary U.S. punishment. To my knowledge, Wacquant does not identify with prison abolition. See Wacquant, "Crafting the Neoliberal State."

57. Bohrman and Murakawa, "Remaking Big Government"; Wacquant, "Crafting the Neoliberal State."

58. Gottschalk describes this as the qualitative dimension of the prison crisis in *Caught.*

59. Wacquant speaks of a "Janus-faced state" in "Crafting the Neoliberal State." Lerman and Weaver have theorized the antidemocratic effects of encounters with the criminal legal system, which generate what they call "custodial citizenship." Lerman and Weaver, *Arresting Citizenship.*

60. Dilts, "Innocent Citizens, Guilty Subjects"; Alexander, *The New Jim Crow.* Whether *The New Jim Crow* is an abolitionist work is a matter of contestation among abolitionists. Alexander does not mention prison abolition in *The New Jim Crow,* but she has identified with abolitionism since its publication. Alexander, "Life After 'The New Jim Crow.'"

61. Brown, "Moralism as Antipolitics," 384.

62. Foucault, "Alternatives to the Prison," 14.

63. For example, Davis, *Are Prisons Obsolete?*

64. I discuss the private industry of so-called video visitation (video calls between incarcerated people and loved ones) in chapter 5 and argue that this technology undermines the right to hug of both incarcerated people and their children.

65. Cho, "Unchecked Growth."

66. Thorpe, "Perverse Politics."

67. Vesla Weaver has powerfully critiqued the marginalization of punishment and policing in the American Politics subfield. See Soss and Weaver, "The Police Are Our Government." Weaver, in contrast, places these front and center, as do Marie Gottschalk, Naomi Murakawa, and Rebecca Thorpe. See *infra,* fn 23, for an overview of abolitionist scholarship outside of political science.

68. Weaver, Prowse, and Piston, "Too Much Knowledge, Too Little Power."

69. On Black freedom dreams, see Kelley, *Freedom Dreams.*

70. Hartman, *Scenes of Subjection.*

71. Andy McAdams cited in Hartman, 132. The claim that there was land owned by no one but the U.S. government obscures Indigenous land claims, and foreshadows tensions between visions of prison abolitionism as a new Reconstruction and the project of decolonization. I discuss these tensions in chapter 3.

72. This is key to Derrick Bell's "racial realism."

73. Murakawa, *The First Civil Right,* 17.

74. Dayan, "Civil Death," 19.

75. Guenther, *Solitary Confinement.*

76. Guenther.

77. See, for example, United Nations Human Rights Office of the High Commissioner, "United States."

78. Lancaster, "How to End Mass Incarceration."

79. Honig and Stears, "The New Realism," 204. This quote discusses realism in art, but it holds for political realism too.

80. Kaba, "The System Isn't Broken," in *We Do This 'til We Free Us,* 13. This text was originally published in *The New Inquiry* in 2015.

81. The right-wing Right on Crime Coalition, for instance, argues the American prison system is broken. See "Case for Reform" at https://rightoncrime.com/about/case-for-reform/.

82. Berlant, *Cruel Optimism.*

83. Surveying U.S. history from the founding through the Civil War and Civil Rights movement to the 1990s, Bell observes that "abstract principles [of equality] lead to legal results that harm blacks and perpetuate their inferior status" (369) and argues that this should lead realists to abandon hope that law can end racism. Such acknowledgment, he says, "enables us to avoid despair, and frees us to imagine and implement racial strategies that can bring fulfillment and even triumph" (374). Racial realists should see law and the courts "as instruments for preserving the status quo [that] *only periodically and unpredictably* serv[e] as a refuge of oppressed people," he says (364, emphasis added).

84. Lancaster, "Response."

85. Bernstein, "Carceral Politics as Gender Justice?"

86. See also Kathi Weeks on abolitionism's revival of structural critique in "Abolition of the Family."

87. Davis, *Abolition Democracy,* 68.

88. Gilmore, *Change Everything.*

89. See https://criticalresistance.org/, https://www.byp100.org/, and https://www.nationalbailout.org/.

90. For example, https://p-nap.org/.

91. For example, https://www.prisonactivist.org/resources/books-magazines-and-publishers.

92. For example, https://southerncoalition.org/justice-system-reform/safe-reentry/ban-the-box-community-initiative-guide/.

93. For example, https://www.facebook.com/columbiaprisondivest/.

94. See https://transformharm.org/.

95. Document on file with the author.

96. Gilmore, *Golden Gulag,* 242.

97. Gorz, *Strategy for Labor,* introduction.

98. Gorz. This example is given by Gorz and recounted by Mathiesen in *The Politics of Abolition.*

99. See, for example, Collins, *Black Feminist Thought.* For Hill Collins, another characteristic of Black Feminist Thought is its focus on negative images of Black womanhood.

100. Williams, *Truth and Truthfulness,* 153, cited in Honig and Stears, "The New Realism," 186.

101. I make this point in "The Revolutionary Politics of Abolition."

102. Mathiesen, *The Politics of Abolition,* 39. Mathiesen explains that the name KROM was nonsensical, but it was chosen as a variation on the names of the Danish prison organization KRIM and the Swedish KRUM. Mathiesen served as chairman and later as board member of the KROM. *The Politics of Abolition,* 46–47.

103. Mathiesen published sections of the book in Norwegian, Swedish, and Finnish between 1971 and 1973, followed by English and German translations in 1974 and 1979. Mathiesen, "The Politics of Abolition," 81. The original publication of the book overlaps with the prison writings of Angela Davis in the United States and the activism of the French Prisons Information Group (GIP), cofounded by Foucault, discussed in chapters 3 and 1, respectively.

104. Mathiesen, *The Politics of Abolition,* chapters 4 and 5.

105. Mathiesen, 110.

106. Mathiesen, 83.

107. Mathiesen, 25.

108. Mathiesen, 211, emphasis added.

109. Mathiesen, 202.

110. Mathiesen, 118.

111. Mathiesen, 118.

112. As Mathiesen explains, such forced labor was permitted under the 1900 Act relating to Vagrancy, Begging, and Drunkenness. It "generally meant induction into Oppstad labour camp, actually a rigorous prison." Mathiesen, 90.

113. Mathiesen, 119, emphasis added.

114. Mathiesen, 212.

115. Rose Braz, "Environmental Challenge Bars Construction of California Prison." See also https://www.justiceashealing.org/nonewwomensprison.

116. See, for instance, New York City mayor Eric Adams's plan to expand involuntary commitment. Gusmano, "New York City's Involuntary Commitment Plan."

117. Of course, abolitionists are "against" the prison, but that tells us very little about what we should do about them, especially given that our society is deeply shaped by confinement, surveillance, and control of various kinds, and that these practices and discourses have shaped our subjectivity and imagination. Similarly, Foucault argues in his late essay "What Is Enlightenment?" that the point is not to be "'for' or 'against' the Enlightenment," an approach he describes as simplistic and authoritarian blackmail. Instead, he says, "we must try to proceed with the analysis of ourselves as beings who are historically determined, to a certain extent, by the Enlightenment," 313.

118. Olson, "The Freshness of Fanaticism"; James, "Airbrushing Revolution for the Sake of Abolition." Before Frederick Douglass could use Constitutionalism to fight against slavery, he had to physically fight his enslavers and flee the plantation where he was forcibly confined. At the same time, Shatema Threadcraft reminds us, we would be wrong to see Douglass's use of physical violence and oratory as exemplary of resistance in general. These are gendered modes of resistance, well suited for the forms of oppression enslaved men faced (control over physical labor, and restriction of self-expression), but less applicable to the intimate oppression specifically imposed on women (control of their sexual, reproductive, and caretaking abilities). See Threadcraft, *Intimate Justice.* I thank Daniel Epstein for bringing James's essay to my attention.

1. Abolition in a Paranoid Key

1. Davis, "Racialized Punishment and Prison Abolition," 96.
2. Foucault, *Discipline and Punish,* 293, 303.
3. GIP, "GIP Manifesto," 64, and "Preface to Intolerable 1," 91.
4. GIP, "GIP Manifesto," 64.
5. GIP, "On Prisons," 67.
6. *Active Intolerance* is coedited by Andrew Dilts and Perry Zurn; *Intolerable* is coedited by Kevin Thompson and Perry Zurn, with translations by Zurn and Erik Beranek.
7. Thompson and Zurn, "Introduction," 4. They write that the GIP offers "an exemplary model for anticarceral work today" (24).
8. Foucault, *Discipline and Punish,* 30. He refers once more to "prisoners' revolts of recent weeks," 268.
9. Bargu, *Starve and Immolate,* 60, emphasis added.
10. Myers, "Resisting Foucauldian Ethics."
11. Foucault, "I Perceive the Intolerable," 77. As Lisa Guenther rightly points out, Foucault too quickly dismisses the importance of prison conditions. In chapter 5, I discuss the importance of comfort for incarcerated people.
12. For the first set of critiques, see Davis, "Racialized Punishment and Prison Abolition"; and James, "Erasing the Spectacle of Racialized State Violence." For the second, see Garland, *Punishment and Modern Society;* and Wacquant, "Crafting the Neoliberal State."
13. *Merriam-Webster.*

14. Foucault, "The Penal System Is a Problem," 82.

15. For Hannah Arendt, forgiveness and promising are both necessary for political life. "Without being forgiven, released from the consequences of what we have done, our capacity to act would, as it were, be confined to one single deed from which we could never recover; we would remain the victims of its consequences forever." *The Human Condition,* 237.

16. The piece was first published as the introductory essay in Sedgwick's edited volume *Novel Gazing: Queer Readings in Fiction* (1997). Later, it appeared as a chapter in her 2003 book *Touching Feeling,* which is the edition I cite in this book.

17. Sedgwick, "Paranoid Reading and Reparative Reading," 125–26.

18. Sedgwick, 124.

19. Sedgwick, 130.

20. Sedgwick, 135. Sedgwick derives this example from DA Miller's 1988 work *The Novel and the Police.*

21. Sedgwick, 138.

22. Sedgwick, 141.

23. Sedgwick, 140.

24. Milo Ward theorizes democratic support for punitive power in "A Democracy of Authorities."

25. Founded after the uprisings of May 1968, the Proletarian Left (GP) advocated violence as both a defensive and an offensive tool of revolutionary "mass struggle against repression." Bourg, *From Revolution to Ethics,* 54. It was criminalized by the French government in 1970. Simone de Beauvoir and others organized to keep the GP's newsletter published after its criminalization, and Daniel Defert, Foucault's partner, joined the GP's "political prisoners" group. Macey, *The Lives of Michel Foucault,* 261. Bourg reports that between June 1968 and March 1972, 1,035 people were imprisoned for crimes related to political action (65). It is easy to overlook the GIP's break with Maoist politics because the group brought together people with various political backgrounds and because its publications regularly use Marxist vocabularies of class oppression. See Hoffman, "Investigations from Marx to Foucault." Foucault and Pierre Vidal-Naquet note that the Maoists' demand for political prisoner status had alienated regular, "common law" prisoners and their families, who saw it as a demand for special treatment. Foucault and Vidal-Naquet, "Inquiry on Prisons," 109. In the preface to its first pamphlet, *Investigations into Twenty Prisons,* the GIP gives a milder and more affirmative account of the hunger strikes by the GP militants, but what it now affirms in the hunger strikes are the same things that Foucault first suggested were missing: a protest that brings together "many" prisoners and provokes, on the outside, "a movement against conditions of detention" such that people on the inside and outside of prisons come together to fight "the same intolerable reality." GIP. "Preface to *Intolerable 1,*" 90–91.

26. Sedgwick, "Paranoid Reading and Reparative Reading," 135.

27. Sedgwick, 135.

28. As Foucault puts it in *History of Sexuality Volume 1*, "We must not think that by saying yes to sex, one says no to power" (157).

29. Foucault, *Discipline and Punish*, 231.

30. Foucault, 205.

31. Foucault, 205.

32. Foucault, "The Means of Correct Training," in *Discipline and Punish.*

33. Foucault, *Discipline and Punish*, 297. Solzhenitsyn's *The Gulag Archipelago* was first published in French in 1974. Foucault's reference to the gulags of the Soviet Union implies carceral continuities between both camps of the Cold War.

34. "I shall not attempt here to reconstitute the whole network that formed first the immediate surroundings of the prison, then spread farther and farther outwards," Foucault writes shortly after introducing the terms "carceral archipelago," "carceral continuum," and "carceral net." *Discipline and Punish*, 297.

35. Foucault, 296.

36. Foucault, 297.

37. Foucault, 27.

38. Foucault, 27.

39. I thank Leigh Claire for this formulation.

40. Foucault, *Discipline and Punish*, 306.

41. Foucault, 306. *Discipline and Punish*, he says in the book's final sentence, "must serve as a historical background to various studies of the power of normalization and the formation of knowledge in modern society" (308).

42. GIP, "On Prisons," 66–67.

43. Foucault, "Par-delà le bien et le mal," 1091.

44. GIP, "Back Cover of *Intolerable 1*," 93.

45. Foucault, "What Is Enlightenment?," 315–16.

46. Foucault, "What Is Called Punishing?," 384. Foucault calls this role that of a "specific intellectual," as opposed to a "universal intellectual" who proclaims universal truths.

47. Sedgwick, "Paranoid Reading and Reparative Reading," 139.

48. Foucault, "I Perceive the Intolerable," 76.

49. GIP, "GIP Manifesto," 64.

50. GIP, "GIP Manifesto," 64.

51. GIP, Intolerable 1.

52. Brich, "The Groupe d'Information sur les Prisons"; and Spivak, "Can the Subaltern Speak?"

53. GIP, "GIP Manifesto" and "On Prisons," 66, emphasis added.

54. Guenther, "Beyond Guilt and Innocence," 233. Guenther's account of the intolerable aligns with the agonistic realist insight that even "the real" is ultimately up for contestation and may well be susceptible to change. Honig and Stears, "The New Realism," 204. Guenther continues: "This potentiality is not inherent in the individual consciousness of a subject who 'perceives the intolerable,' but rather emerges through the *movement* by which embodied subjects call on one another, in unison

and in cacophony, according to the demands of the situation and the instable rhythms of collective organizing" (233).

55. Foucault, "Questions of Method," 84, emphasis added.

56. Foucault, *Discipline and Punish,* 30.

57. "The man described for us, whom we are invited to free, is already in himself the effect of a subjection much more profound than himself," Foucault writes darkly. *Discipline and Punish,* 30.

58. Foucault, "Interview de Michel Foucault," 1507–8. I previously theorized problematization as an activist practice in a journal article by that name; this book's reading of Foucault through the lens of paranoid critique develops a different interpretation.

59. Foucault, "Interview de Michel Foucault," 1507–8.

60. In "Contre les peines de substitution," for instance, Foucault writes that the prison system has been left, for years, "in immobility and sclerosis."

61. Sedgwick, "Paranoid Reading and Reparative Reading," 144.

62. Foucault, "Questions of Method," 82, emphasis added.

63. Sedgwick, "Paranoid Reading and Reparative Reading," 130.

64. See Foucault, *Discipline and Punish;* Davis, *Are Prisons Obsolete?;* and Ben-Moshe, *Decarcerating Disability.*

65. The GIP's manifesto, signed by Foucault, Jean-Marie Domenach, and Pierre Vidal-Naquet on behalf of the GIP, states: "It is not for us to suggest a reform. We wish only to make the reality known."

66. Foucault, "Truth and Power."

67. Foucault, "Par-delà le bien et le mal."

68. Foucault, 1103.

69. Matt Fleischer-Black, "Free Universities."

70. Foucault, "Par-delà le bien et le mal," 1103.

71. Foucault, "On Popular Justice."

72. Foucault, 15.

73. Foucault, 8.

74. Foucault, 8–9.

75. Foucault, 16, translation modified.

76. Foucault, "Par-delà le bien et le mal," 1102.

77. Foucault, "Alternatives to the Prison."

78. Foucault's claim that the prison's failure to rehabilitate is secretly part of its success has received some pushback. Most notably, David Garland has questioned by which standards the prison fails to deliver. If the aim is to separate criminalized people from the general population, or to unleash the state's power to punish, whatever the costs and consequences, he says, then prisons work very well. And if we compare prisons to other "complex institutions" like schools or hospitals, we also wouldn't be surprised to see that a percentage of participants does not meet the institutional objectives, whether that is graduation, cure, or rehabilitation (165). Though Garland does not explore it, the latter is actually a Foucauldian point: Disciplinary practices of examination and categorization *always* identify a group at the wrong end

of the normal curve. Although this is inherent in disciplinary practices of measurement, it is experienced as a failure and often leads to a doubling down on disciplinary techniques. Garland, *Punishment and Modern Society.*

79. Foucault means family expansively, to include relationships between chaplains and incarcerated people, hierarchical social units created in penal institutions, and traditional kinship.

80. Mathiesen offers a similar assessment of prisoner councils in *The Politics of Abolition.*

81. Foucault, "Alternatives to the Prison," 16.

82. Foucault, 17.

83. Foucault, 17.

84. Foucault, "What Is Called Punishing?" 390.

85. Foucault, *Discipline and Punish,* 234, emphasis added.

86. Foucault, 234–35.

87. Taylor, *Foucault, Feminism, and Sex Crimes,* 122.

88. See, for example, Project Nia and the Barnard Center for Research on Women, "What Is Accountability?" https://www.youtube.com/watch?v=QZuJ55iGI14.

89. This is argued, for instance, by Communities Against Rape and Abuse (CARA), discussed in chapter 4.

90. Foucault, "What Is Called Punishing?," 383. The interview took place in December 1983, was edited by Foucault, and was published in February 1984.

91. Hulsman, "The Abolitionist Case."

92. Law, *Resistance Behind Bars;* Thuma, *All Our Trials.*

93. *Intolerable* contains documents regarding several prison revolts: at Melun, Fresnes, Nancy, and Toul prisons.

94. Foucault, "On Attica," 295.

95. Incarcerated women also used menstrual blood. Feldman focuses on men; for an account of the political conflict in Northern Ireland through the lens of gender, with a focus on the tactics of nationalist women, see Aretxaga, *Shattering Silence.* I thank Nadja Eisenberg-Guyot for bringing this book to my attention.

96. Feldman, *Formations of Violence,* 178.

97. Ben-Moshe, *Decarcerating Disability,* 5.

98. Foucault, *Discipline and Punish,* 27.

99. Sedgwick, "Paranoid Reading and Reparative Reading," 133, emphasis in original.

100. Foucault, "What Is Called Punishing?," 384.

101. For English translations of Foucault's writings on the Iranian Revolution, see Afary and Anderson, *Foucault and the Iranian Revolution.*

102. Sedgwick's concept of paranoid reading could thus be read as a complement to Wendy Brown's analysis of melancholy and moralism as a response to lost revolutionary visions. See Brown, "Resisting Left Melancholy" and "Moralism as Antipolitics."

103. Dilts, "How Does It Feel to Be(come) a Problem?"

104. Ahmed, "Feminist Killjoys (and Other Willful Subjects)." See also Ahmed's *The Promise of Happiness.*

105. Dilts, "How Does It Feel to Be(come) a Problem?," 638.

106. Dilts, 639.

107. I thank Perry Zurn for alerting me to the friendships forged in and through the GIP.

108. Dilts, "How Does It Feel to Be(come) a Problem?," 637.

109. Sedgwick, "Paranoid Reading and Reparative Reading," 146.

110. Guenther, "Beyond Guilt and Innocence."

111. Guenther, 236–37.

112. Sedgwick, "Paranoid Reading and Reparative Reading," 130.

113. As Sedgwick observes, "paranoid exigencies . . . are often necessary for nonparanoid knowing and practice" (129).

114. On the link between hope and uncertainty, which distinguishes hope from both optimism and pessimism, see Solnit, "Why Climate Despair Is a Luxury."

115. Sedgwick, "Paranoid Reading and Reparative Reading," 150.

116. Sedgwick, 139. I thank the reviewers of this manuscript for suggesting I include a discussion of Foucault's later work.

117. Chloë Taylor, for instance, reads Foucault as suggesting that "contemporary liberation movements reactivate the Greek model of ethics—giving it a different content—in order to ground their politics in a self-transformative practice." Specifically, she argues for vegetarianism as part of an "ethico-aesthetics of the self." Taylor, "Foucault and the Ethics of Eating," 73.

118. For Ladelle McWhorter, Foucault's notion of political spirituality "puts in question both one's style of existence and one's epistemological regime, one's self-discipline and one's modes of self-awareness, simultaneously in order to cultivate possibilities in both fields simultaneously." McWhorter, "Foucault's Political Spirituality."

119. GIP, "On Prisons," 66.

120. Foucault and Vidal-Naquet, "Inquiry on Prisons," 111.

121. These are taken from "Declaration to the Press and the Public Authorities Coming from the Prisoners at Melun," demands 3, 5, and 7, in *Intolerable,* 224–25.

122. "Toul Prison List of Demands," and "Fresnes," in *Intolerable,* 228–29.

2. The Pull of Purity

1. The Sentencing Project, "Mass Incarceration Trends."

2. Mauer and Huling, *Young Black Americans and the Criminal Justice System,* cited in Human Rights Watch, "Punishment and Prejudice."

3. The Black Panther Party for Self-Defense, for instance, included prison abolition in its ten-point platform. Prison abolitionism was not exclusively a revolutionary project: by the mid-1970s, many mainstream commentators believed that prisons were withering away. Though I don't discuss it in this book, some abolitionism has been religiously motivated. *Instead of Prisons: A Handbook for Abolitionists* (1976) was coauthored by Honey Faye Knopp, who was also a Quaker minister. Angela Davis

observes the prominence of religious abolitionisms in ICOPA, the International Conference on Penal Abolition first held in 1983. Chapter 3 discusses the evolution of Davis's abolitionism over time, from her Black revolutionary Communism in the 1960s to the present.

4. Chapter 4 discusses the work of INCITE! Women and Trans People of Color Against Violence, the initiative Survived and Punished, and other efforts that offer intersectional feminist, queer, and trans* critiques of racial criminalization. See also Mogul et al., *Queer (In)Justice;* Stanley and Smith, *Captive Genders;* and Bey, *Black Trans Feminism.*

5. "The most common path to admission to mental hospitals was involuntary commitment throughout the early part of the twentieth century and well into the 1960s." Harcourt, "Reducing Mass Incarceration," 70. In the early 1960s, close to 90 percent of people institutionalized for diagnoses of "mental retardation" were institutionalized under the age of twenty. More than half of them were institutionalized between the ages of five and fourteen. The George Washington University Institute of Law, Psychiatry and Criminology, "Institutionalization of the Mentally Retarded."

6. Harcourt, "Reducing Mass Incarceration," 54.

7. Exceptions include Emily Thuma and TL Lewis.

8. The Attica Liberation Faction Manifesto of Demands, demand 24.

9. The term was formulated by Lionel Penrose in 1939. Torrey, *Out of the Shadows: Confronting America's Mental Illness Crisis* (John Wiley & Sons, 1997), excerpted at Frontline, "Deinstitutionalization: A Psychiatric 'Titanic,'" https://www.pbs.org/wgbh/pages/frontline/shows/asylums/special/excerpt.html.

10. Harcourt, "Reducing Mass Incarceration," 57, emphasis added.

11. Ben-Moshe, *Decarcerating Disability,* 2.

12. Others examine the fate of people in immigrant detention centers or refugee camps, or of nonhuman animals in the "intensive confinement" of factory farms. The boundaries between "penal," "prison," and "carceral" abolition are fluid; most self-described prison abolitionists in the contemporary United States strictly speaking advocate carceral abolitionism.

13. See work by Noga Rotem and George Shulman. For a theorization of political "impasse," which is where I argue paranoid abolitionism tends to lead, see Shulman, "Fred Moten's Refusals and Consents."

14. In 1960s Norway, prison abolitionist scholar-activist Thomas Mathiesen described this dynamic in the context of forced labor camps for "alcoholic vagrants." Abolitionists successfully lobbied to close these camps, but when their former inhabitants started living on the streets, visible to the general public, a backlash formed, fueled by conservative media reporting on the "pollution" of public space. Mathiesen, *The Politics of Abolition.*

15. Ben-Moshe, *Decarcerating Disability,* 6.

16. Ben-Moshe, 126.

17. Ben-Moshe, 269, 74.

18. Harcourt, "Reducing Mass Incarceration," 61.

19. Geller, "The Rise and Demise of America's Psychiatric Hospitals."

20. Harcourt, "Reducing Mass Incarceration," 64.

21. Pilgrim State Hospital held more than fourteen thousand patients; Rockland State Hospital in New York held nine thousand.

22. Geller, "The Rise and Demise of America's Psychiatric Hospitals."

23. Dowdall 1999, referenced and cited in Harcourt, "Reducing Mass Incarceration," 64.

24. Ben-Moshe, *Decarcerating Disability,* 41.

25. See Edmund Burke Huey, *Backward and Feeble-Minded Children* (1912), cited in https://www.merriam-webster.com/wordplay/moron-idiot-imbecile-offensive-history.

26. See McWhorter, *Racism and Sexual Oppression in Anglo-America.*

27. Cited in Stern, "Sterilized in the Name of Public Health," 1129.

28. Cited in Stern, 1130.

29. Stern, 1128.

30. Ben-Moshe, *Decarcerating Disability,* 3.

31. Ben-Moshe, 3.

32. Quoted in Erickson, "Deinstitutionalization Through Optimism," 6; and Ben-Moshe, *Decarcerating Disability,* 43.

33. Joint Commission on Mental Illness and Health, *Action for Mental Health.*

34. Including that of Bernard Harcourt, discussed later. Ben-Moshe, *Decarcerating Disability,* 44. Harcourt points out, though, that the drugs helped change *public perceptions* of people with psychiatric disabilities. They came to be seen more as patients with conditions amenable to medical treatment than as people who were inherently and irrevocably different. Harcourt, "Reducing Mass Incarceration," 66. See also Shen, "A History of Antipsychotic Drug Development," and Social Security Administration, "History of Monthly Disability Insurance Benefits."

35. Knight, "Unfinished Business," 398.

36. Knight, 395.

37. Until 1991, a Massachusetts court banned public viewings on the grounds that it violated patients' privacy. New England Historical Society, "Titicut Follies."

38. Ben-Moshe, *Decarcerating Disability,* 6.

39. Ben-Moshe, 91.

40. Ben-Moshe, 95.

41. According to Szasz, "The maximum membership of the Association was approximately 1,000. The organization began as a shoe-string operation and, in the absence of interest and funding, remained in that state. In 1980, with the tide of professional and public opinion running irresistibly the other way, the organization was disbanded." Szasz, "The Abolitionist Perspective on Psychiatry."

42. Ben-Moshe, *Decarcerating Disability,* 101–103.

43. Ben-Moshe, 81.

44. Ben-Moshe, 65.

45. Ben-Moshe, 109.

46. American Psychiatric Association, "The Psychiatric Bed Crisis in the United States."

47. Ben-Moshe, *Decarcerating Disability,* 77.

48. Ben-Moshe, 79–81.

49. My account of the past and present field of disability theory is informed by Ben-Moshe, *Decarcerating Disability;* Ben-Moshe, "The State of (Intersectional Critique of) State Violence"; Ben-Moshe and Withers, "Introduction"; and Kafer, *Feminist Queer Crip.*

50. Jasbir Puar theorizes debilitation as "the slow wearing down of populations" where such wearing down is not understood in terms of disability. See *The Right to Maim,* also cited in Ben-Moshe, *Decarcerating Disability,* 29.

51. Harcourt, "Reducing Mass Incarceration."

52. Harcourt, 56.

53. Ben-Moshe, *Decarcerating Disability,* 23.

54. See Fabris, *Tranquil Prisons.*

55. Harcourt, "Reducing Mass Incarceration," 57.

56. I discuss this term further on in the chapter. Let me note for now that Ben-Moshe sometimes uses it in the singular, and sometimes in the plural. For instance, "By 'carceral enclosures,' I am referring not only to physical spaces of containment but to particular logics and discourses that (penal/prison/carceral) abolition opposes" (111). On p. 15, she describes incarceration as "a racist, colonial, gendered logic at its core."

57. Sedgwick, "Paranoid Reading and Reparative Reading."

58. Ben-Moshe, *Decarcerating Disability,* 5.

59. Foucault, *Madness and Civilization.* Foucault invokes his influence on antipsychiatry to refute the claim that his work is politically sterile. Undeniably, many on the Left have found inspiration in Foucault to challenge existing norms and practices. At the same time, his work struggles to support an affirmative politics.

60. GIP, "On Prisons," 67.

61. Foucault, *Abnormal,* referenced and cited in Ben-Moshe, "The Institution Yet to Come."

62. Foucault, *Discipline and Punish,* 300.

63. Ben-Moshe, *Decarcerating Disability,* 5.

64. Ben-Moshe, 15.

65. Critical Resistance offers the following definition on its website: "The prison industrial complex (PIC) is a term we use to describe the overlapping interests of government and industry that use surveillance, policing, and imprisonment as solutions to economic, social and political problems." Critical Resistance, "What Is the PIC? What Is Abolition?"

66. Ben-Moshe, *Decarcerating Disability,* 13.

67. See also Knight, "Unfinished Business" on the "institutional bias" of Medicaid.

68. Ben-Moshe, *Decarcerating Disability,* 38, emphasis added.

69. Ben-Moshe, 126, 116, emphasis in original.

70. Ben-Moshe, 53.

71. Ben-Moshe, 60. The creation of federal support programs (Medicare, Medicaid) helped close large state institutions but also incentivized reliance on smaller institutions. Their "institutional bias" means that "money, in the form of benefits or waivers goes towards institutions, nursing homes, or group homes but not to the person who benefits from these services directly" (44). It follows that "although most people were deinstitutionalized in past decades, the staff, resources, and budgets remained institutionalized" (58).

72. Ben-Moshe, 275. See Foucault, "Alternatives to the Prison," discussed in chapter 1.

73. Sedgwick, "Paranoid Reading and Reparative Reading," 131.

74. Ben-Moshe, *Decarcerating Disability,* 10.

75. In chapter 2, Ben-Moshe offers a more positive assessment of "radical inclusionists" who argue that integrating disabled students into mainstream K–12 education is not about incorporating more people into the status quo but rather "about changing the whole structure of education and its infrastructure so that it will better accommodate all students' abilities, including those who are labeled or identify as disabled." Ben-Moshe, *Decarcerating Disability,* 71.

76. Ben-Moshe also writes that reform "increases the scope of incarceration, and instead of making the system more just, it spreads an unjust system to more people" (16).

77. The term "Dis Inc." "simultaneously captures the corporatization of disability for profit by carceral institutions and the ways disability is subjected to incorporation in society, but only by respectability politics and assimilation (by rehabilitation, approximating normalcy, etc.)" (14). See also Ben-Moshe's remark that "because the goal [of incorporation] is to reduce stigma and assimilate (to be like one's nondisabled universal subject peers), these theories are already rooted in a specific racial, ableist, heteronormative discourse" that "should be dismantled" (81).

78. Ben-Moshe, *Decarcerating Disability,* 71.

79. Ben-Moshe, 10.

80. Ben-Moshe, 131, 53. The term "cripistemologies" was coined by Johnson and McRuer.

81. Ben-Moshe, 86. Wolfensberger's "poignant observations about daily living for those in prison-like 'abnormal settings' had evolved into a set of checklists that disabled people and their caretakers get measured on, such as eating with a fork (as opposed to a spoon or hands) or not having stuffed animals in one's room" (77).

82. In a similar vein, see Cruikshank's *The Will to Empower.*

83. Sedgwick, "Paranoid Reading and Reparative Reading," 141.

84. Ben-Moshe, *Decarcerating Disability,* 3.

85. PHI, "U.S. Home Care Workers." See also Donovan and Alarcón. "Long Hours, Low Pay."

86. Quinn et al., "Healthy Aging Requires a Healthy Home Care Workforce."

87. Erickson, "Deinstitutionalization Through Optimism," 7, 6. The CMHC were meant to be funded by states and localities in the long run.

88. Knight, "Unfinished Business," 400–401.

89. Erickson, "Deinstitutionalization Through Optimism," 7.

90. National Disability Institute, *Financial Inequality.* As the study explains, the causal relationship between disability and poverty runs both ways. People with disabilities often face barriers to education and employment that restrict their ability to earn, and living in poverty has disabling effects. Inadequate access to healthy food and medical care and higher exposure to pollutants all negatively affect health. Knight further discusses the "poverty trap." Medicaid is typically how people with disabilities afford the care they need to live at home, but as a means-tested program, it disincentivizes paid work.

91. Ben-Moshe, *Decarcerating Disability,* 109, emphasis added.

92. *Ben-Moshe,* 15. See also 111: "By 'carceral enclosures,' I am referring not only to physical spaces of containment but to particular logics and discourses that (penal/prison/carceral) abolition opposes."

93. Davis, *Are Prisons Obsolete?,* 25.

94. Carruthers cited in Woodly, *Reckoning,* 105.

95. Knight, "Unfinished Business," 396.

96. A politics of care is theorized as part of an abolitionist politics in Woodly, *Reckoning;* and in the "Critical Exchange," coedited by Woodly and Rachel Brown.

97. Similarly, Knight suggests that recognizing dependency and disability as "normal features of the human condition" might help Americans "see their shared stake in ensuring universal access to coverage for long-term supports and services in the community." Knight, "Unfinished Business," 405.

98. Tronto, *Moral Boundaries.*

99. Kaba, "Everything Worthwhile Is Done with Other People." The quote is from Kaba, who attributes the idea to Mia Mingus.

100. Mingus, "Access Intimacy, Interdependence and Disability Justice," emphasis in original.

3. Reconstructing the State?

1. Davis, *Abolition Democracy,* 68.

2. As Patricia Hill Collins shows, Black feminist thought is often developed in "alternative institutional locations [outside the academy] and among women who are not commonly perceived as intellectuals." Collins, *Black Feminist Thought,* 14.

3. On Angela Davis's life, see *Angela Davis: An Autobiography* (1974); James, "Introduction" to *The Angela Y. Davis Reader*; Roberts, "Angela Davis"; and Kaplan, *Dreaming in French.*

4. "Political Prisoners, Prisons, and Black Liberation" was first published in *If They Come in the Morning . . . Voices of Resistance* (1971). "Reflections on the Black Woman's Role in the Community of Slaves" was first published in *The Black Scholar* (1971). Both are included in *The Angela Y. Davis Reader,* ed. Joy James (1998).

5. Roberts, "Angela Davis," 661.

6. The rare in-depth engagements include work by Joy James and, more recently, Neil Roberts, Sonali Chakravarti, Lisa Beard, Cecilia Sebastian, Bryant William Sculos, and Quinn Lester. See James, "Introduction"; Roberts, "Angela Davis"; Beard, "From Dynamite Hill to the Black Power Mixtape"; Sculos, "Abolitionism & the Critique of Structural Violence"; and Sebastian, "Angela Davis and Critical Theory." My discussion of Davis in this chapter does not consider Joy James's 2023 book *Contextualizing Angela Davis.* I discuss Lester's article, "Whose Democracy in Which State?," later in this chapter.

7. These characterizations of Davis, Ben-Moshe, and Foucault are partial and contestable. Each author is open to other interpretations, which would highlight other characteristics and select different passages or texts. Davis, for instance, could be read through the lens of Black feminist thought, Foucault could be encountered as a theorist of desubjectivation (see, e.g., Huffer's *Mad for Foucault*), and Ben-Moshe could be read as a theorist of intersectionality.

8. I draw in this book on the democratic agonism of Bonnie Honig, inflected by Arendt, Nietzsche, and Derrida and committed to preserving openness and contestability to allow more egalitarian worlds to emerge, rather than the agonism of Chantal Mouffe, grounded in Carl Schmitt's assertion that the political requires the friend/enemy distinction.

9. For Davis and other contemporary abolitionists who reach back to Reconstruction, Du Bois's *Black Reconstruction in America* is the central source. As Joel Olson observes, "in all of his writings Du Bois emphasizes the central role of Black people in history" and "casts [their] achievements in radical-utopian terms" (131). Other historical accounts of Reconstruction include Foner, *Reconstruction.*

10. Foner, *Reconstruction;* also Harris, "How Reconstruction Created American Public Education."

11. Du Bois, *Black Reconstruction,* 184.

12. Cruikshank, *The Will to Empower;* Hartman, *Scenes of Subjection.*

13. Anderson discusses Reconstruction in *The Nation on No Map,* and says: "If we can see the dangers in state-building or the bourgeois values of the nation . . . , we must acknowledge the failures of many projects we'd call our own" (180). Du Bois takes a more agonistic approach when he describes Reconstruction as both splendid and a failure.

14. Dean Spade writes in "No Cops, Courts, or Cages Means No State" that "abolitionists already follow anarchist principles of voluntary association, direct action, and mutual aid" and references "labor and rent strikes, rural and urban land and factory takeovers, fighting the cops to stop eviction attempts, and squatting" as examples of direct action. He has a book devoted to mutual aid: *Mutual Aid: Building Solidarity During This Crisis (and the Next)* (2020). Anderson similarly advocates mutual aid as a political and politicizing response to intentional state neglect and argues that "the demand for autonomy" must be foregrounded in antistate abolition (38). He also advocates creating "liberated zones" or "communes" that allow people to "reject . . . the everyday realities of capitalism in our day-to-day lives," for instance

by squatting, urban gardening, clothing exchanges, and mutual aid. It is crucial, he says, that abolitionist revolutionaries not only build such alternatives but also develop the means to defend them from violent repression, a role he suggests gangs could fulfill. Anderson, *The Nation on No Map,* 108–13 and 135–37.

15. Spade, "No Cops, Courts, or Cages Means No State," 127.

16. On the importance of public goods to democracy, see Honig, *Public Things.*

17. Gilmore and Gilmore, "Restating the Obvious."

18. Davis, *Abolition Democracy,* 31.

19. Roberts, "Angela Davis," 665.

20. Kaplan, *Dreaming in French.* Davis reflects on Marcuse's work and influence in Davis, "Marcuse's Legacies."

21. "After I joined the Communist Party in 1968, I also became a member of the Black Panther Party and worked with a branch of the organization in LA, where I was in charge of political education. However, at one point the leadership decided that members of the BPP could not be affiliated with other parties, at which point I chose to retain my affiliation with the CP. However, I continued to support and to work with the BPP." Davis, *Freedom Is a Constant Struggle,* 8. Joy James adds that Davis was also affiliated with the Student Nonviolent Coordinating Committee (SNCC) in the late 1960s.

22. The three men, John Clutchette, Fleeta Drumgo, and George Jackson, became known as the "Soledad Brothers." Kaplan reports that Davis helped create the Soledad Brothers Defense Committee.

23. On the many threats Davis faced, see Beard, "From Dynamite Hill to the Black Power Mixtape."

24. "The judicial and prison systems are more and more impervious to meaningful reform. Rather they must be transformed in the revolutionary sense" (xiii). And: "Repression is the response of an increasingly desperate imperialist ruling clique to contain an otherwise uncontrollable and growing popular disaffection leading ultimately, we think, to the revolutionary transformation of society" (xiii–xiv). Davis and Aptheker, "Preface."

25. Davis, "Political Prisoners," 47.

26. Davis, "A Letter to Ericka from Angela," 124.

27. Davis, "An Appeal," 145.

28. The GIP's pamphlet *The Assassination of George Jackson* includes contributions by French writer Jean Genet, who had spent time with the Panthers in the United States and was a vocal advocate of the group, as well as by Katharina von Bülow, an editor who had visited both Jackson and Davis in prison and helped publish Jackson's writings in French. Foucault himself would travel to the United States the following year and visit Attica prison, the site of a massive prison uprising that had been brutally repressed. See Kaplan, *Dreaming in French;* and Foucault, "On Attica."

29. On the term counterinsurgency in this context, see Berger, *Captive Nation.*

30. Davis, *Are Prisons Obsolete?,* 11.

31. For this statistic, see Davis, "Racialized Punishment and Prison Abolition," 98, citing Mauer and Huling, *Young Black Americans and the Criminal Justice System,* 1995.

32. Davis does not use the term *colorblindness* in "Race and Criminalization," but it fits her account. In fact, the essay predates by thirteen years Michelle Alexander's key argument in *The New Jim Crow* (2010): that the prison system is at the heart of contemporary U.S. racism, which is embedded in state institutions, a fact that is obscured by ideologies that see ostensibly race-neutral laws as evidence that racism exists only as individual prejudice. Alexander even agrees that racism divides the working class and perpetuates unjust class relations. I discuss *The New Jim Crow,* and its relation to abolition, at greater length in chapter 5.

33. Davis, "Race and Criminalization," 67.

34. Davis, 66.

35. See Brown, "Resisting Left Melancholy."

36. "The History of Critical Resistance," *Social Justice* (2000). The organizing committee for the conference included Bo (rita) d. brown, Ellen Barry, Jennifer Beach, Rose Braz, Julie Browne, Cynthia Chandler, Kamari Clarke, Leslie DiBenedetto Skopek, Gita Drury, Rayne Galbraith, Ruthie Gilmore, Naneen Karraker, Terry Kupers, Rachel Lederman, Joyce Miller, Dorsey Nunn, Dylan Rodríguez, Eli Rosenblatt, Jane Segal, Cassandra Shaylor, Andrea Smith, Nancy Stoller, Julia Sudbury, Robin Templeton, and Suran Thrift, as well as Davis. Davis, *Are Prisons Obsolete?,* 7. In *Golden Gulag,* first published in 2007, Gilmore also remarks on the "proliferation of antiprison groups during the decade when this book was in progress" (242). In 2000, organizing committee member and scholar Julia Sudbury remarks that "in 1999, [CR] became an organization that swings from being an umbrella/resource at the national level to being a grass-roots mobilizing group around issues like the prison slated to be built in Delano, California, and Prop. 21 (juvenile incarceration)." Brown et al., "Reflections on Critical Resistance," 81.

37. James, "Airbrushing Revolution for the Sake of Abolition."

38. Though Davis imagined a revolutionary seizing of power, she never argued that such a revolution would be a one-and-done event. In an interview during her incarceration, she reflects on her visit to Cuba, and notes that "although a revolution is hard to initiate and although it is even harder to sustain to the point of seizing power, the most difficult period of all is the building of the revolutionary society after the seizure of power." She observed "vestiges of cultural racism" against Black people in Cuba, for instance. Davis, "Prison Interviews with Angela Y. Davis," 191. French Marxist André Gorz, meanwhile, argued in the 1960s that a revolutionary insurrection was no longer a realistic possibility in Western Europe and advocated "nonreformist reforms" instead. Ruth Wilson Gilmore follows Gorz in describing revolutionary change as the culmination of many small shifts, asking: "What are the possibilities of nonreformist reform—of changes that, at the end of the day, unravel rather than widen the net of social control through criminalization?" Gilmore, *Golden Gulag,* 242. William C. Anderson, however, depicts incrementalism as inherently liberal and reformist: "People who insist on compromising with the forces that are

determined to exterminate us are only attempting to rearrange the terms of a perpetual crisis. This is the liberal language of reform. As we deteriorate, advocates of an incremental approach to deadly situations put lives at risk." Anderson, *The Nation on No Map,* 5–6.

39. Lester, "Whose Democracy in Which State?" 3083.

40. Perhaps the question is what is meant by the state as an "actor," a personification that implies agency and initiative. Craig and Ruth Wilson Gilmore's definition of the state as a constellation of capacities more readily shows that "the state" is something that can potentially be enlisted for abolitionist ends and that can sometimes be effectively resisted or even, temporarily, defeated. Gilmore and Gilmore, "Restating the Obvious."

41. Davis, *Freedom Is a Constant Struggle,* 4. The question is posed by Frank Barat.

42. *Abolition Democracy,* 10, 110–11.

43. Davis, *Are Prisons Obsolete?,* 104, emphasis added.

44. This point is made by Gilmore and Gilmore, "Restating the Obvious."

45. Davis, *Freedom Is a Constant Struggle,* 125.

46. Neither Foucault nor Ben-Moshe argues that there *is* such a categorical distinction, but in the absence of an account of what abolition is *for,* Ben-Moshe's definition of abolition as the creation of a "noncarceral and nonsegregationist" society encourages avoiding carcerality rather than struggling both with and against it.

47. Thus, Critical Resistance asks: Will we have to fight this ten years from now?

48. Davis, *Are Prisons Obsolete?,* 107, 111.

49. Sedgwick writes that "paranoid exigencies . . . are often necessary for nonparanoid knowing and utterance." Sedgwick, "Paranoid Reading and Reparative Reading," 129.

50. To my knowledge, Davis's first mention of PIC in a publication is in "From the Prison of Slavery to the Slavery of Prison." See also Davis, *Are Prisons Obsolete?,* 85. The term "PIC" is widely used by Critical Resistance.

51. Davis, *Are Prisons Obsolete?,* 85. It is a play on the term "military industrial complex," as used by Mike Davis in the 1990s.

52. This is why Amy Allen characterizes *Are Prisons Obsolete?* as broadly Foucauldian in its genealogical method. Allen, "Justice and Reconciliation."

53. Davis, "Race and Criminalization," 72.

54. Davis, 72, emphasis added.

55. Admittedly, it is still a thin one, as Quinn Lester rightly observes. Lester, "Whose Democracy in Which State?," 3082.

56. Davis, "Racialized Punishment and Prison Abolition," 96–97.

57. Davis, 96.

58. Davis, 97.

59. Davis, 97. In light of Davis's sustained critique of the Israeli occupation, and her insistence that prison abolition requires solidarity with Palestine, we might add the Palestinian territories to this list.

60. On these histories, see, for example, Hayashi, *Democratizing the Enemy;* and Panich, "'Mission Indians' and Settler-Colonialism."

61. See in particular Davis, "Racialized Punishment and Prison Abolition."

62. Davis, 99. According to *Merriam-Webster,* the first definition of *loophole* is "a means of escape, *especially:* an ambiguity or omission in the text through which the intent of a statute, contract, or obligation may be evaded."

63. Davis is featured in the film, but it is Michelle Alexander who is presented as the main spokesperson for this critique of the Thirteenth Amendment.

64. Dorothy Roberts, for instance, argues that the lawmakers who passed the Thirteenth Amendment did not understand it to authorize the enslavement of convicts, only to allow hard labor as part of criminal punishment. Roberts, "Abolition Constitutionalism." I return to this article in chapter 5.

65. Davis cites the Mississippi Black Codes, which declared vagrant "'anyone/who was guilty of theft, had run away [from a job, apparently], was drunk, was wanton in conduct or speech, had neglected job or family, handled money carelessly, and . . . all other idle and disorderly persons.'" Davis, "From the Prison of Slavery to the Slavery of Prison," 76. The significance of mobility for the formerly enslaved, mobility that the Black Codes sought to contain, is discussed by Saidiya Hartman. "By refusing to stay in their place, the emancipated insisted that freedom was a departure, literally and figuratively, from their former condition." Hartman, *Scenes of Subjection,* 128.

66. Du Bois, "The Spawn of Slavery," 86.

67. Davis, "Racialized Punishment and Prison Abolition," 97, 98.

68. See Davis, "Racialized Punishment and Prison Abolition" and her earlier *Women, Race & Class;* "JoAnne Little"; and "Reflections on the Black Woman's Role in the Community of Slaves." Recently, Davis has coauthored *Abolition. Feminism. Now.* with Gina Dent, Erica Meiners, and Beth Richie. For a discussion of Foucault's work centered on sexual violence, see Taylor, *Foucault, Feminism, and Sex Crimes.*

69. Davis, *Are Prisons Obsolete?,* chapter 4.

70. Davis, 25.

71. See Allen, "Slavery, Work, and Property"; and Olson, *The Abolition of White Democracy,* chapter 5.

72. On enslaved women's resistance practices as a general strike, see Weinbaum, "Gendering the General Strike."

73. Du Bois, *Black Reconstruction,* 84.

74. Du Bois, 580.

75. Du Bois, 24.

76. Davis, *Abolition Democracy,* 91–92.

77. Davis, 113.

78. Davis, 70.

79. Davis, 91, emphasis in original.

80. To illustrate this point, Davis juxtaposes the punitive war on drugs, targeted at drug users and sellers of color, with the lenient approach to drunk driving, mostly committed by white men. As Michelle Alexander also observes, affirming a claim by Glenn Loury, "it is nearly impossible to imagine anything remotely similar to mass incarceration happening to young white men." The 1988 Anti-Drug Abuse Act

imposed a five-year mandatory minimum for simple possession of cocaine base, for instance, while drunk drivers typically spend two days in jail and may be sent to drug counseling. Alexander, *The New Jim Crow,* 205–7. Ruth Wilson Gilmore, though, cautions against reifying the Black-white binary, and argues that we might see the formation of a "convict race" that comprises people of many racial and ethnic identities. Gilmore, *Golden Gulag,* 244.

81. Davis, *Abolition Democracy,* 68.

82. Davis, *Freedom Is a Constant Struggle,* 6.

83. Davis, *Abolition Democracy,* 124.

84. Davis, *Freedom Is a Constant Struggle,* 29. "For example when the Occupy movement emerged in 2011, that was a really exciting moment. Had we previously done the organizing that would have allowed us to take advantage of that moment, we could have really used that opportunity to build, organize formations—whether we're talking about party formations [or not]—and we would have a much stronger anticapitalist movement today."

85. This is similar to how Hannah Arendt describes the American revolutionaries in *On Revolution.*

86. See Kilgore, "The Myth of Slave Labor Camps in the US"; Gilmore, "The Worrying State of the Anti-Prison Movement"; and Gilmore, *Golden Gulag.*

87. Gilmore and Gilmore, "Restating the Obvious."

88. Du Bois, "The Spawn of Slavery," 91.

89. Du Bois, 90–91.

90. Olson, *The Abolition of White Democracy,* 142.

91. Davis, "Political Prisoners, Prisons, and Black Liberation," 48, 50.

92. Davis, *Are Prisons Obsolete?,* 107–8, emphasis added. Later, she remarks that "decriminalization would advance the abolitionist strategy of decarceration—that is, the consistent reduction in the numbers of people who are sent to prison—with the ultimate aim of dismantling the prison system as the *dominant mode* of punishment." Davis, 110, emphasis added.

93. "Imprisonment is increasingly used as a strategy of deflection of the underlying social problems—racism, poverty, unemployment, lack of education, and so on." Davis, *Freedom Is a Constant Struggle,* 6. See also Davis, *Abolition Democracy,* 92. This is a softening of claims she made in the 1970s, when she argued that "the majority of criminal offenses bear a direct relationship to property" and alleged the "virtual absence" of rape "in the socialist world," implying that the establishment of socialism will be enough to make most crime disappear. Davis, "Political Prisoners, Prisons, and Black Liberation," 45; and "Rape, Racism, and the Capitalist Setting," 129. In "Political Prisoners, Prisons, and Black Liberation," Davis asserts that crime is "spontaneously produced by a capitalist organization of society." She similarly describes a "society *fraught with irreconcilable antagonisms,* which engendered repressive penal institutions as one of its bulwarks" in "An Appeal" 144, emphasis added. In 1998, Davis added an author's note to her statement in "Rape, Racism, and

the Capitalist Setting," stating that "information regarding rape in the then socialist countries was not readily available at the time this essay was written. Today I would argue for a relationship between sexual violence and capitalist economies that is far more complex than this analysis acknowledges."

94. Already in "Race and Criminalization," Davis critiques the treatment of poor Black and Brown people as disposable, a disposability that is rooted in racism and facilitated by the prison as an abstract site that disappears people. "The persisting neo-Malthusian approach to population control, which, instead of seeking to solve those pressing social problems that result in real pain and suffering in people's lives, calls for the elimination of those suffering lives—finds strong resonances in the public discussion about expurgating the 'nation' of crime" (63).

95. Davis, *Are Prisons Obsolete?*, 107.

96. James, "Introduction," in *The New Abolitionists,* xxxvi note 1.

97. The "restraint of the dangerous few" is advocated by the *Instead of Prisons* handbook, which Ben-Moshe critiques. Ben-Moshe, *Decarcerating Disability,* 279.

98. Hartman, *Scenes of Subjection,* especially chapter 5.

99. Priscilla Yamin cited in Bruyneel, *Settler Memory.*

100. Cited in Bruyneel, 62–63. Merritt continues: "The number of adult descendants of the original Homestead Act recipients living in the year 2000 was estimated to be around 46 million people, about a quarter of the US adult population. If that many white Americans can trace their legacy of wealth and property ownership to a single entitlement programme, then the perpetuation of black poverty must also be linked to national policy" (63).

101. There has been growing attention in recent years to the relationship between prison abolition and decolonial political projects. See, for example, Nichols, "The Colonialism of Incarceration"; and Curley et al., "Decolonisation Is a Political Project."

102. Bruyneel, *Settler Memory,* 66.

103. For example, Davis, *Freedom Is a Constant Struggle.*

104. Bruyneel, *Settler Memory,* 66.

105. Bruyneel, 69.

106. Bruyneel, 75.

107. https://www.pbs.org/wgbh/americanexperience/features/death-numbers/.

108. Lester, "Whose Democracy in Which State?," 3083.

109. Du Bois, *Black Reconstruction,* 631, cited in Lester, "Whose Democracy in Which State?," 3084.

110. Lester, "Whose Democracy in Which State?," 3082.

111. Davis, "Political Prisoners, Prisons, and Black Liberation," 50.

112. Davis, "The Making of a Revolutionary" (1993), cited in James's introduction to *The Angela Y. Davis Reader.* James, "Introduction," 7. Both in the 1970s and in the 2010s, Davis rejects the demand that freedom struggles be nonviolent, and she critiques the violence/nonviolence binary for obscuring the politics around whether violence is or is not recognized, legitimated, or else labeled "terrorist." Davis, *Freedom Is a Constant Struggle.* For a critique of how the violence/nonviolence binary

constrains receptions and understandings of Black political thought, see also Beard, "From Dynamite Hill to the Black Power Mixtape."

113. Kaba, "Everything Worthwhile Is Done with Other People." Her invocation of a "third Reconstruction" may be a reference to Dr. William J Barber's 2016 book by that name. In the interview, Kaba reflects not only on the conditions under which abolition democracy might realistically come into being, but also on the democratic shortcomings and remainders of Reconstruction, specifically its relationship to settler-colonialism. "I'm thinking a lot about blackness in the 21st century," she says. "Because there are Native people, indigenous people the world over, having survived eliminationist policies, having survived genocide . . . Where are we in relationship to them? We need deep solidarity and co-strugglership with folks. But while we need that more than ever, we're in a conversation right now over land trust around reparations in the US and other parts of the world, when we are not on our land. There were people here."

114. Anderson, *The Nation on No Map,* 120–21, 136.

115. Spade, "No Cops, Courts, or Cages Means No State," 124.

116. Anderson, *The Nation on No Map,* 35, 38.

117. Anderson, 35–36.

118. Anderson, 11.

119. Spade, "No Cops, Courts, or Cages Means No State," 127, emphasis added.

120. Hartman, "Black in Anarchy," xiv.

121. Kaba, "Hope Is a Discipline." I return to this text in the conclusion.

122. Anderson, *The Nation on No Map,* 27.

4. What About the Rapists?

1. See the initiative Survived and Punished: https://survivedandpunished.org/.

2. Generation FIVE focuses on ending child sexual abuse; Chen et al.'s *The Revolution Starts at Home* focuses on partner abuse in activist communities.

3. Chen et al., *The Revolution Starts at Home,* 2.

4. The term "abolition feminism" has emerged in the past few years and serves as an umbrella term for feminist approaches and experiments that combine feminist and abolitionist concerns and that are typically grounded in anticapitalist, Women of Color feminism. These approaches might earlier have been called "community accountability," "restorative justice," or "transformative justice."

5. McLeod, "Envisioning Abolition Democracy," 1637.

6. See, for example, Gilmore and Gilmore, "Restating the Obvious."

7. According to longtime abolitionist and INCITE! cofounder Mimi Kim, the language of community accountability not only emphasized "the community" but also eschewed "justice," perceived to be both embedded in the criminal justice system and to promise too much. "Transformative Justice in the Era of #DefundThePolice," Barnard webinar with Shira Hassan and Mimi Kim, October 21, 2020. Author's notes. The two terms continue to overlap, however.

8. Kim, "From Carceral Feminism," 227.

9. brown, *We Will Not Cancel Us,* 5, 44. In the same book, brown endorses Gilmore's claim that abolition involves "building life-affirming institutions" (1). Gilmore's abolitionism, however, involves *both* state *and* nonstate institutions.

10. "Transformative Justice in the Era of #DefundThePolice," Barnard webinar with Shira Hassan and Mimi Kim, October 21, 2020. Author's notes. See also Shira Hassan in "What Is Transformative Justice?" Barnard video.

11. Davis, *Freedom Is a Constant Struggle,* 138. She continues: "Carceral feminisms do the work of the state as surely as they focus on state violence and repression as the solution to heteropatriarchy and as the solution, more specifically, to sexual assault."

12. Kaba, *We Do This 'til We Free Us, Part III.* Similarly, in her book on transformative justice, adrienne maree brown states: "I want us to abolish *the state,* including the ways we support them to dominate us." brown, 61, emphasis added. The conflation also happens in scholarly publications. In a coauthored journal article, Brady Heiner and Sarah Tyson note that the feminist antiviolence movement was coopted by the state in the period that neoliberal restructuring expanded the state's punitive arm and shrank its welfare arm, but they praise community efforts that work outside of the state altogether. "The continuum of alternatives to law enforcement and prisons that we . . . discuss," they write, "have been largely developed by people who have lived and continue to live close to state violence and, thus, do not see the police *or other mechanisms of the state* as potential solutions to the violence in their lives." Heiner and Tyson, "Feminism and the Carceral State," 14, emphasis added.

13. INCITE! and Critical Resistance, "Statement."

14. On settler-colonialism and the carceral state, see Nichols, "The Colonialism of Incarceration"; and Smith, *Conquest.*

15. Van Dam, "Less than 1% of Rapes Lead to Felony Convictions."

16. Jane Gordon argues that rather than oppose "good" political institutions to "bad" states, we should consider that states are forms of political institutions, and that both "can enjoy and lack fuller and more fractured legitimacy." Gordon, *Statelessness and Contemporary Enslavement.*

17. As was discussed in chapter 3, Critical Resistance was founded in 1997 and came to prominence with the 1998 conference "Critical Resistance: Beyond the Prison Industrial Complex" in Berkeley. INCITE! organized its first conference in 2000, and the two organizations wrote an influential joint statement in 2001.

18. For a historical account that inscribes INCITE! in decades of Black feminist antiviolence work, see Richie, *Arrested Justice,* especially chapter 5.

19. According to INCITE, the conference "The Color of Violence: Violence Against Women of Color" "was initially conceptualized as a small gathering for impassioned women of color activists" but turned into a massive event, whose two thousand participants included Mimi Kim, Loretta Ross, Andrea Smith, and Angela Davis. INCITE!, "History."

20. The Combahee River Collective statement uses the language of "oppression" rather than "violence," however, for instance in its famous claim that "the major systems of oppression are interlocking." See Taylor, *How We Get Free.*

21. According to the Sentencing Project, "the rate of growth for female imprisonment has been twice as high as that of men since 1980." Budd, "Fact Sheet."

22. INCITE!, "History."

23. Andrew Dilts interprets this statement as exemplary of an abolitionist practice of mutual "holding to account." Dilts, "Crisis, Critique, Abolition."

24. Tilly, "Warmaking and Statemaking as Organized Crime," 171.

25. Tilly, 172.

26. Craig and Ruth Gilmore, for instance, show that the neoliberal state derives its legitimacy from its claim to offer forceful "protection" from threats that must be made when they are not readily found. And Loïc Wacquant interprets the late-twentieth-century expansion of punishment and retraction of welfare as a "remasculinization" of the state. Gilmore and Gilmore, "Restating the Obvious"; Wacquant, *Punishing the Poor;* and "Crafting the Neoliberal State." See also Davis, "Political Prisoners, Prisons, and Black Liberation."

27. Gilmore, "In the Shadow of the Shadow State," 43.

28. Richie, *Arresting Justice,* 138. Gilmore uses the term "organized abandonment"; "strategic divestment" is Richie's.

29. See Gottschalk, *Caught,* especially the chapter "Catch and Keep."

30. Goodmark, "Reimagining VAWA."

31. See, for example, Kim, "From Carceral Feminism to Transformative Justice."

32. Tjaden and Thoennes, "Extent, Nature, and Consequences of Rape Victimization."

33. The same study found that only about 20 percent of victims report to the police. Other studies offer lower estimates.

34. See Goodmark, "Hands Up at Home."

35. Hoppe et al., "Mandatory Arrest for Domestic Violence and Repeat Offending," 256.

36. See Richie, *Arrested Justice.* One initiative by Survived and Punish is named "No Perfect Victims."

37. Hoppe et al., "Mandatory Arrest for Domestic Violence and Repeat Offending"; and Coalition to End Domestic Violence, "Justice Denied."

38. The National Domestic Violence Hotline, "Law Enforcement Experience Report."

39. The National Domestic Violence Hotline.

40. Christie, "Conflicts as Property," 3.

41. Christie, 7, emphasis in original.

42. Christie, 7.

43. Christie, 8. In democratic theory, the status of the people as both authors and subjects of the law presents a paradox, since good laws are needed to make good citizens but good citizens are needed to make good laws. Rousseau solved this chicken-or-egg problem by appealing to a foreign lawgiver, but agonists see it as a permanent feature of democratic politics. For Bonnie Honig, it is "a fundamental problem of democracy [that] power must rest with the people but the people are

never so fully who they need to be (unified, democratic) that they can be counted upon to exercise their power democratically." Honig, *Emergency Politics,* xvi. I return to what Honig calls the "paradox of politics" at the end of the chapter.

44. Christie, 4.

45. Young, "The Logic of Masculinist Protection."

46. See, for instance, James, ed., *Warfare in the American Homeland.*

47. Both books were published with the now-defunct South End Press. They were republished by Duke University Press in 2016 and 2017 respectively.

48. The movement includes the group Generation FIVE, based in Oakland, which published a call to action in 2007, "Toward Transformative Justice," followed in 2017 by "Ending Child Sexual Abuse," both available as free online PDFs. The #MeToo movement emerged that year, and in essays and other online publications, abolition feminists affirmed the importance of fighting sexual violence but cautioned against using the criminal legal system to do so, popularizing the term "carceral feminism" to describe punitive approaches. Abolitionist organizer and thinker Mariame Kaba launched the website www.transformharm.org in 2019 to serve as an online resource hub for abolition feminist approaches to harm, followed in 2021 by her book *We Do This 'til We Free Us,* a collection of essays and interviews. Print books keep coming, including *Abolition. Feminism. Now.* by Erica Meiners, Gina Dent, Angela Davis, and Beth Richie.

49. The example dates back to the early 2000s, but CARA's important place in early articulations of abolition feminism and the group's rich descriptions of its work make it an instructive case. CARA member Alisa Bierria helped write the joint INCITE! CR statement, and CARA's work was featured in both INCITE! anthologies as well as in the 2011 zine *The Revolution Starts at Home.*

50. Bierria, "Pursuing a Radical Antiviolence Agenda Inside/Outside a Non-Profit Structure," 153.

51. Bierria, 151–52.

52. All citations are taken from the version published in *Color of Violence.* The essay was also republished in *The Revolution Starts at Home.*

53. I have argued that the term *carceral feminism,* typically used as an epithet, can be overly broad and thereby oversimplify the politics of prison abolition. See my article "What Is Carceral Feminism?"

54. Chen et al., *The Revolution Starts at Home,* 2.

55. CARA, 266.

56. This list of principles is compiled from CARA's accountability principles in the essay "Taking Risks."

57. CARA 266.

58. CARA, 250.

59. CARA uses the language of "aggressor" and "survivor." I largely follow that usage here, but I also sometimes speak of "offenders" (a term Christie uses) and "victims." The latter term to me seems accurate and, like Duff, I do not find it inherently disempowering. On that latter point, see Duff, "Feminism Against Crime Control."

60. CARA, "Taking Risks," 253, 264.

61. "The change that the organizing group is making is not just the transformation of the particular aggressor, but also the transformation of our culture" (255). And: "A consciousness of rape culture prepares us for the need to organize beyond the accountability of an individual aggressor. We also realize we must organize for accountability and transformation of institutions that perpetuate rape culture such as the military, prisons, and the media" (253).

62. CARA, "Taking Risks," 251.

63. CARA, 254.

64. CARA, 254.

65. Credibility is mentioned when CARA discusses the potential positive roles the aggressor's community could play. Friends and family, they say, "have more credibility with the aggressor; it is harder for her to refuse accountability if she is receiving the demand for accountability from people she cares about" (255).

66. CARA, 259. While CARA demanded that Dan be allowed to stay at the organization but forbidden from working with young people, Dan ultimately simply resigns.

67. CARA, 261. The victims belong to a close-knit punk community, and after Lou responds to a confrontation with one of the victims by justifying his behavior, a small group forms to seek accountability. The group takes several actions: First, they circulate flyers that describe Lou's behavior, reveal his identity, and call for a boycott of his club, turning to anonymous emails after Lou threatens to sue for libel. Next, they publish a statement that includes the specific demands cited here. The public shaming and the boycott lead to negotiations over a face-to-face meeting with Lou, but the negotiations ultimately break down and the meeting doesn't happen. Frustrated and exhausted, the group "switched tactics and focused more on community-building, education, and prevention" of sexual violence (262).

68. CARA, 263. The demands are that the aggressor, Juan, "step down from leadership positions in Unido, that he pursue counseling and that his friends support him to go to appropriate counseling, and that Unido pursue intensive educational work on sexual violence." The organization agrees to the demands and CARA reports that Juan "was supported [by "friends and community"] to go to culturally specific counseling addressing power and control issues, particularly for aggressors of sexual violence" (264).

69. CARA, 253.

70. Young, "The Logic of Masculinist Protection," 21.

71. Kaba, "Whether Darren Wilson Is Indicted or Not, the Entire System Is Guilty" in *We Do This 'til We Free Us*, 56, emphasis added.

72. CARA, "Taking Risks," 262.

73. Smith, "Beyond Restorative Justice," 266ff. As feminist abolitionist organizations INCITE! and Sista II Sista acknowledge, activists must not only oppose corporate and state power but also "'make power' by creating those structures within

our organizations, movements, and communities that model the world we are trying to create" (268).

74. The first section of the Fourteenth Amendment reads: "All persons born or naturalized in the United States, and subject to the jurisdiction thereof, are citizens of the United States and of the State wherein they reside. No State shall make or enforce any law which shall abridge the privileges or immunities of citizens of the United States; nor shall any State deprive any person of life, liberty, or property, without due process of law; nor deny to any person within its jurisdiction the equal protection of the laws."

75. CARA, "Taking Risks," 265. "Critically engaging an account of sexual assault means actively considering it in multiple contexts. For example, we come to this work with an understanding that we live in a culture in which sexual violence is, sadly, a regular occurrence. We consider how institutional oppression informs people's choices within the situations in question. We look at people's patterns of behavior."

76. CARA, 266. When CARA later posits building "systems" as part of revolutionary movement-building, then, it seems to have local activist initiatives in mind. "Revolutionary movement-building will only happen if we can *build the systems* and practices that affirm our liberation-based values of connection, agency, respect, self-determination, and justice" (266).

77. CARA writes, for instance: "Our understanding of community accountability ultimately transcends the idea of simply holding an abusive community member responsible for his or her actions, but also includes the vision of the community itself being accountable for supporting a culture that allows for sexual violence. This latter accountability process truly necessitates active and constant re-creating and re-affirming a community that values liberation for everyone" (303n3).

78. CARA, 254.

79. It cites differences in "values, politics, cultures, and attitudes," (250). Another reason might be CARA's appreciation of the instrumental role of demand making in opening avenues for reconciliation between victims and aggressors, regardless of the specific content of the demands.

80. In chapter 3, I discuss how Angela Davis reconceives the temporality of revolution from a dramatic seizing of power (in the 1960s and early '70s) to a decentralized, incremental process (in the 1990s and onward). On abolition as a horizon, see also Chua, "Abolition Is a Constant Struggle."

81. Foucault, "Alternatives to the Prison."

82. Foucault, 92. Criminal records and sex offender registries, for instance, limit where people may live and work and impose other restrictions and requirements for years after incarceration, sometimes indefinitely, measures that all make people more vulnerable to rearrest.

83. Foucault, "Alternatives to the Prison," 23, translation modified.

84. CARA, "Taking Risks," 255.

85. Kaba, *We Do This 'til We Free Us,* 62. On what we "cannot not want" in the realm of justice, see Dilts, "Justice as Failure."

86. Heiner and Tyson, "Feminism and the Carceral State," 4.

87. Heiner and Tyson, 27.

88. Christie, "Conflicts as Property," 4. Bianchi concurs, he rejects what he calls the "medical model." Bianchi, "Abolition," 115.

89. The last two quotes are from adrienne maree brown's *We Will Not Cancel Us,* 28, 51.

90. Duff, "Restorative Punishment and Punitive Restoration." I thank Christopher Berk for bringing this argument to my attention.

91. Duff, 88.

92. Duff, 90.

93. Gordon, *Statelessness and Contemporary Enslavement,* 124–25.

94. Gordon, 15, emphasis added.

95. Davis, "Racialized Punishment and Prison Abolition," 102. The "major theorists of prison abolition" she mentions by name are all Western European: either Norwegian (sociologists Thomas Mathiesen and Nils Christie), Dutch (Louk Hulsman, Herman Bianchi, Willem de Haan, René van Swaaningen, and Rolf de Folter, all legal scholars or criminologists), or British (criminologist Stanley Cohen). She dedicates two sentences to critiquing Mathiesen, and another two to critiquing Willem de Haan. In *Are Prisons Obsolete?* (2003), Davis softens her initial stance and approvingly if very briefly cites Bianchi's scholarship on restorative justice. Bianchi and others "have suggested that crime needs to be defined in terms of tort and, instead of criminal law, should be reparative law [*sic*]," she says. "In his words, '[The lawbreaker] is thus no longer an evil-minded man or woman, but simply a debtor, a liable person whose human duty it is to take responsibility for his or her acts, and to assume the duty of repair.'" Bianchi also proposes institutions that would protect people accused of serious wrongdoing when they are at risk of violence or harm from angry community members. There is a long history of churches offering sanctuary, he points out, and community justice efforts would require the creation of secular institutions that would fulfill a similar function. I would add that all efforts to obtain community accountability and repair outside the criminal legal system would benefit from a kind of generalized sanctuary from criminal prosecution, such as the assurance that confessions to wrongdoing made in the context of such processes, for instance, would not be admissible as evidence in criminal court. Davis, *Are Prisons Obsolete?,* 113–14, citing Bianchi, "Abolition," 117.

96. Davis, "Race and Criminalization," 71; and "Racialized Punishment and Prison Abolition," 103.

97. For example, Hulsman, "Critical Criminology and the Concept of Crime"; and "The Abolitionist Case."

98. This point is also made by Bianchi: Citizens must be "re-skilled" in coping with problems in the community (124). And by Louk Hulsman, who replaces the concept of crime with that of "problematic situations": "events which are in a negative way deviating from the order in which we see and feel our lives rooted." Such situations cannot be eradicated, he says, which is why he prioritizes trying "to influence societal

structures in such a way that people can cope and deal with problems in a way which permits growth and learning and avoids alienation" (73). The criminal legal system is one of the most inflexible formalized systems of social control, he says. In informal settings, people have greater flexibility to "bestow . . . meaning on what is going on," which "increases the possibilities to reach by negotiation a common meaning of problematic situations. It provides also possibilities for learning" (77). Hulsman, "Critical Criminology and the Concept of Crime."

99. Christie, "Conflicts as Property," 10, emphasis in original.

100. Christie, 10.

101. Christie, 10.

102. If the court is modeled on civil law, then "preponderance of the evidence" could be an appropriate standard, rather than the determination of guilt "beyond reasonable doubt." What evidence is required could depend on what sanctions are considered, for example, in Christie's proposal, whether a judge is authorized to impose punishment.

103. Christie, "Conflicts as Property," 9.

104. Bianchi, "Abolition," 124. He envisions that "for the coming decades we have to live with the reality that two different systems will operate side by side." Outside of courts, he envisions that "neighborhood centres" and/or "boards of citizens" would handle minor and slightly more serious cases of injury. For serious cases (he alludes to rape and murder), he proposes sanctuaries for those involved: "the actor needs some protection in order to survive for the later negotiations" (123). If there's no individual victim (from traffic violations to environmental offences to the preparation of war), remedies should either be administrative (revoking a driver's license) or they should be determined by political bodies (e.g., parliament).

105. See Arendt in *On Revolution* on the powerlessness of constitutions that are imposed on conquered peoples.

106. Gilmore, "In the Shadow of the Shadow State," 45, attributing the term "shadow state" to Jennifer Wolch.

107. Gilmore, 44.

108. For example, Generation FIVE, Sista II Sista, Philly Stands Up, API Chaya, CAT 911. Also see transformharm.org.

5. The Power of New Rights

1. See Arendt, "The End of the Nation-State and the Decline of the Rights of Man," in *Origins of Totalitarianism*.

2. Bell, "Racial Realism," 363.

3. Bell, 369.

4. *Students for Fair Admissions, Inc. v. President and Fellows of Harvard College*. Official Reports of the Supreme Court 600 (2023): 181–411.

5. Bell, "Racial Realism," 373–74.

6. Bell, 378.

7. Bell, 378.

8. Bell, 377.

9. Connecting political theory to literary genres, Honig argues that the gothic romance is best suited to democracy because it teaches a healthy suspicion of heroic figures, who may turn out to be villains. "What [female gothics] provide us with is not a sense of paralyzing paranoia in the face of monstrous forces beyond our control, nor a clear distinction between the forces of good and evil, but a healthy caution to be wary of authorities and powers that seek to govern us, claiming to know what is in our best interests," she writes, recommending an ambivalent relationship to democratic sites of belonging. See Honig, *Democracy and the Foreigner,* chapter 5: "The Genres of Democracy," 118, 121.

10. Working the tensions is also what Dorothy Roberts calls for. She describes her position as animated by a *tension* "between recognizing the relentless antiblack violence of Constitutional doctrine, on one hand, and demanding the legal recognition of black people's freedom and equal citizenship" on the other. Prison abolitionists, Roberts argues, should see "the abolitionist history of the Reconstruction Amendments as a *usable past* to help move toward a radical future." Roberts, "Abolition Constitutionalism," 10, 11.

11. Prolepsis means "the representation or assumption of a future act or development as if presently existing or accomplished." It is used to describe emergent rights claims by Lisa Guenther, "Beyond Guilt and Innocence," 232.

12. Roberts, "Abolition Constitutionalism," 9.

13. Roberts, 72–73.

14. Roberts, 109.

15. Honig, *Emergency Politics,* 62, emphasis omitted.

16. These concerns are articulated, respectively, by Ben-Moshe, *Decarcerating Disability;* Dean Spade; and Michelle Alexander, *The New Jim Crow.*

17. See, for example, Ross and Solinger, *Reproductive Justice;* and Sins Invalid, "Skin, Tooth, and Bone." Ross attended the founding conference of INCITE! discussed in chapter 4.

18. Ben Golder's explanation for Foucault's increased use of rights claims in the late 1970s and early 1980s is that rights discourse became increasingly prominent in this period. I would add that Foucault also moves away from paranoid thinking in this time. There is a significant shift between *The History of Sexuality Volume 1* (1976), which diagnoses unsuspected and troubling power operations at work in sexuality and the regulation of our biological existence, and *The Use of Pleasure* and *The Care of the Self* (1984), which theorize ancient Greek and Roman techniques for cultivating self-mastery in the face of sexual and other desires. Golder, *Foucault and the Politics of Rights,* 156.

19. Cited in Golder, *Foucault and the Politics of Rights,* 12, emphasis added.

20. GIP, "GIP Manifesto."

21. Daniel Defert described the survey as speaking "less to the experience or misery of prisoners than to their rights. The right to defend themselves against the courts. The right to information, visits, and mail. The right to hygiene and nourishment.

The right to a decent salary for their work and the right to be able to work after they get out. The right to maintain a family. . . . The questionnaire is a way of declaring these rights and affirming our will to advance them." Defert, "When Information Is a Struggle," 71. The GIP helped secure the right to uncensored newspapers in prison. Guérin, *Prisonniers en révolte,* 96–98.

22. Foucault, "To Escape Their Prison," 235.

23. Golder, *Foucault and the Politics of Rights,* 6.

24. See Bennett, "'The State Was Patiently Waiting for Me to Die.'"

25. Foucault, "Va-t-on extrader Klaus Croissant?," cited in Golder, *Foucault and the Politics of Rights,* 85.

26. Foucault, "Va-t-on extrader Klaus Croissant?," 365. In an interesting echo of Nils Christie's critique of criminal legal processes, discussed in chapter 4, Foucault opposes this kind of legal representation to "having a lawyer who speaks about you . . . with the prosecutor as if you were absent or as if your role in the process is merely that of a passive object, asked little more than to confess or to be silent" (365).

27. Foucault, "Va-t-on extrader Klaus Croissant?," 364.

28. Olson, *The Abolition of White Democracy.*

29. Olson, 127.

30. Olson, 127. See also Andrew Dilts's analysis, indebted to Judith Shklar, of American citizenship as a kind of racial standing preserved through felon disenfranchisement. Dilts, "Innocent Citizens, Guilty Subjects."

31. Olson, *The Abolition of White Democracy,* 128.

32. Olson, 130.

33. Olson, 129.

34. Olson, 130.

35. Davis, *Abolition Democracy,* 99, emphasis added.

36. Davis, 80.

37. Davis, 80.

38. Alexander, *The New Jim Crow.* Critics have taken issue with the book's focus on the War on Drugs (Gottschalk), its attribution of mass incarceration to a conservative backlash (Forman Jr.), and its centering of Black men (Ben-Moshe). See also Walker, "The New Jim Crow?."

39. Since the publication of *The New Jim Crow,* Alexander has come to identify with abolitionism. In a 2016 interview, she states: "I consider myself a prison abolitionist, in the sense that I think we will eventually end the prisons as we know them," a prediction she follows with the normative claim that prisons as we know them *should* be eliminated. Alexander, "Life After 'The New Jim Crow.'"

40. Alexander, *The New Jim Crow,* 202.

41. Alexander, 259.

42. Alexander, 259.

43. Alexander's critique of the professionalization and legalism of civil rights organizations in the late twentieth and early twenty-first centuries resonates with feminist critiques of the professionalization of the antiviolence movement, discussed in chapter 4.

44. Alexander, *The New Jim Crow,* 244–45.

45. Witters, "In U.S., an Estimated 46 Million Cannot Afford Needed Care." Roberts et al., "Contributors to the Black-White Life Expectancy Gap in Washington D.C." According to the U.S. Department of Agriculture, 12.8 percent of U.S. households, approximately seventeen million people, experienced food insecurity in 2022. U.S. Department of Agriculture, Economic Research Service, "Food Security in the U.S." On felon disenfranchisement, see Uggen et al., "Locked Out 2022," and on other measures of democratic decline, see, for example, Williamson, "Understanding Democratic Decline in the United States."

46. Davis expects that harmful behaviors would diminish, and Marie Gottschalk suggests that "men—especially white men—who expect their economic situation to deteriorate are considerably more punitive" than those with better economic outlooks. Davis, *Abolition Democracy;* and Gottschalk, *Caught,* 28, referencing Michael T. Costelloe et al., "Public Attitudes Toward Criminals."

47. Davis and Olson insist on *direct* political participation, while the Universal Declaration of Human Rights is satisfied with electoral participation. Article 21 states that "everyone has the right to take part in the government of his country, directly or through freely chosen representatives."

48. For Mathiesen, prison abolitionists find themselves in a bind. If their proposals make sense according to the premises of dominant discourse, they are reformist rather than abolitionary, but if they depart from these premises, they are easily dismissed as nonsensical and irrelevant. The challenge, for him, is how to make abolitionism a "competing contradiction": something that challenges existing frameworks and seeks to displace them. As I discussed in the introduction, Mathiesen privileges uncertainty and negative reforms. Mathiesen, *The Politics of Abolition.*

49. Honig, *Emergency Politics,* 47.

50. Olson, "The Freshness of Fanaticism," 693. Like Honig, Olson argues that the perception that something is obviously wrong or right is produced through "political struggles that make such morality so obvious and so much a part of common sense as to appear timeless" (696). His examples are slavery and abortion; the same is arguably true for prisons.

51. On slavery abolitionism and feminism, see Davis, *Women, Race, Class;* and Williams, "The Female Anti-Slavery Movement." On abolitionism and vegetarianism, see Sinha, *The Slave's Cause,* 13. As Ilana Newman discusses in the undergraduate thesis "You Are What You Eat," the Grimké sisters practiced the Graham diet, which was vegetarian and largely plant-based.

52. Olson, *The Abolition of White Democracy,* 141.

53. Lartey, "'Concrete Coffins.'" According to the *Texas Tribune,* "of Texas' more than 100 state prisons and jails, nearly 75 percent are uncooled in inmate housing areas." The offices of prison personnel, in contrast, are typically air-conditioned. McCullough, "Judge Approves Settlement."

54. *Keith Cole et al. v. Brad Livingston et al.,* Civil Action No. 4:14-CV-1698 (2016), referencing 37 Tex. Admin. Code §259.160.

55. McCullough, "As the Death Toll." The average of fourteen deaths was found in Skarha et al., "Provision of Air Conditioning." Other reports on the perils of hot prisons include *Reckless Indifference* by the Human Rights Clinic of the University of Texas School of Law, and, under the auspices of the Marshall Project, Chammah, "'Cooking Them to Death.'"

56. This description is featured in Human Rights Clinic, *Reckless Indifference, 10.*

57. Cited in McGuaghy, "Louisiana Death Row Inmates Testify."

58. Burnett, "Texas Prisoners Sue over 'Cruel' Conditions."

59. *Keith Cole et al v. Brad Livingston et al.*, Civil Action No.4 :14-CV-1698 (2016). Cole's fellow plaintiffs are: Jackie Brannum, Richard Elvin King, Lavar Santee, Fred Wallace, and Marvin Ray Yates.

60. Keith Cole, cited in Burnett, "Texas Prisoners Sue over 'Cruel' Conditions."

61. David Fathi, cited in Zimmerman, "Extreme Heat Tests Prisons."

62. This is the "objective" component of cruel and unusual punishment. The "subjective" component is that prison officials display "deliberate indifference" to such conditions. *Farmer v. Brennan,* 511 US 825 (1994), p. 825.

63. Foucault, "Lecture of 17 March 1976," in *Society Must Be Defended.*

64. See also Spade, *Normal Life.*

65. Gilmore, *Golden Gulag,* 247.

66. Gilmore, 244–45.

67. The GIP devoted its fourth and final booklet in the *Intolerable* series to prison suicides. These, it argued, were not simply suicides that took place *in* prison but suicides *of* the prison [*suicides de prison*], produced by the institution and a symptom of its violence. The booklet reproduces a series of letters written from prison by a man, H.M., who was sent to solitary for committing "homosexual acts" and ultimately hanged himself there. The prison makes the life of this queer man unlivable. Deleuze, writing for the GIP, emphasizes H.M.'s frantic search for escape, which ended in death. See *Intolerable 4. Prison Suicides* in *Intolerable,* edited by Thompson and Zurn.

68. Patterson, "The Dose–Response"; and Fenster, "New Data."

69. *Rhodes v. Chapman,* 452 US 337 (1981).

70. Christopher Ivey cited in Blinder, "In US Jails, a Constitutional Clash Over Air-Conditioning," emphasis added.

71. McCullough, "Judge Approves Settlement." The Tribune article does describe Cole's reasons for refusing to sign, but it says he vocally dissented during the hearing and mentions his dismay that it did not contain a clause protecting the plaintiffs from retaliation, a clause that "our attorneys positively, absolutely stated that they were going to add." Cole is serving a life sentence, but another incarcerated person reported that his parole had been revoked because of the lawsuit.

72. McCullough, "Despite Budget Surplus."

73. Guenther, *Solitary Confinement,* 132, citing Ann Keramet Reiter, "The Most Restrictive Alternative: A Litigation History of Solitary Confinement in US Prisons, 1960–2006," in *Studies in Law, Politics, and Society,* ed. Austin Sarat, vol. 57 (Emerald Group, 2012), 100.

74. This is how a U.S. District Court in 2016 interpreted the duties imposed on prison officials by the Eighth Amendment. *Keith Cole et al. v. Brad Livingston et al.*, Civil Action No. 4:14-CV-1698 (2016), p. 12.

75. Dayan, *The Story of Cruel and Unusual*, 5.

76. *Rhodes v. Chapman* (1981).

77. Mbembe, "Necropolitics"; Bargu, *Starve and Immolate.*

78. In chapter 3, I discussed the anarchist abolitionisms of William C. Anderson and Dean Spade.

79. The term "basic comfort" is proposed by former GIP activist Antoine Lazarus in Foucault, "Luttes Autour des Prisons," cited in Guenther, "Beyond Guilt and Innocence," 234. See also Foucault, "Il y a un an à peu près," cited in Guenther, "Beyond Guilt and Innocence," 233–34.

80. The list of demands is available online at: https://prisonerhungerstrikesolidarity.wordpress.com/education/the-prisoners-demands-2/.

81. Guenther, "Beyond Guilt and Innocence," 234.

82. Guenther, *Solitary Confinement*, 126.

83. Posthumanism is a privileged term in *Solitary Confinement;* "creaturely politics" dominates in Guenther's more recent piece "Beyond Guilt and Innocence."

84. See especially chapter 6, "Beyond Dehumanization: A Posthumanist Critique of Intensive Confinement," in *Solitary Confinement*, 125–60.

85. Angela Davis, for instance, described veganism in a public address as part of a revolutionary perspective that confronts and refuses the infliction of suffering that is typically normalized and obscured. To my knowledge, her published works on prison abolition do not mention veganism. Davis, "On Revolution," 27th Empowering Women of Color Conference (2012), cited in Dickstein et al., "Veganism as Left Praxis."

86. Alexander, *The New Jim Crow*, 149.

87. Weeks, *The Problem with Work*, 12.

88. Gilmore, *Golden Gulag*, 243.

89. The right to hug is discussed in Stillman, "Do Children Have a 'Right to Hug' Their Parents?"

90. A report by the Prison Policy Initiative, "Screening Out Family Time," explains that video visitation technology goes back to the 1990s but reached a "critical mass" in 2014. By 2015, "more than 500 facilities in 43 states and the District of Columbia [were] experimenting with video visitation" (4). https://static.prisonpolicy.org/visitation/ScreeningOutFamilyTime_January2015.pdf.

91. The Prison Policy Initiative report from 2015 notes: "While virtually no state prisons ban in-person visitation, we found that 74% of jails banned in-person visits when they implemented video visitation" (11).

92. Stillman, "Do Children Have a 'Right to Hug' Their Parents?"

93. The Prison Policy Initiative found that at the Knox County Detention Facility in Tennessee, "Eliminating In-Person Visits Did Not Result in a Substantial Drop in Contraband." See https://www.prisonpolicy.org/graphs/Contraband.html/. The PPI

report, "Screening Out Family Time," also references a study by "Grassroots Leadership and the Texas Criminal Justice Coalition," which found that "disciplinary cases for possession of contraband in Travis County, Texas increased 54% after the county completed its transition to video-only visitation" (16). A local activist group, "Face to Face Knox," found that the elimination of in-person visits was followed by increased assault rates at the jail. Stillman, "Do Children Have a 'Right to Hug' Their Parents?"

94. I thank Kirstine Taylor for discussing this point with me.

95. San Francisco Children of Incarcerated Parents Partnership, *A Bill of Rights*, Right 5, emphasis added.

96. San Francisco Children of Incarcerated Parents Partnership, *A Bill of Rights*, Right 5.

97. Threadcraft, *Intimate Justice.*

98. Environmental Protection Agency, *Reduce Urban Heat Island Effect.* https://www.epa.gov/green-infrastructure/reduce-urban-heat-island-effect/.

99. Milman, "'Silent Killer'"; Davis, "The Radical Politics of Shade."

100. Davis, "The Radical Politics of Shade," 38.

101. We must stop greenhouse gas emissions, but even the most drastic cuts will not prevent the rise of global temperatures on the short term. As Davis writes, "The inevitability of global warning [*sic*] makes this mitigation of summer heat even more urgent" (38).

102. Davis coined the term "PIC" in "Hell Factories in the Field." The right to shade has been taken up by researchers studying street vendors in India and Pakistan. The studies show the vital importance of shade trees for street vendors, who are in turn an important resource for poor people who rely on them for food. Basu and Nagendra, "The Street as Workspace."

103. Davis, "The Radical Politics of Shade," 38.

104. Bloch, "Shade."

105. See Lisa Beard's wonderful reading of June Jordan through the lens of abolitionism and Black feminist thought: "June Jordan's Political Theory of Redesign."

106. Bloch, "Shade."

107. National Conference of State Legislatures, "Right to Work Resources."

108. Cited in Lyiscott, "The Tyranny of White Comfort."

Conclusion

1. Solnit, "Why Climate Despair Is a Luxury."

2. Kaba, "Hope Is a Discipline." All quotes from Kaba in this conclusion are taken from this interview.

Bibliography

Afary, Janet, and Kevin B. Anderson. *Foucault and the Iranian Revolution: Gender and the Seductions of Islamism.* University of Chicago Press, 2005.

Ahmed, Sara. "Feminist Killjoys (and Other Willful Subjects)." *Cahiers du Genre* 53 (2012): 77–98. https://doi.org/10.3917/cdge.053.0077.

Ahmed, Sara. *The Promise of Happiness.* Duke University Press, 2010.

Alexander, Michelle. "Life After 'The New Jim Crow.'" Interview with Brentin Mock. *Bloomberg News,* September 30, 2016. https://www.bloomberg.com/news/articles/2016-09-30/mass-incarceration-can-t-be-fixed-by-legislation-alone.

Alexander, Michelle. *The New Jim Crow: Mass Incarceration in the Age of Colorblindness.* The New Press, 2010.

Allen, Amy. "Justice and Reconciliation: The Death of the Prison?" Human Studies 30, no. 4 (2007): 311–21. https://doi.org/10.1007/s10746-007-9062-9.

Allen, Amy. "Slavery, Work, and Property: DuBois' Black Marxism." *Columbia Center for Contemporary Critical Thought,* November 29, 2020. https://blogs.law.columbia.edu/abolition1313/amy allen slavery work and property duboiss black marxism.

American Psychiatric Association. "The Psychiatric Bed Crisis in the United States: Understanding the Problem and Moving Toward Solutions." *The American Journal of Psychiatry* 179, no. 8 (2022). https://ajp.psychiatryonline.org/doi/10.1176/appi.ajp.22179004.

Anderson, William C. *The Nation on No Map: Black Anarchism and Abolition.* AK Press, 2021.

Arendt, Hannah. *The Human Condition.* 2nd ed. University of Chicago Press, 2018.

Arendt, Hannah. *On Revolution.* Penguin, 1990.

Arendt, Hannah. *The Origins of Totalitarianism.* A Harvest Book, 1976.

Aretxaga, Begoña. *Shattering Silence: Women, Nationalism, and Political Subjectivity in Northern Ireland.* Princeton University Press, 1997.

The Attica Liberation Faction. "The Attica Liberation Faction Manifesto of Demands and Anti-Depression Platform." *Race & Class* 53, no. 2 (2011): 28–35. https://doi.org/10.1177/0306396811414338.

Artières, Phillipe, and Groupe d'Information sur les Prisons. *Intolérable*. Gallimard, 2013.

Bargu, Banu. *Starve and Immolate: The Politics of Human Weapons*. Columbia University Press, 2014.

Basu, Sukanya, and Harini Nagendra. "The Street as Workspace: Assessing Street Vendors' Rights to Trees in Hyderabad, India." *Landscape and Urban Planning* 199 (2020). https://doi.org/10.1016/j.landurbplan.2020.103818.

Beard, Lisa. "From Dynamite Hill to the Black Power Mixtape: Angela Davis on the Violence/Nonviolence Binary and the Mediation of Black Political Thought." *Political Theory* 51 no. 1 (2023): 645–73. https://doi.org/10.1177/00905917231155291.

Beard, Lisa. "June Jordan's Political Theory of Redesign." *American Political Science Review* (2024): 1–13. https://doi.org/10.1017/S0003055424000698.

Beckett, Katherine. *Making Crime Pay: Law and Order in Contemporary American Politics*. Oxford University Press, 1999.

Bell, Derrick. "Racial Realism." *Connecticut Law Review* 24, no. 2 (1992): 363–79.

Ben-Moshe, Liat. *Decarcerating Disability: Deinstitutionalization and Prison Abolition*. University of Minnesota Press, 2020.

Ben-Moshe, Liat. "The Institution Yet to Come: Analyzing Incarceration Through a Disability Lens." In *The Disability Studies Reader*, edited by Lennard J. Davis. Routledge, 2016.

Ben-Moshe, Liat. "The State of (Intersectional Critique of) State Violence." *Women's Studies Quarterly* 46, no. 3&4 (2018): 306–11.

Ben-Moshe, Liat, and AJ Withers, eds. "Introduction." In *Radical Disability Politics*. Routledge, 2019.

Ben-Moshe, Liat, Allison C. Carey, and Chris Chapman, eds. *Disability Incarcerated: Imprisonment and Disability in the United States and Canada*. Palgrave Macmillan, 2014.

Ben-Moshe, Liat, Rebecca C. Cory, Mia Feldbaum et al., eds. *Building Pedagogical Curb Cuts: Incorporating Disability in the University Classroom and Curriculum*. Syracuse University Press, 2005.

Bennett, Nolan. "'The State Was Patiently Waiting for Me to Die': Life Without the Possibility of Parole as Punishment." *Political Theory* 49, no. 2 (2020): 165–89. https://doi.org/10.1177/0090591720927800.

Berger, Dan. *Captive Nation: Black Prison Organizing in the Civil Rights Era*. University of North California Press, 2016.

Berlant, Lauren. *Cruel Optimism*. Duke University Press, 2011.

Bernstein, Elizabeth. "Carceral Politics as Gender Justice? The 'Traffic in Women' and Neoliberal Circuits of Crime, Sex, and Rights." *Theory and Society* 41 (2012): 233–59.

Bey, Marquis. *Black Trans Feminism*. Duke University Press, 2022.

Bianchi, Herman. "Abolition: Assensus and Sanctuary." In *Abolitionism: Towards a Non-repressive Approach to Crime*, edited by Herman Bianchi and René van Swaaningen. Free University Press, 1985.

Bickford, Susan, and Elizabeth Markovits. "Clear Eyes, Full Hearts: Toward an Affective Realism." Paper presented at the American Political Science Association Conference, 2022.

Bierria, Alisa. "Pursuing a Radical Antiviolence Agenda Inside/Outside a Non-Profit Structure." In *The Revolution Will Not Be Funded: Beyond the Non-Profit Industrial Complex.* South End Press, 2007.

The Black Panther Party for Self Defense. "The Black Panther Party's Ten Point Program 1972." *Black Panther Party Alumni Legacy Network.* Accessed January 14, 2025. https://bppaln.org/10-point-platform.

Blinder, Alan. "In US Jails, a Constitutional Clash Over Air-Conditioning." *New York Times,* August 15, 2016. http://www.nytimes.com/2016/08/16/us/in-us-jails-a-constitutional-clash-over-air-conditioning.html?_r=0.

Bloch, Sam. "Shade." *Places Journal.* April 2019. https://placesjournal.org/article/shade-an-urban-design-mandate.

Bohrman, Rebecca, and Naomi Murakawa. "Remaking Big Government: Immigration and Crime Control in the United States." In *Global Lockdown: Race, Gender, and the Prison-Industrial Complex,* edited by Julia Sudbury. Routledge, 2014.

Bourg, Julian. *From Revolution to Ethics: May '68 and Contemporary French Thought.* McGill-Queen's University Press, 2007.

Braz, Rose. "Environmental Challenge Bars Construction of California Prison." *Prison Legal News,* November 15, 2001. https://www.prisonlegalnews.org/news/2001/nov/15/environmental-challenge-bars-construction-of-california-prison/.https://www.justiceashealing.org/nonewwomensprison.

Braz, Rose, et al. "The History of Critical Resistance." *Social Justice* 27, no. 3 (2000): 6–10. http://www.jstor.org/stable/29767223.

Brennan Center for Justice. "America's Faulty Perception of Crime Rates." Last modified November 29, 2022. https://www.brennancenter.org/our-work/analysis-opinion/americas-faulty-perception-crime-rates.

Brich, Cecile. "The Groupe d'Information sur les Prisons: The Voice of Prisoners? Or Foucault's?" *Foucault Studies* 5 (2008): 26–47.

brown, adrienne maree. *We Will Not Cancel Us: And Other Dreams of Transformative Justice.* AK Press, 2020.

Brown, Rita (Bo), et al. "Reflections on Critical Resistance." *Social Justice* 27, no. 3 (2000): 180–94. http://www.jstor.org/stable/29767241.

Brown, Wendy. "Moralism as Antipolitics." In *Materializing Democracy: Toward a Revitalized Cultural Politics,* edited by Russ Castronovo and Dana D. Nelson. Duke University Press, 2002.

Brown, Wendy. "Resisting Left Melancholy." *Boundary* 2, 26, no. 3 (1999): 19–27. http://www.jstor.org/stable/303736.

Bruyneel, Kevin. *Settler Memory: The Disavowal of Indigeneity and the Politics of Race in the United States.* University of North Carolina Press, 2021.

Budd, Kristen M. "Fact Sheet: Incarcerated Women and Girls." *The Sentencing Project.* July 24, 2024. https://www.sentencingproject.org/fact-sheet/incarcerated-women-and-girls.

Bureau of Justice Statistics. "Correctional Populations in the United States, 2013." U.S. Department of Justice, Office of Justice Programs, 2013. https://bjs.ojp.gov/library/publications/correctional-populations-united-states-2013.

Bureau of Justice Statistics. "Correctional Populations in the United States, 2019." U.S. Department of Justice, Office of Justice Programs, 2019. https://bjs.ojp.gov/sites/g/files/xyckuh236/files/media/document/cpus19st.pdf.

Bureau of Justice Statistics. "Female Murder Victims and Victim-Offender Relationship, 2021." U.S. Department of Justice, Office of Justice Programs, 2021. https://bjs.ojp.gov/female-murder-victims-and-victim-offender-relationship-2021.

Bureau of Justice Statistics. "Recidivism of Prisoners Released in 24 States in 2008: A 10-Year Follow-Up Period (2008–2018)." Department of Justice, Office of Justice Programs, 2021. https://bjs.ojp.gov/BJS_PUB/rpr24s0810yfup0818/Web%20content/508%20compliant%20PDFs.

Bureau of Justice Statistics. "Suicide in Local Jails and State and Federal Prisons, 2000–2019." U.S. Department of Justice, Office of Justice Programs, 2021. https://bjs.ojp.gov/sites/g/files/xyckuh236/files/media/document/sljsfp0019st.pdf.

Burnett, John. "Texas Prisoners Sue over 'Cruel' Conditions." *NPR*, September 12, 2016. https://www.npr.org/2016/09/12/493608371/with-no-air-conditioning-texas-prisoners-live-in-cruel-conditions-suit-alleges.

Camp, Jordan. *Incarcerating the Crisis: Freedom Struggles and the Rise of the Neoliberal State.* University of California Press, 2016.

CARA. "Taking Risks: Implementing Grassroots Community Accountability Strategies." In *Color of Violence: The INCITE! Anthology.* South End Press, 2006.

Carrier, Nicolas, and Justin Piché. "The State of Abolitionism." *Champ pénal/Penal Field,* 12 (2015). https://doi.org/10.4000/champpenal.9164/.

Cavadino, Mick, et al. *The Penal System: An Introduction,* 5th ed. SAGE, 2013.

Chambliss, William J. "The Politics of Crime Statistics." In *The Blackwell Companion to Criminology,* edited by Colin Sumner. Blackwell, 2004.

Chammah, Maurice. "'Cooking Them to Death': The Lethal Toll of Hot Prisons." *The Marshall Project,* November 11, 2017. https://www.themarshallproject.org/2017/10/11/cooking-them-to-death-the-lethal-toll-of-hot-prisons.

Chen, Ching-In, and Jai Dulani, Leah Lakshmi Piepzna-Samarasinha, eds. *The Revolution Starts at Home: Confronting Intimate Violence Within Activist Communities.* South End Press, 2011.

Cho, Eunice Hyunhye. "Unchecked Growth: Private Prison Corporations and Immigration Detention, Three Years Into the Biden Administration." *ACLU,* August 7, 2023. https://www.aclu.org/news/immigrants-rights/unchecked-growth-private-prison-corporations-and-immigration-detention-three-years-into-the-biden-administration.

Christie, Nils. "Conflicts as Property." *The British Journal of Criminology* 17, no. 1 (1977): 1–15. https://doi.org/10.1093/oxfordjournals.bjc.a046783.

Chua, Charmaine. "Abolition Is a Constant Struggle: Five Lessons From Minneapolis." *Theory & Event* 23, no. 4 Supplement (2020): S-127–47. https://doi.org/10.1353/tae.2020.0072.

Coalition to End Domestic Violence. "Justice Denied: Arrest Policies for Domestic Violence." Accessed January 13, 2025. https://endtodv.org/wp-content/uploads/2021/04/Arrest-Policies.pdf.

Collins, Patricia Hill. *Black Feminist Thought: Knowledge, Consciousness, and the Politics of Empowerment.* Taylor and Francis, 1990.

Columbia Prison Divest. Facebook page. Accessed January 7, 2025. https://www.facebook.com/columbiaprisondivest.

Costelloe, Michael T., Ted Chiricos, and Marc Gertz. "Public Attitudes Toward Criminals: Exploring the Relevance of Crime Salience and Economic Insecurity." *Punishment and Society* 11, no. 1 (2009): 25–49. https://doi.org/10.1177/1462474508098131.

Crenshaw, Kimberlé. "From Private Violence to Mass Incarceration: Thinking Intersectionally About Women, Race, and Social Control." *Journal of Scholarly Perspectives* 9, no. 1 (2013): 21–50.

Critical Resistance. "What Is the PIC? What Is Abolition?" Accessed January 10, 2025. https://criticalresistance.org/mission-vision/not-so-common-language/.

Cruikshank, Barbara. *The Will to Empower: Democratic Citizens and Other Subjects.* Cornell University Press, 1999.

Curley, Andrew, Pallavi Gupta, Lara Lookabaugh, et al. "Decolonisation Is a Political Project: Overcoming Impasses Between Indigenous Sovereignty and Abolition." *Antipode* 54, no. 2 (2022): 1043–62. https://doi.org/10.1111/anti.12830.

Davis, Angela Y. "A Letter to Ericka from Angela." In *If They Come in the Morning . . . Voices of Resistance.* Verso, 2016.

Davis, Angela Y. "An Appeal." In *If They Come in the Morning . . . Voices of Resistance.* Verso, 2016.

Davis, Angela Y. *Abolition Democracy: Beyond Empire, Prisons, and Torture.* Seven Stories Press, 2005.

Davis, Angela Y. *Angela Davis: An Autobiography.* Random House, 1974.

Davis, Angela Y. *Are Prisons Obsolete?*. Seven Stories Press, 2003.

Davis, Angela Y. *Freedom Is a Constant Struggle.* Penguin Books, 2022.

Davis, Angela Y. "From the Prison of Slavery to the Slavery of Prison." In *The Angela Y. Davis Reader,* edited by Joy James. Blackwell, 1998.

Davis, Angela Y. "JoAnne Little: The Dialectics of Rape." In *The Angela Y. Davis Reader,* edited by Joy James. Blackwell, 1998.

Davis, Angela Y. "Marcuse's Legacies." In *Herbert Marcuse: A Critical Reader,* edited by John Abromeit and W. Mark Cobb. Routledge, 2003.

Davis, Angela Y. "Political Prisoners, Prisons, and Black Liberation." In *If They Come in the Morning . . . Voices of Resistance.* Verso, 2016.

Davis, Angela Y. "Prison Interviews with Angela Y. Davis." In *If They Come in the Morning . . . Voices of Resistance.* Verso, 2016.

Davis, Angela Y. "Race and Criminalization: Black Americans and the Punishment Industry." In *The Angela Y. Davis Reader,* edited by Joy James. Blackwell, 1998.

Davis, Angela Y. "Racialized Punishment and Prison Abolition." In *The Angela Y. Davis Reader,* edited by Joy James. Blackwell, 1998.

Davis, Angela Y. "Rape, Racism, and the Capitalist Setting." In *The Angela Y. Davis Reader,* edited by Joy James. Blackwell, 1998.

Davis, Angela Y. "Reflections on the Black Woman's Role in the Community of Slaves." *The Black Scholar* 3, no. 4 (1971): 2–15. http://www.jstor.org/stable/41203704.

Davis, Angela Y. *Women, Race & Class.* Vintage, 1983.

Davis, Angela Y., and Bettina Aptheker. "Preface." In *If They Come in the Morning . . . Voices of Resistance.* Verso, 2016.

Davis, Angela Y., Gina Dent, Erica R. Meiners, et al. *Abolition. Feminism. Now.* Haymarket Books, 2022.

Davis, Mike. "Hell Factories in the Field: A Prison-Industrial Complex." *Nation,* February 20, 1995.

Davis, Mike. "The Radical Politics of Shade." *Capitalism, Nature, Socialism* 8, no. 3 (1997): 35–39. https://doi.org/10.1080/10455759709358747.

Dayan, Colin. "Civil Death." In *The Law Is a White Dog: How Legal Rituals Make and Unmake Persons.* Princeton University Press, 2011.

Dayan, Colin. *The Story of Cruel and Unusual.* MIT Press, 2024.

Defert, Daniel. "When Information Is a Struggle." In *Intolerable: Writings from Michel Foucault and the Prisons Information Group (1970–1980),* edited by Kevin Thompson and Perry Zurn. Translated by Erik Beranek and Perry Zurn. University of Minnesota Press, 2021.

Dickstein, Jonathan, Jan Dutkiewicz, Jinshnu Guha-Majumdar, et al. "Veganism as Left Praxis." *Capitalism, Nature, Socialism* 33, no. 2 (2020): 1–20. https://doi.org/10.1080/10455752.2020.1837895.

Dilts, Andrew. "Crisis, Critique, Abolition." In *A Time for Critique,* edited by Bernard E. Harcourt and Didier Fassin. Columbia University Press, 2019.

Dilts, Andrew. "How Does It Feel to Be(come) a Problem? Active Intolerance and the Abolitionist Killjoy." *Theory & Event* 24, no. 2 (2021): 637–43. https://dx.doi.org/10.1353/tae.2021.0035.

Dilts, Andrew. "Innocent Citizens, Guilty Subjects." In *Punishment and Inclusion: Race, Membership, and the Limits of American Liberalism.* Fordham University Press, 2014.

Dilts, Andrew. "Justice as Failure." *Law, Culture and the Humanities* 13, no. 2 (2017): 184–92. https://doi.org/10.1177/1743872115623518.

Dilts, Andrew, and Perry Zurn, eds. *Active Intolerance: Michel Foucault, the Prisons Information Group, and the Future of Abolition.* Palgrave Macmillan, 2016.

Donovan, Liz and Muriel Alarcón. "Long Hours, Low Pay: Loneliness and a Booming Industry." *New York Times,* September 25, 2021. https://www.nytimes.com/2021/09/25/business/home-health-aides-industry.html.

Du Bois, W. E. B. *Black Reconstruction in America.* Free Press, 1998.

Du Bois, W. E. B. "The Spawn of Slavery: The Convict Lease System in the South." *The Missionary Review of the World* (1901): 737–45.

Duff, Koshka. "Feminism Against Crime Control: On Sexual Subordination and State Apologism." *Historical Materialism* 26, no. 2 (2018): 123–48. https://doi.org/10.1163/1569206x-00001649.

Duff, RA. "Restorative Punishment and Punitive Restoration." In *Restorative Justice and the Law,* edited by Lode Walgrave. Willan Publishing, 2002.

Enns, Peter K. *Incarceration Nation: How the United States Became the Most Punitive Democracy in the World.* Cambridge University Press, 2016.

Environmental Protection Agency. "Reduce Urban Heat Island." *EPA.* Last updated on October 17, 2024. https://www.epa.gov/green-infrastructure/reduce-urban-heat-island-effect.

Erickson, Blake. "Deinstitutionalization Through Optimism: The Community Mental Health Act of 1963." *American Journal of Psychiatry Residents' Journal* 16, no. 4 (2021). https://doi.org/10.1176/appi.ajp-rj.2021.160404.

Fabris, Erick. *Tranquil Prisons: Chemical Incarceration Under Community Treatment Orders.* University of Toronto Press, 2011.

Feldman, Allen. *Formations of Violence.* Chicago University Press, 1991.

Fenster, Andrea. "New Data: Solitary Confinement Increases Risk of Premature Death After Release." *Prison Policy Initiative,* October 13, 2020. https://www.prisonpolicy.org/blog/2020/10/13/solitary_mortality_risk.

Filipas, Henrietta H., and Sarah E. Ullman. "Child Sexual Abuse, Coping Responses, Self-Blame, Posttraumatic Stress Disorder, and Adult Sexual Revictimization." *Journal of Interpersonal Violence* 16, no. 10 (2001): 1015–41.

Fleischer-Black, Matt. "Free Universities." In *American Countercultures,* edited by Gina Misiroglu. Routledge, 2015.

Foner, Eric. *Reconstruction: America's Unfinished Revolution, 1863–1877.* Harper and Row, 1988.

Foucault, Michel. *Abnormal: Lectures at the College de France 1974–1975.* Translated by Graham Burchell. St Martin's Press, 2003.

Foucault, Michel. "Alternatives to the Prison: Dissemination or Decline of Social Control?" *Theory, Culture & Society* 26, no. 6 (2009): 12–24. https://doi.org/10.1177/0263276409353775.

Foucault, Michel. "Contre les peines de substitution." Libération, September 18, 1981.

Foucault, Michel. "Débat avec les Maos." In *Dits et écrits: Tome 1, 1954–1975.* Editions Gallimard, 2001.

Foucault, Michel. "Declaration to the Press and the Public Authorities Coming from the Prisoners at Melun." In *Intolerable: Writings from Michel Foucault and the Prisons Information Group (1970–1980),* edited by Kevin Thompson and Perry Zurn. Translated by Erik Beranek and Perry Zurn. University of Minnesota Press, 2021.

Foucault, Michel. *Discipline and Punish: The Birth of the Prison.* Translated by Alan Sheridan. Vintage-Random House, 1995.

Foucault, Michel. "To Escape Their Prison." In *Intolerable: Writings from Michel Foucault and the Prisons Information Group (1970–1980),* edited by Kevin Thompson and Perry Zurn. Translated by Erik Beranek and Perry Zurn. University of Minnesota Press, 2021.

Foucault, Michel. "Interview de Michel Foucault." In *Dits et écrits: Tome 2, 1976–1988.* Editions Gallimard, 2001. Foucault, Michel. *The History of Sexuality Volume 1: An Introduction.* Translated by Robert Hurley. Vintage, 1990.

Foucault, Michel. *The History of Sexuality Volume 2: The Use of Pleasure.* Translated by Robert Hurley. Vintage, 1990.

Foucault, Michel. *The History of Sexuality Volume 3: The Care of the Self.* Translated by Robert Hurley. Vintage, 1988.

Foucault, Michel. "I Perceive the Intolerable." In *Intolerable: Writings from Michel Foucault and the Prisons Information Group (1970–1980),* edited by Kevin Thompson and Perry Zurn. Translated by Erik Beranek and Perry Zurn. University of Minnesota Press, 2021.

Foucault, Michel. "Is It Really Important to Think?" Interview by Dider Eribon. Translated by Thomas Keenan. *Philosophy & Social Criticism* 9, no. 1 (1982): 30–40. https://doi.org/10.1177/019145378200900102.

Foucault, Michel. *Madness and Civilization.* Translated by Richard Howard. Vintage, 1988.

Foucault, Michel. "On Attica." In *Intolerable: Writings from Michel Foucault and the Prisons Information Group (1970–1980),* edited by Kevin Thompson and Perry Zurn. Translated by Erik Beranek and Perry Zurn. University of Minnesota Press, 2021.

Foucault, Michel. "On Popular Justice." In *Power/Knowledge: Selected Interviews and Other Writings 1972-1977,* edited by Colin Gordon. Pantheon, 1980.

Foucault, Michel. "Par-delà le bien et le mal." In *Dits et écrits: Tome 1, 1954–1975.* Editions Gallimard, 2001.

Foucault, Michel. "The Penal System Is a Problem That Has Interested Me for Some Time." In *Intolerable: Writings from Michel Foucault and the Prisons Information Group (1970–1980),* edited by Kevin Thompson and Perry Zurn. Translated by Erik Beranek and Perry Zurn. University of Minnesota Press, 2021.

Foucault, Michel. "The Political Function of the Intellectual." Translated by Colin Gordon. *Radical Philosophy* 17, no. 13 (1977): 126–33.

Foucault, Michel. "Questions of Method." In *The Foucault Effect: Studies in Governmentality,* edited by Graham Burchell and Colin Gordon. University of Chicago Press, 1991.

Foucault, Michel. *Society Must Be Defended: Lectures at the College de France,* edited by Mauro Bertani and Alessandro Fontana. Translated by David Macey. Picador, 1997.

Foucault, Michel. "Truth and Power." In *Power/Knowledge: Selected Interviews and Other Writings 1972-1977,* edited by Colin Gordon. Pantheon, 1980.

Foucault, Michel. "Va-t-on extrader Klaus Croissant?" In *Dits et écrits: Tome 2, 1976–1988.* Editions Gallimard, 2001.

Foucault, Michel. "What Is Called Punishing?" In *Essential Works of Foucault 1954–1984: Power.* New Press, 2000.

Foucault, Michel. "What Is Enlightenment?" In Ethics: Subjectivity and Truth, edited by Paul Rabinow. Translated by Robert Hurley and others. The New Press, 1997.

Foucault, Michel, and John K. Simon. "Michel Foucault on Attica: An Interview." *Telos* (1974): 154–61. https://doi.org/10.3817/0374019154.

Foucault, Michel, and Pierre Vidal-Naquet. "Inquiry on Prisons: Let Us Break Down the Bars of Silence." In *Intolerable: Writings from Michel Foucault and the Prisons Information Group (1970–1980)*, edited by Kevin Thompson and Perry Zurn. Translated by Erik Beranek and Perry Zurn. University of Minnesota Press, 2021.

Foucault, Michel, and the Prisons Information Group. *Intolerable: Writings from Michel Foucault and the Prisons Information Group (1970–1980)*, edited by Kevin Thompson and Perry Zurn. Translated by Erik Beranek and Perry Zurn. University of Minnesota Press, 2021.

Galston, William. "Realism in Political Theory." *European Journal of Political Theory* 9, no. 4 (2010): 385–411. https://doi.org/10.1177/1474885110374001.

Garland, David. *Punishment and Modern Society: A Study in Social Theory.* Oxford University Press, 1991.

Geller, Jeffrey. "The Rise and Demise of America's Psychiatric Hospitals: A Tale of Dollars Trumping Sense." *Psychiatric News* 54, no. 6 (2019). https://doi.org/10.1176/appi.pn.2019.3b29.

generation FIVE. "Ending Child Sexual Abuse: A Transformative Justice Handbook." *Transform Harm.* June 17, 2017. https://transformharm.org/tj_resource/ending-child-sexual-abuse-eng.

generation FIVE. "Toward Transformative Justice: A Liberatory Approach to Child Sexual Abuse and Other Forms of Intimate and Community Violence." *Transform Harm,* December 4, 2007. https://transformharm.org/tj_resource/toward-transformative-justice-a-liberatory-approach-to-child-sexual-abuse-and-other-forms-of-intimate-and-community-violence.

The George Washington University Institute of Law, Psychiatry and Criminology. "Institutionalization of the Mentally Retarded." National Association for Retarded Children, 1967. https://mn.gov/mnddc/parallels2/pdf/60s/67/67-IMR-NAC.pdf.

Ghandnoosh, Nazgol, and Celeste Barry. "One in Five: Racial Disparity in Imprisonment — Causes and Remedies." December 7, 2023. https://www.sentencingproject.org/reports/one-in-five-racial-disparity-in-imprisonment-causes-and-remedies.

Gilmore, Ruth Wilson. *Change Everything: Racial Capitalism and the Case for Abolition.* Haymarket, 2024.

Gilmore, Ruth Wilson. "Fatal Couplings of Power and Difference: Notes on Racism and Geography." In *Abolition Geography: Essays Towards Liberation.* Verso, 2022.

Gilmore, Ruth Wilson. *Golden Gulag: Prisons, Surplus, Crisis, and Opposition in Globalizing California.* University of California Press, 2007.

Gilmore, Ruth Wilson. "In the Shadow of the Shadow State." In *The Revolution Will Not Be Funded: Beyond the Non-Profit Industrial Complex,* edited by INCITE!. South End Press, 2007.

Gilmore, Ruth Wilson. "The Worrying State of the Anti-Prison Movement." *Social Justice Journal* 23 (2015). https://socialjusticejournal.org/the-worrying-state-of-the-anti-prison-movement.

Gilmore, Ruth Wilson, and Craig Gilmore. "Restating the Obvious." In *Indefensible Space: the Architecture of the National Insecurity State,* edited by Michael Sorkin. Routledge, 2008.

GIP. "Back Cover of Intolerable 1." In *Intolerable: Writings from Michel Foucault and the Prisons Information Group (1970–1980),* edited by Kevin Thompson and Perry Zurn. Translated by Erik Beranek and Perry Zurn. University of Minnesota Press, 2021.

GIP. "Declaration to the Press and the Public Authorities Coming from the Prisoners at Melun." In *Intolerable: Writings from Michel Foucault and the Prisons Information Group (1970–1980),* edited by Kevin Thompson and Perry Zurn. Translated by Erik Beranek and Perry Zurn. University of Minnesota Press, 2021.

GIP. "Fresnes." In *Intolerable: Writings from Michel Foucault and the Prisons Information Group (1970–1980),* edited by Kevin Thompson and Perry Zurn. Translated by Erik Beranek and Perry Zurn. University of Minnesota Press, 2021.

GIP. "GIP Manifesto." In *Intolerable: Writings from Michel Foucault and the Prisons Information Group (1970–1980),* edited by Kevin Thompson and Perry Zurn. Translated by Erik Beranek and Perry Zurn. University of Minnesota Press, 2021.

GIP. "Investigation in 20 Prisons." In *Intolerable: Writings from Michel Foucault and the Prisons Information Group (1970–1980),* edited by Kevin Thompson and Perry Zurn. Translated by Erik Beranek and Perry Zurn. University of Minnesota Press, 2021.

GIP. "On Prisons." In *Intolerable: Writings from Michel Foucault and the Prisons Information Group (1970–1980),* edited by Kevin Thompson and Perry Zurn. Translated by Erik Beranek and Perry Zurn. University of Minnesota Press, 2021.

GIP. "Preface to Intolerable 1." In *Intolerable: Writings from Michel Foucault and the Prisons Information Group (1970–1980),* edited by Kevin Thompson and Perry Zurn. Translated by Erik Beranek and Perry Zurn. University of Minnesota Press, 2021.

GIP. "Toul Prison List of Demands." In *Intolerable: Writings from Michel Foucault and the Prisons Information Group (1970–1980),* edited by Kevin Thompson and Perry Zurn. Translated by Erik Beranek and Perry Zurn. University of Minnesota Press, 2021.

Golder, Ben. *Foucault and the Politics of Rights.* Stanford University Press, 2015.

Goodmark, Leigh. "Hands Up at Home: Militarized Masculinity and Police Officers Who Commit Intimate Partner Abuse." *BYU Law Review* 2015, no. 5 (2015): 1183–246.

Goodmark, Leigh. "Reimagining VAWA: Why Criminalization Is a Failed Policy and What a Non-Carceral VAWA Could Look Like." *Violence Against Women* 27, no. 1 (2020): 84–101. https://doi.org/10.1177/1077801220949686.

Gordon, Jane. *Statelessness and Contemporary Enslavement.* Routledge, 2020.

Gorz, André. *Strategy for Labor: A Radical Proposal.* Beacon Press, 1964.

Gottschalk, Marie. *Caught: The Prison State and the Lockdown of American Politics.* Princeton University Press, 2016.

Goubert, Anaïs, Julie Yixia, and Eileen Appelbaum. "Home Health Care: Latinx and Black Women Are Overrepresented, but All Women Face Heightened Risk of Poverty." *Center for Economic and Policy Research.* October 27, 2021. https://cepr.net/home-health-care-latinx-and-black-women-are-overrepresented-but-all-women-face-heightened-risk-of-poverty.

Guenther, Lisa. "Beyond Guilt and Innocence: The Creaturely Politics of Prisoner Resistance Movements." In *Active Intolerance,* edited by Perry Zurn and Andrew Dilts. Palgrave Macmillan, 2016.

Guenther, Lisa. *Solitary Confinement: Social Death and Its Afterlives.* University of Minnesota Press, 2013.

Guérin, Anne. *Prisonniers en révolte: quotidien carceral, mutineries et politique pénitentiaire en France (1970–1980).* Agone, 2013.

Gusmano, Michael. "New York City's Involuntary Commitment Plan: Fulfilling a Moral Obligation?" The Hastings Center, December 13, 2022. https://www.thehastingscenter.org/new-york-citys-involuntary-commitment-plan-fulfilling-a-moral-obligation.

Harcourt, Bernard. "Reducing Mass Incarceration: Lessons from the Deinstitutionalization of Mental Hospitals in the 1960s." *Ohio State Journal of Criminal Law* 9 (2011): 53–88.

Harney, Stefano, and Fred Moten. *The Undercommons: Fugitive Planning and Black Study.* Minor Compositions, 2013.

Harris, Adam. "How Reconstruction Created American Public Education." *The Atlantic,* November 13, 2023. https://www.theatlantic.com/magazine/archive/2023/12/reconstruction-education-black-students-public-schools/675816.

Hartman, Saidiya. "Black in Anarchy." Foreword to *The Nation on No Map: Black Anarchism and Abolition,* by William C. Anderson. AK Press, 2021.

Hartman, Saidiya. *Scenes of Subjection: Terror, Slavery, and Self-Making in Nineteenth-Century America.* Oxford University Press, 1997.

Hassan, Shira, and Mimi Kim. "Transformative Justice in the Era of #DefundPolice: Lessons from the Past, Strategizing for the Future." *Barnard Center for Research on Women,* October 21, 2020. Video. https://bcrw.barnard.edu/videos/transformative-justice-in-the-era-of-defundpolice-lessons-from-the-past-strategizing-for-the-future/.

Hayashi, Brian Masaru. *Democratizing the Enemy: The Japanese American Internment.* Princeton University Press, 2008.

Heiner, Brady T., and Sarah K. Tyson. "Feminism and the Carceral State: Gender-Responsive Justice, Community Accountability and the Epistemology of Antiviolence." *Feminist Philosophy Quarterly* 3, no. 1 (2017): 1–37. https://doi.org/10.5206/fpq/2016.3.3.

Hoffman, Marcelo. "Investigations from Marx to Foucault." In *Active Intolerance: Michel Foucault, the Prisons Information Group, and the Future of Abolition,* edited by Perry Zurn and Andrew Dilts. Palgrave Macmillan, 2016.

Honig, Bonnie. *Democracy and the Foreigner.* Princeton University Press, 2009.

Honig, Bonnie. *Emergency Politics: Paradox, Law, Democracy.* Princeton University Press, 2011.

Honig, Bonnie. *Political Theory and the Displacement of Politics.* Cornell University Press, 1993.

Honig, Bonnie. *Public Things: Democracy in Disrepair.* Fordham University Press, 2017.

Honig, Bonnie, and Marc Stears. "The New Realism: From Modus Vivendi to Justice." In *Political Philosophy Versus History? Contextualization and Real Politics in Contemporary Political Thought,* edited by Jonathan Floyd and Marc Stears. Cambridge University Press, 2011.

Hoppe, Susan J., Yan Zhang, Brittany E. Hayes, et al. "Mandatory Arrest for Domestic Violence and Repeat Offending: A Meta–analysis." *Aggression and Violent Behavior* 53 (2020). https://doi.org/10.1016/j.avb.2020.101430.

Huey, Edmund Burke. *Backward and Feeble-Minded Children.* Warwick and York, 1912.

Huffer, Lynne. *Mad for Foucault: Rethinking the Foundations of Queer Theory.* Columbia University Press, 2009.

Hulsman, Louk. "The Abolitionist Case: Alternative Crime Policies." *Israel Law Review* 25, no. 3–4 (1991): 681–709. https://doi.org/10.1017/S0021223700010694.

Hulsman, Louk. "Critical Criminology and the Concept of Crime." *Contemporary Crises* 10 (1986): 63–80. https://doi.org/10.1007/BF00728496.

Human Rights Clinic, University of Texas School of Law. *Reckless Indifference: Deadly Heat in Texas Prisons.* March 2015. https://law.utexas.edu/wp-content/uploads/sites/11/2015/04/2015-HRC-USA-Reckless-Indifference-Report.pdf.

Human Rights Watch. "Punishment and Prejudice: Racial Disparities in the War on Drugs." May 2000. https://www.hrw.org/legacy/reports/2000/usa/.

INCITE! Women of Color Against Violence. *Color of Violence: The INCITE! Anthology.* South End Press, 2006.

INCITE! Women of Color Against Violence. "History." Accessed January 13, 2025. https://incite-national.org/history.

INCITE! Women of Color Against Violence. *The Revolution Will Not Be Funded: Beyond the Non-Profit Industrial Complex.* South End Press, 2007.

INCITE! Women of Color Against Violence, and Critical Resistance. "CR and INCITE! Statement on Gender Violence and the Prison Industrial Complex." In *Color of Violence: The INCITE! Anthology.* South End Press, 2006.

James, Joy. "Airbrushing Revolution for the Sake of Abolition." Black Perspectives, July 20, 2020. https://www.aaihs.org/airbrushing-revolution-for-the-sake-of-abolition/2020.

James, Joy. "Erasing the Spectacle of Racialized State Violence." In *Resisting State Violence: Radicalism, Gender, and Race in US Culture.* University of Minnesota Press, 1996.

James, Joy. "Introduction." In *The Angela Y. Davis Reader,* edited by Joy James. Blackwell, 1998.

James, Joy. "Introduction." In *The New Abolitionists: (Neo)Slave Narratives and Contemporary Prison Writings,* edited by Joy James. SUNY Press, 2005.

James, Joy, ed. *The Angela Y. Davis Reader*. Blackwell, 1998.

James, Joy, ed. *Warfare in the American Homeland: Policing and Prison in a Penal Democracy.* Duke University Press, 2007.

Johnson, Gaye Theresa, and Alex Lubin, "Angela Davis: An Interview on the Futures of Black Radicalism." *Verso* (blog post). June 23, 2020. https://www.versobooks.com/blogs/news/3421-angela-davis-an-interview-on-the-futures-of-black-radicalism.

Joint Commission on Mental Illness and Health. *Action for Mental Health: Final Report of the Joint Commission on Mental Illness and Health*. Basic Books/Hachette Book Group, 1961. https://doi.org/10.1037/11140-000.

Kaba, Mariame. "Everything Worthwhile Is Done with Other People." *Adi Magazine*. Fall 2019. https://adimagazine.com/articles/mariame-kaba-everything-worthwhile-is-done-with-other-people/.

Kaba, Mariame. "Hope Is a Discipline." Discussion with Brian Sonenstein and Kim Wilson. *Beyond Prisons*. Episode 19, January 2018. https://www.beyond-prisons.com/home/hope-is-a-discipline-feat-mariame-kaba.

Kaba, Mariame. *We Do This 'til We Free Us: Abolitionist Organizing and Transformative Justice*. Haymarket, 2021.

Kafer, Alison. *Feminist Queer Crip*. Indiana University Press, 2013.

Kaplan, Alice. *Dreaming in French: The Paris Years of Jacqueline Kennedy, Susan Sontag, and Angela Davis*. University of Chicago Press, 2013.

Kelley, Robin. *Freedom Dreams: The Black Radical Imagination*. Beacon Press, 2002.

Kilgore, James. "The Myth of Slave Labor Camps in the US." *Counterpunch*, August 9, 2013. https://www.counterpunch.org/2013/08/09/the-myth-of-prison-slave-labor-camps-in-the-u-s.

Kim, Mimi. "From Carceral Feminism to Transformative Justice: Women-of-Color Feminism and Alternatives to Incarceration." *Journal of Ethnic & Cultural Diversity in Social Work* 27, no. 1 (2018): 1–15. https://doi.org/10.1080/15313204.2018.1474827.

Kirkner, Anne, et al. "A Qualitative Study of Sexual Assault Disclosure Impact and Help-Seeking on Support Providers." *Violence and Victims* 33, no. 4 (2018): 721–38. https://doi.org/10.1891/0886-6708.VV-D-17-00059.

Knight, Amber. "Unfinished Business: Deinstitutionalization and Medicaid Policy." *Politics Groups and Identities* 9, no. 6 (2021): 395–408. https://doi.org/10.1080/21565503.2020.1854324.

Knopp, Honey Fay, and Mark Morris, eds. *Instead of Prisons: A Handbook for Abolitionists*. Prison Research Education Action Project, 1977.

Lancaster, Roger. "How to End Mass Incarceration." *Jacobin*, August 18, 2017. https://jacobin.com/2017/08/mass-incarceration-prison-abolition-policing.

Lancaster, Roger. "Response: A Word on Words," *Jacobin*, October 2, 2017. https://jacobin.com/2017/10/mass-incarceration-prison-abolition.

Lartey, Jamiles. "'Concrete Coffins': Surviving Extreme Heat Behind Bars." *The Marshall Project*, July 22, 2023. https://www.themarshallproject.org/2023/07/22/texas-heat-prison-louisiana.

Law, Victoria. *Resistance Behind Bars: The Struggles of Incarcerated Women*. PM Press, 2009.

Lee, Rosalyn, Xiangming Fan, and Feijun Luo. "The Impact of Parental Incarceration on the Physical and Mental Health of Young Adults." *Pediatrics* 131, no. 4 (2013): 1188-1195.

Lerman, Amy E., and Vesla Weaver. *Arresting Citizenship: The Democratic Consequences of American Crime Control*. University of Chicago Press, 2014.

Lester, Quinn. "Whose Democracy in Which State?: Abolition Democracy from Angela Davis to W. E. B. Du Bois." *Social Science Quarterly* 102, no. 7 (2021): 3081–86. https://doi.org/10.1111/ssqu.13019.

Locke, John. *Second Treatise of Government*. In *Two Treatises of Government*, edited by Peter Laslett. Cambridge University Press, 1988.

Lyiscott, Jamila. "The Tyranny of White Comfort: Centering Black Students in the Face of Hateful Legislation." *Medium*, February 8, 2022. https://medium.com/@jamila.lyiscott/the-tyranny-of-white-comfort-centering-black-students-in-the-face-of-hateful-legislation-94b2a6fe74e6.

Macey, David. *The Lives of Michel Foucault*. Vintage Press, 1995.

Machiavelli, Niccolò. *The Prince*. Translated by Harvey Mansfield. University of Chicago Press, 1998.

MacKinnon, Catharine. *Toward a Feminist Theory of the State*. Harvard University Press, 1991.

Macktoom, Soha, Nausheen H. Anwar, and Jamie Cross. "Hot Climates in Urban South Asia: Negotiating the Right to and the Politics of Shade at the Everyday Scale in Karachi." *Urban Studies Online*, September 12, 2023. https://www.urbanstudiesonline.com/hot-climates-in-urban-south-asia-negotiating-the-right-to-and-the-politics-of-shade-at-the-everyday-scale-in-karachi.

Mauer, Marc, and Tracy Huling, *Young Black Americans and the Criminal Justice System: Five Years Later*. The Sentencing Project, 1995.

Mathiesen, Thomas. *The Politics of Abolition*. John Wiley and Sons, 1974.

Mathiesen, Thomas. "The Politics of Abolition." Contemporary Crises 10 (1986): 81-94.

Mbembe, Achille. "Necropolitics." *Public Culture* 15, no. 1 (2003): 11–40. https://muse.jhu.edu/article/39984.

McCullough, Jolie. "As the Death Toll in Stifling Texas Prisons Climbs, Congressional Democrats Ask for Investigation." *Texas Tribune*, August 21, 2023. https://www.texastribune.org/2023/08/21/texas-prison-heat-deaths/.

McCullough, Jolie. "Despite Budget Surplus, Texas Legislature Makes Little Money Available for Prison Air Conditioning." *Texas Tribune*, May 26, 2023. https://www.texastribune.org/2023/05/26/texas-prisons-air-conditioning/.

McCullough, Jolie. "Judge Approves Settlement Mandating Air Conditioning at Hot Texas Prison." *Texas Tribune*, May 8, 2018. https://www.texastribune.org/2018/05/08/settlement-air-condition-hot-texas-prison-gets-final-judicial-approval/.

McGuaghy, Lauren. "Louisiana Death Row Inmates Testify to 'Indescribable' Heat at Angola Prison." *NOLA*, August 6, 2013. http://www.nola.com/crime/baton-rouge/index.ssf/2013/08/louisiana_death_row_inmates_te.html.

McLeod, Allegra M. "Envisioning Abolition Democracy." *Harvard Law Review* 132, no. 6 (2019): 1613–49.

McWhorter, Ladelle. "Foucault's Political Spirituality." *Philosophy Today* 47, no. 5 (2003): 39–44. https://doi.org/10.5840/philtoday200347supplement6.

McWhorter, Ladelle. *Racism and Sexual Oppression in Anglo-America: A Genealogy*. Indiana University Press, 2009.

Merriam-Webster. "The History of 'Moron,' 'Idiot,' and 'Imbecile': Why Are These Words Offensive?" *Merriam-Webster.* Accessed January 12, 2025. https://www.merriam-webster.com/wordplay/moron-idiot-imbecile-offensive-history.

Merriam-Webster. "Pessimism." Accessed January 14, 2025. https://www.merriam-webster.com/dictionary/pessimism.

Miller, D. A. *The Novel and the Police.* University of California Press, 1989.

Milman, Oliver. "'Silent Killer': Experts Warn of Record US Deaths from Extreme Heat." *The Guardian,* August 1, 2023. https://www.theguardian.com/us-news/2023/aug/01/heat-related-deaths-us-temperatures-heatwave.

Mingus, Mia. "Access Intimacy, Interdependence and Disability Justice." *Leaving Evidence,* April 12, 2017. https://leavingevidence.wordpress.com/2017/04/12/access-intimacy-interdependence-and-disability-justice.

Mogul, Joey L., Andrea J. Ritchie, and Kay Whitlock. *Queer (In)Justice: The Criminalization of LGBT People in the United States.* Beacon Press, 2011.

Muhammad, Khalil Gibran. *The Condemnation of Blackness: Race, Crime, and the Making of Modern Urban America.* Harvard University Press, 2019.

Murakawa, Naomi. *The First Civil Right: How Liberals Built Prison America.* Oxford University Press, 2014.

Myers, Ella. "Resisting Foucauldian Ethics: Associative Politics and the Limits of the Care of the Self." *Contemporary Political Theory* 7, no. 2 (2008): 125–46. https://doi.org/10.1057/palgrave.cpt.2007.25.

National Conference of State Legislatures. "Right to Work Resources." *NCSL,* Last updated December 19, 2023. https://www.ncsl.org/labor-and-employment/right-to-work-resources.

National Disability Institute. *Financial Inequality: Disability, Race, and Poverty in America.* February 8, 2017. https://www.nationaldisabilityinstitute.org/wp-content/uploads/2019/02/disability-race-poverty-in-america.pdf.

The National Domestic Violence Hotline. "Law Enforcement Experience Report." Accessed January 13, 2025. https://www.thehotline.org/wp-content/uploads/media/2022/09/2209-Hotline-LES_FINAL.pdf.

New England Historical Society. "*Titicut Follies:* A Documentary Film of a Madhouse So Shocking It Was Banned." Accessed January 10, 2025. https://newenglandhistoricalsociety.com/titicut-follies-documentary-film-madhouse-shocking-banned.

Newman, Ilana. "You Are What You Eat: The Grimké-Weld Family and the Graham Diet." Thesis, Wesleyan University, 2018.

Nichols, Robert. "The Colonialism of Incarceration." *Radical Philosophy Review* 17, no. 2 (2014): 435–55. https://doi.org/10.5840/radphilrev201491622.

Olson, Joel. *The Abolition of White Democracy.* University of Minnesota Press, 2004.

Olson, Joel. "The Freshness of Fanaticism: The Abolitionist Defense of Zealotry." *Perspectives on Politics* 5, no. 4 (2007): 685–701. https://doi.org/10.1017/S1537592707072179.

Page, Jennifer, and Desmond King. "Truth and Reconciliation for the US Policing and Punishment Regime: A Transitional Justice Perspective." *Du Bois Review* 19, no. 2 (2022): 209–31. https://doi.org/10.1017/S1742058X21000357.

Panich, Lee M. "'Mission Indians' and Settler-Colonialism: Rethinking Indigenous Persistence in Nineteenth-Century Central California." In *Indigenous Persistence in the Colonized Americas: Material and Documentary Perspectives on Entanglement,* edited by Russell N. Sheptak and Heather Law Pezzarossi. University of New Mexico Press, 2019.

Patterson, Evelyn J. "The Dose–Response of Time Served in Prison on Mortality: New York State, 1989–2003." *American Journal of Public Health* 103 (2013): 523–28. https://doi.org/10.2105/AJPH.2012.301148.

PBS. "The Civil War by the Numbers." *American Experience.* Accessed January 12, 2025. https://www.pbs.org/wgbh/americanexperience/features/death-numbers/.

Pettit, Philip. "Republican Theory and Criminal Punishment." *Utilitas* 9, no. 1 (1997): 59–79. https://doi.org/10.1017/S0953820800005136.

PHI. "U.S. Home Care Workers: Key Facts." September 6, 2017. https://www.phinational.org/wp-content/uploads/legacy/phi-home-care-workers-key-facts.pdf.

Pineda, Erin. *Seeing Like an Activist: Civil Disobedience and the Civil Rights Movement.* Oxford University Press, 2021.

Prison Activist Resource Center. "Books, Magazines, and Publishers." Accessed January 7, 2025. https://www.prisonactivist.org/resources/books-magazines-and-publishers.

Prison Neighborhood Arts/Education Project (PNAP). Accessed January 7, 2025. https://p-nap.org.

Prisoner Hunger Strike Solidarity. "Prisoners' Demands." *Prisoner Hunger Strike Solidarity,* April 3, 2011. https://prisonerhungerstrikesolidarity.wordpress.com/education/the-prisoners-demands-2.

Prison Policy Initiative. "Eliminating In-Person Visits Did Not Result in a Substantial Drop in Contraband." *Prison Policy Initiative.* Accessed January 13, 2025. https://www.prisonpolicy.org/graphs/Contraband.html.

Prison Policy Initiative. "Race and Ethnicity." Accessed January 7, 2025. https://www.prisonpolicy.org/research/race_and_ethnicity.

Puar, Jasbir K. *The Right to Maim: Debility, Capacity, Disability.* Duke University Press, 2017.

Quinn, M. M., P. K. Markkanen, C. J. Galligan, et al. "Healthy Aging Requires a Healthy Home Care Workforce: the Occupational Safety and Health of Home Care Aides." *Current Environmental Health Reports* 8, no. 3 (2021): 235-44. https://doi.org/10.1007/s40572-021-00315-7.

Rabuy, Bernadette, and Daniel Kopf. "Detaining the Poor: How Money Bail Perpetuates an Endless Cycle of Poverty and Jail Time." *Prison Policy Initiative,* May 10, 2016. https://www.prisonpolicy.org/reports/incomejails.html.

Rabuy, Bernadette, and Peter Wagner. "Screening Out Family Time." *Prison Policy Initiative,* January 2015. https://static.prisonpolicy.org/visitation/ScreeningOutFamilyTime_January2015.pdf.

Rawls, John. *A Theory of Justice.* Belknap Press, 2005.

Richie, Beth. *Arrested Justice: Black Women, Violence, and America's Prison Nation.* NYU Press, 2012.

Richie, Beth. "Queering Antiprison Work: African American Lesbians in the Juvenile Justice System." In *Global Lockdown*, edited by Julia Sudbury. Routledge, 2014.

Right on Crime Coalition. "Case for Reform." Accessed May 20, 2025. https://rightoncrime.com/about/case-for-reform/.

Roberts, Dorothy E. "Abolition Constitutionalism." *Harvard Law Review* 133, no. 1 (2019): 1–122.

Roberts, Max, Eric N. Reither, Sojung Lim. "Contributors to the Black-White Life Expectancy Gap in Washington D.C." *Scientific Reports* 10 (2020). https://doi.org/10.1038/s41598-020-70046-6.

Roberts, Neil. "Angela Davis: Abolitionism, Democracy, Freedom." In *African American Political Thought*, edited by Melvin Rogers and Jack Turner. University of Chicago Press, 2021.

Robinson, Cedric J. *Black Marxism: The Making of the Black Radical Tradition*. University of North Carolina, 2021.

Ross, Loretta, and Rickie Solinger. *Reproductive Justice: An Introduction*. University of California Press, 2017.

Rothstein, Richard. *The Color of Law: A Forgotten History of How Our Government Segregated America*. Liveright, 2017.

San Francisco Children of Incarcerated Parents Partnership. "Bill of Rights." San Francisco Children of Incarcerated Parents Partnership, Summer 2005. https://sfonline.barnard.edu/children/SFCIPP_Bill_of_Rights.pdf.

Schulman, Sarah. *Conflict Is Not Abuse: Overstating Harm, Community Responsibility, and the Duty of Repair*. Arsenal Pulp Press, 2016.

Sculos, Bryant W. "Abolitionism & the Critique of Structural Violence: The Case for Reading Angela Davis as a Militant Pacifist." Paper presented at the Western Political Science Association Annual Meeting, 2024.

Sebastian, Cecilia. "Angela Davis and Critical Theory, from Kant to Abolition." *Polity* 56, no. 2 (2024): 207–29. https://doi.org/10.1086/729280.

Sedgwick, Eve Kosofsky. "Paranoid Reading and Reparative Reading, or, You're So Paranoid, You Probably Think This Essay Is About You." In *Touching Feeling: Affect, Pedagogy, Performativity*, Duke University Press, 2003.

The Sentencing Project. "Americans with Criminal Records: Poverty and Opportunity Profile." November 2015. https://www.sentencingproject.org/wp-content/uploads/2015/11/Americans-with-Criminal-Records-Poverty-and-Opportunity-Profile.pdf.

The Sentencing Project. "Mass Incarceration Trends." May 21, 2024. https://www.sentencingproject.org/reports/mass-incarceration-trends/.

Shen, W. W. "A History of Antipsychotic Drug Development." *Comprehensive Psychiatry* 40, no. 6 (1999): 407–14. https://doi.org/10.1016/s0010–440x(99)90082–2.

Shulman, George. "Fred Moten's Refusals and Consents: The Politics of Fugitivity." *Political Theory* 49, no. 2 (2021): 272–313.

Sinha, Manisha. *The Slave's Cause: A History of Abolition*. Yale University Press, 2017.

Sins Invalid. "Skin, Tooth, and Bone: A Disability Justice Primer." Reproductive Health Matters 25, no. 50 (2017): 149–50. https://doi.org/10.1080/09688080.2017.1335999.

Skarha, Julianne, Amite Dominick, Keith Spangler, et al. "Provision of Air Conditioning and Heat-Related Mortality in Texas Prisons." JAMA Network Open 1;5 (2022): 1-10. https://doi.org/ 10.1001/jamanetworkopen.2022.39849.

Sleat, Matt. "Introduction: Politics Recovered—on the Revival of Realism in Contemporary Political Theory." In *Politics Recovered: Realist Thought in Theory and Practice*, edited by Matt Sleat. Columbia University Press, 2018.

Smith, Andrea. "Beyond Restorative Justice." In *Restorative Justice and Violence Against Women*, edited by James Ptacek. Oxford University Press, 2009.

Smith, Andrea. *Conquest: Sexual Violence and American Indian Genocide*. Duke University Press, 2005.

Social Security Administration. "History of Monthly Disability Insurance Benefits." Last modified in 1986. https://www.ssa.gov/history/1986dibhistory.html#:~:text=Monthly%20disability%20insurance%20benefits%20were,was%20disabled%20before%20age%2018.

Solnit, Rebecca. "Why Climate Despair Is a Luxury." New Statesman, July 17, 2023. https://www.newstatesman.com/environment/2023/07/rebecca-solnit-climate-despair-hope.

Soss, Joe, and Vesla Weaver. "Police Are Our Government: Politics, Political Science, and the Policing of Race–Class Subjugated Communities." *Annual Review of Political Science* 20, no. 1 (2017): 565–91. https://doi.org/10.1146/annurev-polisci-060415-093825.

Southern Coalition for Social Justice. "Ban the Box Community Initiative Guide." Accessed January 7, 2025. https://southerncoalition.org/justice-system-reform/safe-reentry/ban-the-box-community-initiative-guide.

Spade, Dean. *Mutual Aid: Building Solidarity During This Crisis (and the Next)*. Verso, 2020.

Spade, Dean. "No Cops, Courts, or Cages Means No State." *Contemporary Political Theory* 23, no. 1 (2023): 123–28. https://doi.org/10.1057/s41296-023-00640-6.

Spade, Dean. *Normal Life: Administrative Violence, Critical Trans Politics, and the Limits of Law*. Duke University Press, 2015.

Spivak, Gayatri Chakravorty. "Can the Subaltern Speak?" In Imperialism, edited by Peter H. Cain and Mark Harrison. Routledge, 2004.

Stanley, Eric, and Nat Smith, eds. *Captive Genders: Trans Embodiment and the Prison Industrial Complex*. AK Press, 2011.

Stern, Alexandra Minna. "Sterilized in the Name of Public Health." *American Journal of Public Health* 95 (2011): 1128–38. https://doi.org/10.2105/AJPH.2004.041608.

Stillman, Sarah. "Do Children Have a 'Right to Hug' Their Parents?" *New Yorker*, May 13, 2024. https://www.newyorker.com/magazine/2024/05/20/the-jails-that-forbid-children-from-visiting-their-parents.

Survived & Punished. "Survived & Punished: End the Criminalization of Survival." Accessed January 13, 2025. https://survivedandpunished.org.

Survived and Punished. "About Us." Accessed January 7, 2025. https://survivedandpunished.org/about.

Szasz, Thomas. "The Abolitionist Perspective on Psychiatry." Accessed January 10, 2025. https://www.szasz.com/abolitionist.html.

Taylor, Chloë. "Foucault and the Ethics of Eating." *Foucault Studies* no. 9 (2010): 71–88. https://doi.org/10.22439/fs.v0i9.3060.

Taylor, Chloë. *Foucault, Feminism, and Sex Crimes: An Anti-Carceral Analysis.* Routledge, 2019.

Taylor, Keeanga-Yamahtta, ed. *How We Get Free: Black Feminism and the Combahee River Collective.* Haymarket Books, 2017.

Taylor, Keeanga-Yamahtta. *Race For Profit: How Banks and the Real Estate Industry Undermined Black Homeownership.* University of North Carolina Press, 2019.

Terwiel, Anna. "Problematization as an Activist Practice: Reconsidering Foucault." *Theory and Event* 23, no. 1 (2020): 66–84. https://dx.doi.org/10.1353/tae.2020.0003.

Terwiel, Anna. "The Revolutionary Politics of Abolition." *Polity* 55, no. 4 (2023).

Terwiel, Anna. "What Is Carceral Feminism?" *Political Theory* 48, no. 4 (2020): 421–42.

Terwiel, Anna. "What Is the Problem with High Prison Temperatures? From the Threat to Health to the Right to Comfort." *New Political Science* 40, no. 1 (2018): 70–83.

13th. Directed by Ava DuVernay. Forward Movement, 2016.

Thompson, Kevin, and Perry Zurn. "Introduction: Legacies of Militancy and Theory." In *Intolerable: Writings from Michel Foucault and the Prisons Information Group (1970–1980),* edited by Kevin Thompson and Perry Zurn. Translated by Erik Bernanek and Perry Zurn. University of Minnesota Press, 2021.

Thorpe, Rebecca. "Perverse Politics: The Persistence of Mass Imprisonment in the Twenty-First Century." *Perspectives on Politics* 13, no. 3 (2015): 618–37. https://doi.org/10.1017/S1537592715001218.

Threadcraft, Shatema. *Intimate Justice: The Black Female Body and the Body Politic.* Oxford University Press, 2016.

Threadcraft, Shatema. "North American Necropolitics and Gender: On #BlackLivesMatter and Black Femicide." *South Atlantic Quarterly* no. 3 (2017): 553–79. https://doi.org/10.1215/00382876-3961483.

Thuma, Emily L. *All Our Trials: Prisons, Policing, and the Feminist Fight to End Violence.* University of Illinois Press, 2019.

Tilly, Charles. "Warmaking and Statemaking as Organized Crime." In *Bringing the State Back In,* edited by Peter B. Evans, Dietrich Rueschemeyer, and Theda Skocpol. Cambridge University Press, 2010.

Tjaden, Patricia, and Nancy Thoennes. "Extent, Nature, and Consequences of Rape Victimization: Findings from the National Violence Against Women Survey." *National Institute of Justice,* January 2006.

TransformHarm.org. Accessed January 7, 2025. https://transformharm.org/.

Tronto, Joan. *Moral Boundaries: A Political Argument for an Ethic of Care.* Routledge, 1993.

Uggen, Christopher, Ryan Larson, Sarah Shannon, et al. "Locked Out 2022: Estimates of People Denied Voting Rights." *The Sentencing Project,* October 25, 2022. https://www.sentencingproject.org/reports/locked-out-2022-estimates-of-people-denied-voting-rights.

United Nations General Assembly. Universal Declaration of Human Rights. December 10, 1948. https://www.un.org/en/about-us/universal-declaration-of-human-rights.

United Nations Human Rights Office of the High Commissioner. "United States: Prolonged Solitary Confinement Amounts to Psychological Torture." Press release, February 28, 2020. https://www.ohchr.org/en/press-releases/2020/02/united-states-prolonged-solitary-confinement-amounts-psychological-torture.

U.S. Department of Agriculture, Economic Research Service. "Food Security in the U.S.—Key Statistics & Graphics." *ERS USDA*. Last updated January 8, 2025. https://www.ers.usda.gov/topics/food-nutrition-assistance/food-security-in-the-u-s/key-statistics-graphics.

Van Dam, Andrew. "Less than 1% of Rapes Lead to Felony Convictions. At Least 89% of Victims Face Emotional and Physical Consequences." *Washington Post,* October 6, 2018.

Vera Institute. "How the United States Punishes People for Being Poor." September 21, 2023. https://www.vera.org/news/how-the-united-states-punishes-people-for-being-poor.

Wacquant, Loïc. "Crafting the Neoliberal State: Workfare, Prisonfare, and Social Insecurity." *Sociological Forum* 25, no. 3 (2010): 197–220. https://doi.org/10.1111/j.1573-7861.2010.01173.x.

Wacquant, Loïc. *Punishing the Poor: The Neoliberal Government of Social Insecurity.* Duke University Press, 2009.

Walker, Anders. "The New Jim Crow? Recovering the Progressive Origins of Mass Incarceration." Hastings Constitutional Law Quarterly 41, no. 4 (2014): 845–74.

Ward, Milo. "A Democracy of Authorities: Broken Windows Policing and the Neoconservative Political Theory of Law and Order." *Perspectives on Politics,* published online 2025: 1–18. https://doi.org/10.1017/S1537592724002688.

Weaver, Vesla, Gwen Prowse, and Spencer Piston. "Too Much Knowledge, Too Little Power: An Assessment of Political Knowledge in Highly Policed Communities." *The Journal of Politics* 81, no. 3 (July 2019): 1153–66.

Weeks, Kathi. "Abolition of the Family." *Feminist Theory* 24, no. 3 (2021): 433–53. https://doi.org/10.1177/14647001211015841.

Weeks, Kathi. *The Problem with Work: Feminism, Marxism, Antiwork Politics, and Postwork Imaginaries.* Duke University Press, 2011.

Weinbaum, Alys. "Gendering the General Strike. W. E. B. Du Bois's *Black Reconstruction* and Black Feminism's 'Propaganda of History.'" *South Atlantic Quarterly* 112, no. 3 (2013): 437–63. https://doi.org/10.1215/00382876-2146395.

Wilderson, Frank B. *Afropessimism.* W. W. Norton, 2020.

Williams, Bernard. *In the Beginning Was the Deed: Realism and Moralism in Political Argument.* Princeton University Press, 2009.

Williams, Carolyn. "The Female Anti-Slavery Movement: Fighting Against Racial Prejudice and Promoting Women's Rights in Antebellum America." In *The Abolitionist Sisterhood,* edited by Jean Fagan Yellin and John C. Van Horne. Cornell University Press, 1994.

Williamson, Vanessa. "Understanding Democratic Decline in the United States." *Brookings,* October 17, 2023. https://www.brookings.edu/articles/understanding-democratic-decline-in-the-united-states.

Witters, Dan. "In U.S., an Estimated 46 Million Cannot Afford Needed Care." *Gallup,* March 31, 2021. https://news.gallup.com/poll/342095/estimated-million-cannot-afford-needed-care.aspx.

Woodly, Deva R. *Reckoning: Black Lives Matter and the Democratic Necessity of Social Movements.* Oxford University Press, 2021.

Woodly, Deva, and Rachel Brown, eds. "Critical Exchange: The Politics of Care." *Contemporary Political Theory* 20, no. 4 (2021): 890–925. https://doi.org/10.1057/s41296-021-00515-8.

Young, Iris Marion. "The Logic of Masculinist Protection: Reflections on the Current Security State." *Signs: Journal of Women in Culture and Society* 29, no. 1 (2003): 1–25. https://doi.org/10.1086/375708.

Zimmerman, Ann. "Extreme Heat Tests Prisons." *Wall Street Journal,* October 17, 2013. https://www.wsj.com/articles/extreme-heat-tests-prisons-1382050799.

Index

ANNA TERWIEL is assistant professor of political science at Trinity College.